MY FRIEND, MY FRIEND

My Friend, My Friend

THE STORY OF THOREAU'S RELATIONSHIP
WITH EMERSON

Harmon Smith

University of Massachusetts Press   *Amherst*

Copyright ©1999 by Harmon Smith
All rights reserved
Printed in the United States of America
LC 98-53492
ISBN 1-55849-186-4

Designed by Jack Harrison
Set in Adobe Garamond with Deepdene display by Graphic Composition
Printed and bound by BookCrafters
Library of Congress Cataloging-in-Publication Data
Smith, Harmon D.
My friend, my friend : the story of Thoreau's relationship with Emerson / Harmon Smith.
p. cm.
Includes bibliographical references and index.
ISBN 1-55849-186-4 (cloth : alk. paper)
1. Thoreau, Henry David, 1817–1862—Friends and associates.
2. Emerson, Ralph Waldo, 1803–1882—Friends and associates.
3. Friendship—United States—History—19th century.
4. Authors, American—19th century—Biography. I. Title.
PS3053.S65   1999
810.9′003—dc21
[b]   98-53492
CIP

British Library Cataloguing in Publication data are available.

For Vickie,
who understands

Contents

List of Illustrations   ix

Preface   xi

Introduction   1

1   An Extraordinary Young Man   5

2   A Troubled Dream   25

3   The Beautiful and the Brave   38

4   The Womb of Zeus   52

5   One of the Family   63

6   Into the World   80

7   A Beautiful Asylum   95

8   At Home with Lidian   112

9   Separate Paths   129

10   Undercurrents   144

11   Between Narrow Walls   158

12   The Final Years   167

Notes   185

Selected Bibliography   201

Index   213

Illustrations

Following page 62

The center of Concord village in 1841

The shopping center of Concord, ca. 1865

Crayon portrait of R. W. Emerson by Samuel Worcester Rowse

Crayon portrait of H. D. Thoreau by Samuel Worcester Rowse

Lidian Emerson with her son Waldo

Ellen Sewell

The Emerson home in Concord

Caroline Sturgis Tappan, ca. 1850

Samuel Gray Ward

Margaret Fuller

Waldo Emerson

Portrait of John Thoreau Jr.

Following page 128

Ellen Tucker Emerson

Edward and Edith Emerson

Lidian Emerson

R. W. Emerson
H. D. Thoreau
Ellery Channing
Ellen Channing
H. D. Thoreau
Sophia Thoreau
R. W. Emerson

Preface

Thoreau's friendship with Emerson played a crucial role in Thoreau's life, a vital one in Emerson's. This book deals with the human side of the story. It follows the progress of their relationship from their first meeting on an April afternoon in 1837 until Thoreau's death twenty-five years later.

Emerson's biographers, confronted by their subject's crowded life, have generally chosen to devote limited space to the friendship, at most a chapter with additional references scattered throughout the book. Thoreau's biographers have dealt with the subject at greater length but often seem determined to establish his independence of Emerson, perhaps assuming incorrectly that to admit the extent of Emerson's influence on him might somehow diminish his accomplishments. Immersion in this literature can only produce a fragmented view of the friendship, however. If the dynamics of the relationship are to be understood, there is a wealth of additional material to be consulted in published and unpublished letters and in journals, memoirs, and monographs. My aim has been to explore the relationship of the two men in depth, in order to define the role it played in their work and in their lives.

I have had a great deal of help and support with this project. For reading the manuscript and offering wise counsel, I thank Robert Barnes, Thomas Blanding, Earl Brecher, Charlotte Collins, Victoria Givotovsky, Joseph Groell, Helen Hunt, Alice Jones, Harry Jones, Elliot Nichols, Peter Nichols, and Sally Nichols. Martin Kessler provided me with invaluable support during the early days of the writing of this book. Joel Myerson's comments on an early draft led me to explore subsidiary friendships of the two men, which added substantial interest to the story. Ronald W. Hoag, editor of the Thoreau Society's *Concord Saunterer,* published chapter 8 at an important time in the development of the book. Eleanor M. Tilton let me see typescripts of her new volumes of Emerson letters before they were published. Elizabeth Witherell sent me transcripts of additional Thoreau letters that will appear in the new Princeton edition of his correspondence. I especially thank Bruce Wilcox whose sustained interest and thoughtful guidance as editor and publisher led to a greatly strengthened book. I also thank Marcia Moss of the Concord Free Public Library and the staffs of the Houghton Library at Harvard, the Massachusetts Historical Society, the Berg Collection of the New York Public Library, the Morgan Library, and the Middlebury College Library. And I express my deep appreciation to my wife, Victoria Beller Smith, and my daughter, Gwendolyn Smith Dunaif, for their advice, patience, and support during the years that I worked on this project.

MY FRIEND, MY FRIEND

Introduction

From the beginning Henry Thoreau's friendship with Ralph Waldo Emerson was the subject of considerable comment among the people who knew them. Emerson's wife, Lidian, was the first to express interest in the attraction that Thoreau, then twenty years old, exerted upon her husband. She had rarely known "Mr. E.," as she called Emerson, to be so eager to share his walks with anyone as he was with young Henry Thoreau. Visitors to Concord soon noticed that Henry had begun to speak like Emerson, to use the same gestures, even to comb his hair the same way. When Emerson traveled to England to lecture, an acquaintance with whom he spent considerable time while there was amazed by how his talk centered on the young friend he had left behind. They were, Thoreau proclaimed, like gods to each other.[1]

When Thoreau was introduced to Emerson in 1837, Emerson had already published *Nature* and was gaining recognition as a leading radical thinker in the small intellectual world that found its center in Boston and Cambridge. Henry Thoreau, fourteen years Emerson's junior, had not yet finished his senior year at Harvard. Nothing in the background or experience of either man could have foretold that they would become such close friends so quickly, or that their intimacy would span a quarter of a century until Thoreau's death.

Emerson, who had been born into an established New England family, had recently inherited enough money to be independent; Thoreau's father made pencils for a living, and his mother ran a boarding house to help pay the bills. Two years earlier Emerson had married for the second time and had acquired a large house in Concord for himself and his new wife; Thoreau was attending Harvard with scholarship support and living in a dormitory in Cambridge. Emerson possessed a personal magnetism that drew people to him; Thoreau's closest friend was his older brother, and he did not make friends easily. Yet very quickly these two men discovered they had an affinity for each other, which was all that mattered.

The day Emerson met Thoreau he recognized that he was in the presence of "an extraordinary young man." Although Thoreau had so far produced only a few immature poems, Emerson saw a potential in him that was not apparent to the rest of the world. Emerson's belief in his young friend's ability was a major factor in Thoreau's long, slow development as a writer. The financial assistance Emerson provided over the years gave Thoreau the time to develop into an author of great originality. Without the support of Ralph Waldo Emerson, it is doubtful that Henry Thoreau could have become one of America's major literary figures. In fact, if Emerson had not befriended him, it is unlikely that Thoreau would have had a significant literary career.[2]

From the beginning Emerson showed his concern for Thoreau's future by treating him as a member of the family. On their second meeting he opened his library to him. Soon he invited him to move into the Emerson home, where Thoreau remained for two years. When Thoreau decided to strike out on his own, Emerson arranged for him to tutor the son of his brother William on Staten Island where he was only a ferry ride from the literary marketplace in New York City. Later, having acquired land on Walden Pond, Emerson allowed Thoreau to erect a cabin there where he could write undisturbed. It was Lidian Emerson who persuaded Thoreau to abandon his solitary existence at Walden to stay with her and her children while Emerson traveled abroad for a year.

In time the closeness of the relationship between Thoreau and Emerson became a source of tension in itself. Emerson found Thoreau's natural combativeness more and more difficult to deal with as the years passed. Thoreau became restive as Emerson continued to insist on his role as mentor despite the evident maturing of Thoreau's talent. Emerson's penchant for taking up talented young men—most notably, Ellery Channing, Samuel Gray Ward, and Giles Waldo—periodically threatened Thoreau's privileged status. Thoreau's growing attachment to Lidian Emerson openly alarmed Emerson. By the summer of 1848 when Emerson returned home from his trip to England, it was clear that a fissure was opening between them.

The friends were not alone on the stage as this drama was being played out. Emerson's presence in Concord drew an astonishing number of visitors to the town. Bronson Alcott and Margaret Fuller were among the first to come. They were followed by Caroline Sturgis and Ellery Channing. These friends often stayed for a week or two in the room that the Emersons called the Pilgrim's Chamber. At the same time an increasing flow of writers, intellectuals, and eccentrics from all walks of life had begun to cross Emerson's doorstep. Despite Thoreau's reclusiveness, Emerson insisted on his meeting as many of them as possible, a circumstance that greatly broadened his experience without causing him to step outside the village.

These were years of intellectual ferment in New England, particularly in Emerson's circle. Along with Margaret Fuller, Henry Hedge, and George Ripley, Thoreau and Emerson were in the forefront of the development of the new transcendental thought that swept the region in the 1830s and early 1840s. Reared at a time when a repressive Calvinism dominated society's view of life, they found in the "Newness," as they called it, a welcome release from these constraints. Emerson and his group believed so strongly in the importance of exploring these new ideas that they established a quarterly magazine, the *Dial,* to give young writers a chance to present their views. Under the editorship of Margaret Fuller, then Emerson himself with Thoreau as his occasional assistant, the *Dial* appeared regularly for four years.[3]

The decade that began with Emerson's publication of *Nature* in 1836 and concluded with Thoreau's withdrawal from Walden in 1847 was one of the most productive in American literary history. It was then that Emerson completed and issued his *Essays,* first and second series, and produced his major collection of poems. At the same time Thoreau became fully engaged with his journal, drafted *A Week on the Concord and Merrimack Rivers,* and began work on *Walden.* These were among the major works of the period we know today as the American Renaissance.

Although Thoreau and Emerson were deeply involved in their work, they did not allow themselves to be distracted from the demands of friendship. They thought about it constantly and wrote about it at length. For both men, however, friendship presented a dilemma, since their expectations of it were never fully met by the reality. This was as true in their own relationship as it was in their relationships with others. They dreamed of ideal friendship while experiencing the human variety.

Emerson, Thoreau, and their circle may have thought of themselves as dedicated to the life of the mind, but that didn't exempt them from the needs and passions everyone else is prey to. Henry Thoreau was as close to his brother, John, as to anyone, yet he allowed himself to fall in love with the same woman and to propose to her, which led inevitably to a breach between them. Emerson's constant attention to Margaret Fuller aroused such jealousy in his wife, Lidian, that she could not hide it from her family and friends. Margaret Fuller permitted her feelings for Emerson to cross the line from friendship to a deeper attachment, as Emerson himself did with Caroline Sturgis. Ellery Channing, who settled in Concord to be near Emerson, evolved from a young man very much in love with his young wife into an abusive husband and father.

It was the relationship between Thoreau and Emerson, however, that caught the imagination of their contemporaries, although it perplexed them as much as it interested them. What these observers did not know—could not know—without access to the journals to which the men confided their most private thoughts was that much of the behavior that puzzled them grew from a lack of understanding on the part of the friends themselves of each other's true feelings. While the bond that united Thoreau and Emerson remained strong, the interests and desires that lay behind it were often tragically at variance.

The years immediately before and after the publication of *Walden* witnessed a growing estrangement between the friends. Thoreau was wounded by his perception of Emerson's response to his first book, *A Week on the Concord and Merrimack Rivers,* but could not bring himself to discuss his feelings openly. Emerson was affronted by Thoreau's cold behavior and withdrew into the majesty of his growing reputation. Misunderstanding piled on misunderstanding. It took a crisis in Emerson's health in 1858 to enable them to put aside their accumulated grievances and begin once again to enjoy the companionship that meant so much to both of them.

Since the thoughts and feelings of Thoreau and Emerson are so well documented in their journals and letters, it is possible to trace the pattern of their emotional involvement with each other in great detail. What emerges is more than the record of the relationship between two men. It is an intimate look at the nature of friendship itself.

1

An Extraordinary Young Man

In the 1830s, Concord, Massachusetts, was a small rural village with about two thousand inhabitants. Although the town was situated only nineteen miles from Boston, it took from two and a half to three hours to get there traveling in a stagecoach over rough country roads, a fact that increased its attractiveness for Ralph Waldo Emerson. Immersed in the effort to complete *Nature,* his first book, Emerson moved to Concord in 1834 to escape the multiple distractions of the city as he struggled to get his ideas down on paper.

Emerson had recently taken legal action to obtain his late wife's portion of her father's estate, a sizable inheritance that would have come to her if she had lived until her twenty-first birthday. This sudden accession of wealth had allowed Emerson to withdraw from the ministry, which had occupied his young adult years, and to devote himself to lecturing and writing. The money also enabled him to buy a commodious house in Concord when he decided to remarry only eighteen months after settling down in the country.

Emerson's second wife, Lidian Jackson Emerson, didn't share her husband's enthusiasm for small town life. Brought up in the more sophisticated community of Plymouth, Massachusetts, she found little in a rural village to engage her interest. Happily for Lidian, her sister, Mrs. Lucy Brown, was free to come to Concord to keep her company for long periods. A warm, sympathetic woman, Mrs. Brown had seen her world collapse around her a few years earlier when her husband, after dissipating her assets, had deserted her.

Shortly after the Emersons' marriage, Mrs. Brown and her two small children moved in with the newlyweds for twenty-two weeks. A year later, when Lidian invited her to return to Concord for a second lengthy stay, it was mutually agreed that it would be in everyone's interest if she obtained independent quarters. Before her arrival, arrangements were made for her to board with Mr. and Mrs. John Thoreau, who lived in a rented house on Main Street.

Of the Thoreaus' four children only Sophia, then seventeen, was living at home that winter. Two others, John and Helen, were teachers in nearby towns where they boarded during the school year. A fourth, Henry, was just completing his senior year at Harvard. Recognizing that Henry possessed unusual abilities, the whole Thoreau family, including two maiden aunts, had been struggling for three and a half years to meet the cost of sending him to college. Mrs. Thoreau said of Lucy Brown that she had never known a woman to take "such a friendly interest in every one." It's not surprising, therefore, that the Thoreaus' new boarder quickly became friendly with Sophia Thoreau and also developed a strong interest in young Henry, who was the focus of so much attention in the family.[1]

One day in March, Lucy Brown accompanied Sophia Thoreau to the Concord Lyceum to hear Emerson repeat a lecture on manners that he had recently delivered in Boston.[2] At that time attending lectures was a principal means of recreation in the United States, and Emerson, who was then thirty-four, was already noted for his compelling presence on the speaker's platform. "His coming into the room had the magic of sunlight," one contemporary recalled.[3] His smile seemed "to proclaim him the translated inhabitant of some higher sphere." His voice had "the appeal of silver trumpets." People in Concord came to his lectures whether they agreed with what he had to say or not, just to enjoy the performance.[4]

As Sophia Thoreau was listening to Emerson, she was surprised and delighted to hear him present a thought identical to one her brother Henry had expressed in a passage he had written not long before. Leaning toward Mrs. Brown, Sophia excitedly informed her of the coincidence. Although Henry was then living in a dormitory in Cambridge, Sophia had no trouble locating the manuscript in question when she and Lucy Brown returned to the Thoreaus' house after the lecture. Impressed by what she read, Mrs. Brown decided to share the discovery with her sister.

The paper, which Lidian Emerson immediately passed along to her husband, caught Emerson's attention. He was always pleased when young men displayed "a lively interest" in his ideas. Here was a youth who offered more than that, whose mode of perception followed the same path as his own. Although Emerson was acquainted with the Thoreau family, he had not been formally introduced to Henry. He suggested that Mrs. Brown bring Henry to meet him when the young man was in Concord visiting his parents.[5]

Over the years Henry Thoreau had had many opportunities to observe Emerson. After Emerson's ordination in 1829, he had preached frequently in Concord and since resigning his ministry had lectured there regularly. But Henry had not yet read *Nature,* and he immediately proceeded to do that. *Nature* was a serious attempt on Emerson's part to come to grips with the meaning of existence. It brought together for the first time in a single volume ideas Emerson had developed over the previous decade in journal entries, letters, sermons, and lectures. The lesson that he had carried to the world in his book was that man is an independent being who must find understanding and a correct path for action within himself rather than "impotently relying upon a dead past." In a society that was still struggling to free itself from a strict Calvinism in which predetermination was a central doctrine this was a revolutionary position.[6]

Nature did not present an argument that was necessarily easy to penetrate. As Edward Everett Hale noted shortly after its publication, there was "a good deal in it" that did not readily reveal itself to the understanding of readers who were not serious students of philosophy. But Henry Thoreau's response was different from theirs. To his great joy he found that a careful reading of *Nature* permitted him to come to grips with an inner inclination that he hadn't previously found the means of expressing. That the book was "radically anarchic, overthrowing all the authority of the past" delighted him. Emerson's bold claim that "man may discover his own divine attributes in the mirror held up to him by nature" came as a welcome illumination. He had learned that there was a new way to view experience, one that suited him perfectly. The book, he said later, had opened "a new era" in his life.[7]

On Sunday April 9, 1837, Henry set out with Mrs. Brown for the ten-minute walk from the Thoreaus' house on Main Street to the Emersons'. The large white house in which Emerson lived with his wife, his mother, his infant son, and three female servants stood on two acres on the Post Road leading to Cambridge and Boston. Only eight years old, the house had been built with higher ceilings and taller windows than those favored earlier in New England. It was an impressive residence that left no doubt of the owner's social position.[8]

Emerson recognized at once that the Harvard senior who presented himself at his door was not an ordinary youth. To his classmates Henry may have seemed "impassive," "cold and unimpressible" as he moved about the campus with his eyes on the path in front of him. But when he encountered an adult like Emerson whose superior intellectual powers were immediately evident, he suddenly became animated. The ideas that crowded his mind came tumbling out as he tested them against the experience and knowledge of his companion. Never shy, Henry became assertive as he talked, occasionally allowing a youthful self-confidence to carry him too far. Emerson was impressed by this "youthful giant" who seemed "sent to work revolutions." He noted approvingly that Henry seemed completely at home in speaking of society, books, and religion. What perplexed him was how this brilliant young man had sprung from such a simple background. His view of Thoreau's parents and their circle would always be colored by an element of condescension. He could find no explanation for the appearance in their midst of an outstanding mind like Henry's.[9]

Later that day, as Emerson looked back on his meeting with Henry Thoreau, he found himself wondering about the young man. Would he have the staying power to fulfill his promise? Given the straitened circumstances of Henry's life, it would require a great deal of hard work and drive to do so. Thinking of others in whom he had seen the spark flicker brightly then die, Emerson jotted in his journal, "An extraordinary young man is sure to defeat expectation." Then he crossed out the words, unable to sustain such a pessimistic view of his new acquaintance.[10]

In later years Emerson would reflect that his own "special parish" was "young men seeking their way." Although born into an established New England family, he had been brought up in poverty, his father having died suddenly when Emerson was five years old. He understood the difficulties faced by bright young men of limited means in a materialistic society, especially if they hoped to pursue literary interests. When he detected talent in one of them, he would go to great lengths to help him find his bearings in "the tough world." Emerson didn't know it yet, but in reflecting in his journal on his meeting with Henry Thoreau he had taken the first tentative step on the journey that would see his young neighbor emerge as the principal protégé of his long and active life.[11]

While Henry couldn't have foreseen this outcome either, the meeting clearly opened a dazzling prospect for him. Since Emerson arguably possessed the most original mind in New England, the possibility that Henry's acquaintance with him might grow into a deeper relationship over the years radically changed the outlook for his future. Henry returned to his dormitory in Cambridge at the end of the spring vacation determined to gain a broader understanding of Emerson's ideas. In the remaining months of the school year he withdrew *Nature* from the library once more. Later he bought a copy for himself, gave it to a friend, and purchased another. *Nature* had an immediate influence on Henry's thinking. Echoes of Emerson's views can readily be detected in the essays he wrote that spring for his English professor, Edward Tyrell Channing.[12]

If it hadn't been for Lucy Brown, Emerson might easily have lost sight of his youthful neighbor. During the remainder of her stay in Concord, Mrs. Brown maintained a link between them by bringing Henry's poems to Emerson to read. Emerson not only admired the work of professional practitioners of the art, he also enjoyed the poetry produced in response to an inner need by sensitive people lacking a developed talent, which he called poetry "of the portfolio." Even when placed in this category, Henry's early work appears crude and amateurish. Still, Emerson continued to read the poems, partly to please his sister-in-law, partly because he was attracted by Henry's attitude toward experience.[13]

Emerson's continued interest in Henry led Mrs. Thoreau to hope that he would help with a potentially difficult situation facing the family. Although Henry had been the recipient of "exhibition money" in his freshman and sophomore years, he had been dropped from the awards list in his junior year, and Mrs. Thoreau was fearful that he would be missing from the list again when it was announced later in the spring. Emerson obligingly wrote a letter to his Harvard classmate Josiah Quincy, who was now president of the university. Although Quincy warned in his reply to Emerson that "an unfavorable opinion had been entertained" by Henry's instructors "of his disposition to exert himself," Emerson's letter was apparently decisive. On

June 15, it was announced that Henry Thoreau had been granted $25.00, a substantial sum at a time when tuition, room, and board cost $179.00 a year.[14]

Three weeks later, Henry returned to Concord for the Independence Day weekend. Emerson had departed for Plymouth a few days earlier to recuperate from an illness but had left behind a poem to be sung on the Fourth of July during the dedication of a monument to the town's Revolutionary War heroes. As Henry gathered with his neighbors on the green for the ceremony, slips of paper with "The Concord Hymn" printed on them were passed among them. Henry joined with the crowd in singing the "Hymn" to the tune of "Old Hundred," a popular song of the period. Later, he inserted his copy of the poem into a scrapbook that he kept for the rest of his life.[15]

Although in 1837 Harvard's school year ended on July 12, graduation ceremonies were not scheduled to take place until the end of August. For Henry, who had strongly disliked living away from home, the intervening six-week vacation was a period of great contentment. Adding to his pleasure during these weeks was the presence in the house of his sister Helen and brother, John, who were also there on vacation from their teaching jobs.

The relationship between Henry and John was unusually close despite the marked differences in their personalities. While Henry had been a solemn child, content to sit on the sidelines, John had always chosen to be in the thick of things. He liked the rough and tumble of boys' games and, with his talent for telling stories that made the other children laugh, was usually at the center of an admiring group. Although Henry was the greater walker of the two, John liked to accompany him into the countryside where they would search tirelessly for Indian relics. A favorite pastime of theirs as youngsters had been to pretend that they were Indians, assuming Indian names and talking in a mock Indian dialect. That summer they fell into the practice once again. One day Henry was so carried away by the pretense that he burst into "an extravagant eulogy on those savage times," waving his arms wildly and shouting from the hillside they were climbing. It was a happy, carefree period, the last during which the brothers would be free enough of responsibility to be able to play at being boys again.[16]

In midsummer the close connection between the Thoreau and Emerson households was severed by Mrs. Brown's departure from Concord. Emerson, who had returned home from Plymouth during the second week in July, was occupied at his desk much of the time during August working on a speech he had been asked to deliver at Harvard's commencement. Since his talk would be the main address at the two-day event, Emerson had decided to make it the occasion of a major statement. He wanted to provide a sense of direction to the young men of Henry's graduating class who would be entering a world that was changing rapidly as the country's westward expansion accelerated.

On August 30, the opening day of the exercises, Henry Thoreau was one of twenty-two classmates who spoke briefly. Despite the fact that his assigned topic was "the commercial spirit," he managed during the course of it to hint at the ideas that Emerson had expressed in *Nature*. Emerson's address, which was delivered the following day, has become famous under the title of "The American Scholar." His message to the graduating class of 1837 was that its members should look to nature itself as the new frontier not the territories that were opening up in the West. In his view, genius could best express itself by searching out nature's latent messages and bringing them into consciousness. He was proposing "a new calling with its own rewards," one in which success was "identical with self-realization." For a young man with Henry's personality and inclinations there could not have been any more welcome advice.[17]

2

Early in September Henry Thoreau began work as the sole instructor in the one-room schoolhouse in Concord that he had attended as a child. In the small brick building, grades one through twelve sat together on wooden benches arranged along three sides of the room. The grade that was reciting stood before Henry's elevated desk while the other students remained in their seats, where they were supposed to be studying. The temptation to test the resolve of their fledgling teacher was often more than they could resist, however, and there was a great deal of rowdiness.

During the second week of Henry's tenure, Deacon Cyrus Snow, a member of Concord's school committee, stopped in to see how the new instructor was doing. Dismayed by the level of noise in the room, Deacon Snow insisted that Henry administer corporal punishment when his charges ignored the rules. Henry's response to this demand created quite a stir in the village. After following the deacon's orders for a day, he suddenly announced his resignation. It went "against his conscience," he declared, to maintain discipline in this manner.[18]

Emerson, who knew what it was like to work in a public school of the period, sympathized with Henry's situation. Teaching in a "hot, steaming, stoved, stinking, dirty AB[C] spelling school," as he described his own experience, had been one of the factors that had directed him toward the ministry four years after his graduation from Harvard. "Better tug at the oar, dig the mine, or saw wood; better sow hemp, or hang with it, than sow the seed of instruction," he had written at the time. Since job opportunities were limited for a young man without a profession in the 1830s, Emerson accepted the fact that Henry would have to begin searching for another teaching assignment. But he was concerned that the pressure on him to find and hold a new job would lead him to abandon his higher aspirations. He thought Henry should take an optimistic view of this period of "cold eclipse" and use it as an opportunity to pursue his literary interests.[19]

Toward the end of October another meeting in Emerson's study was arranged between the two men to discuss the situation. The room, which lay to the right when one entered the front hall of the house, was painted a dark red. In addition to Emerson's writing table and favorite chair, there were chairs and a comfortable sofa for visitors. But for Henry Thoreau the most attractive feature of the room was that it housed Emerson's library. Emerson had slowly built up a substantial private collection, to which he had recently added a major acquisition: a twenty-two-volume edition of Goethe's works in German.

Emerson considered Goethe's to be "the pivotal mind in modern literature," indeed he thought him "the most modern of the moderns." Although in his final term at Harvard Henry had studied German literature under the newly appointed instructor Henry Wadsworth Longfellow, his exposure to Goethe had apparently been limited to a reading of *Wilhelm Meister*. Henry had nevertheless worked hard while in college to master the German language, and it was immediately agreed that he would borrow Emerson's copy of *Torquato Tasso,* Goethe's play about the author and poet whose most famous work was *Jerusalem Delivered*. On their first opportunity to talk since Henry's graduation the young man and his older neighbor made the auspicious discovery that their interests coincided neatly.[20]

On this visit Henry found himself being treated not simply as a promising student but as a young man whose literary interests deserved respect. From an early age Emerson had committed his thoughts to paper on an almost daily basis. Scraps of poetry, observations of daily life, religious and philosophical speculations followed one another across the pages of his journal in the order in which they entered his mind. It was the repository from which he had drawn the raw materials for *Nature* and that he continued to mine for his lectures. "Do you keep a journal?" he asked Henry.[21] When he learned that it was not the young man's practice, he strongly advised him to begin at once. Henry heeded Emerson's advice. Returning home, he opened a clean notebook, entered the date, and began recording the "visits of truth" to his mind.[22]

Friendships flower when people have natural occasions to meet. Henry's interest in Emerson's books and Emerson's willingness to permit him to borrow from his library at will provided them with the opportunity to come together regularly in a casual way. Soon Emerson was inviting him along on his walks through the countryside surrounding the village. After a day spent in his study Emerson liked to set out along the road leading to Walden Pond or to climb up to the cliffs overlooking Fairhaven Bay, but he usually walked alone. In a letter to Mrs. Brown written at this time Lidian mentioned that Emerson had begun asking Henry to join him and pointed out that this was "a thing he would propos[e to] few; as you well know." She added that her husband had "taken to Henry with great interest" and thought him "[un]-common in mind & character."[23]

One afternoon early in December, Emerson called for Henry at the Thoreau home and was surprised to discover that the young man had left for Boston earlier in the day. Emerson was scheduled to deliver his first lecture of the season that evening at the city's Masonic Temple, and he had presented Henry with a pass. Lacking the money to take the stagecoach, Henry had set out on foot to cover the nineteen miles. This news affected Emerson strongly. A few days later, when Emerson decided to spare Lidian the weekly trip to Boston by repeating his lectures at home, he invited Henry to become a regular member of the party.

The group that gathered at the Emersons' on those winter evenings was small. The only addition to the family circle besides Henry Thoreau was Elizabeth Hoar, accompanied occasionally by one of her brothers. The daughter of Concord's leading citizen, former congressman Samuel Hoar, Elizabeth had been engaged to Emerson's younger brother Charles. Since the death of Charles two years earlier at the age of twenty-six, Elizabeth had grown closer to Emerson and his wife. It was said that "for generations the Concord people had been instructed from the cradle to the grave to fear God and the Hoar family." Although Elizabeth's reserve suggested an awareness of her position, it was a facade that masked a genuine humility. Emerson, impressed by her faithfulness to the memory of her fiancé, called her a "lovely nun." The fineness of her perception, her good sense in practical matters, her command of classical Greek, all commended her to him strongly.[24]

In December and January, Emerson delivered ten lectures in Boston and repeated all but two at home. Entitled "Human Culture," the series offered revolutionary advice to the youth of New England. In these lectures, as in *Nature* and "The American Scholar," Emerson was participating in a dialogue that had been moving in widening circles throughout New England in recent years, particularly among Unitarian clergymen like himself. With them he shared a growing dissatisfaction with the pessimism that pervaded Calvinism and the rationalism that dominated Unitarian thought. As one of their number, James Freeman Clarke, put it, they were "revolted" at the Lockean attempt "to explain soul out of sense, deducing mind from matter." It was Coleridge, interpreting Kant, who had led them to an awareness of the possibility that "though knowledge begins *with* experience it does not come *from* experience."[25] They were convinced that man had "an innate ability" to see beyond "mere sensory experience" to arrive at truth; in other words, to transcend it. Although Emerson and his colleagues described themselves as simple explorers of the "the Newness," conservative Bostonians picked up on this distinction and mockingly called them transcendentalists in an effort to ridicule them.[26]

The bright, sensitive young men and women who crowded into Boston's Masonic Temple were captivated by Emerson's message but did not seriously attempt to live up to it. Henry Thoreau was different. Sitting in Emerson's study beside Lidian and Elizabeth Hoar, he absorbed the words as if they were scripture. The choice of vocation, Emerson said, was the most important decision confronting any young person. His advice was to "do nothing to get money which is not worth your doing in its own account." If, to be true to one's inner dictates, it was necessary to give up the hope of material comfort and "doom" oneself "to endless lowness," then that reality should be embraced, not avoided. "We do not sufficiently discriminate between what appears and what is," he insisted. Men who believe that "bread and flesh" are "real" and "thought and will," "less real" are misguided. Let others "seem," he added. Trust yourself to "being." Open your senses and let God think through you. Then you will attain true culture. As Henry Thoreau's life would demonstrate, he took these words to heart.[27]

In the dead of winter few of Emerson's friends or acquaintances braved the stagecoach ride to Concord to visit him. By February when Lidian was away for a few weeks visiting Lucy Brown in Plymouth, Emerson was thrown almost completely on Henry for company. "My good Henry Thoreau made this else solitary afternoon sunny with his simplicity & clear perception," he noted after one visit. "Strait & decorous" himself, he enjoyed Henry's youthful exuberance. Not only was Henry's intellect of a high order, he was fun to be with. "I delight much in my young friend," he wrote on another occasion that month, "who seems to have as free & erect a mind as any I have ever met." For his part, Henry began to refer to Emerson in his journal as "My friend," an epithet he would reserve for him through thick and thin for a quarter of a century.[28]

3

During the long, cold winter months Henry Thoreau applied himself seriously "to the cultivation of general literature" under Emerson's watchful eye. Henry's taste in books was certainly of the highest order; he was reading the *Iliad* in Greek, for instance. But nothing about the prose or poetry he was writing suggested that he had unusual gifts. In fact, many of his contemporaries had displayed greater facility at an earlier age. Henry's journal entries read like those of a diligent student who wanted to please his teacher. And the poems that survive from this period seem no better than those that Mrs. Brown had carried to the Emerson house the previous summer. Still, Henry kept working. Emerson's suggestion that he "write out the history of his college life" as a prose exercise seems to have been ignored, but a few weeks later he began to compose a lecture that he delivered before the Concord Lyceum.[29]

Although Henry realized that benefiting from Emerson's guidance as he pursued his literary interests was an important opportunity for him, neither he nor Emerson expected the situation to last much longer. Emerson suggested in a letter to Mrs. Brown that she should visit Concord soon if she wanted to see Henry, because he would not always be there. Since Henry had as yet had no success in finding a school that would hire him in any of the nearby towns, pressure had been building within his family for him to look for work farther afield.

Breaking away from Emerson just as their relationship was showing so much promise was only part of the problem Henry faced, however. As his family and friends would recognize in time, he had a "peculiar interest" in Concord, one that reached beyond the normal attachment to home.[30] Going away to college had been his parents' idea, not his. Although he had lived in dormitory rooms for four years, his "heart and soul," he insisted, had remained behind "among the scenes of his boyhood." While still a student, Henry had asked his mother what he ought to do after graduation, and she had suggested that he "buckle on [his] knapsack" and "set out to seek his fortune." At the thought of this, tears had flooded his eyes and hurried down his cheeks.[31]

The root of Henry's "peculiar interest" in Concord lay in his bond with his mother. Mrs. Thoreau was a forceful woman whose energies were focused on her children. Since Henry, with his exceptional intelligence, stood out among them, it seemed natural to everyone that her interest should center on him. Unfortunately, as he grew older, Henry was unable to move beyond his deep-seated attachment to her. If this had meant simply that he would remain in Concord to be near her, it would not have mattered greatly. But the situation was more complicated than that. Whenever Henry was attracted to another woman, the repressed guilt associated with his feelings for his mother would rise up to torment him, a circumstance that would act to narrow his experience significantly in the years to come. He not only stayed close to home; he stayed single as well.

Given the strength of Henry's feelings, it was not surprising that the possibility of his having to settle hundreds of miles away put great stress on him emotionally. Nevertheless, in the spring of 1838 it looked as if he had hit on a solution that would make it easier for him to deal with moving away. His brother, John, was then teaching in Taunton, Massachusetts, about forty miles south of Concord. Henry wrote to him proposing that he leave his job when the present school term ended and accompany Henry to the west, possibly as far as Louisville, Kentucky. A family friend who had recently settled there had assured Henry that he knew of "a dozen" teaching jobs in the vicinity that either of the brothers would be fitted for.[32]

It wasn't long before Henry received encouraging news. John wrote that he expected to be released from his school in the middle of May and suggested that they set out together immediately after he had taken a week's vacation. Preparations for the journey began at once. In order to go, Henry had to borrow money, and it was Emerson who lent it to him. On April 2, Emerson entered the following item in his account book: "Cash to H. D. Thoreau, for which I took his note in interest, $100.00." Henry also took the precaution of obtaining a letter of recommendation from Josiah Quincy, Harvard's president, who declared that in college "his rank was high as a scholar in all the branches," which was somewhat of an exaggeration, and "his morals and general conduct [were] unexceptionable and exemplary," which was undoubtedly true. Mrs. Thoreau began readying her son's clothes.[33]

Just as John was expected home, a note arrived from Josiah Quincy telling Henry of an opening in a school in Alexandria, Virginia, for "a person who has had experience in school keeping." In his note Quincy stressed the importance of this qualification by underscoring the words. Despite the paucity of Henry's experience, he applied, with the inevitable result. He did not get the job, and in the meantime, John who understandably needed to secure his own income for the coming months had found employment in West Roxbury. While nothing prevented Henry from setting out on his own for Louisville where there was work to be had, he left instead for Maine where he had cousins living in Bangor. Although in his quest for a job Henry visited eleven Maine towns in quick succession, he returned home after two weeks still unemployed. In pursuing his search in established communities in Maine where qualified applicants were available he had once again made a choice where the odds were on the side of failure.[34]

By now it must have been clear to everyone that Henry would not be leaving Concord. For some time, Emerson had been attempting to find a teacher who would establish a school in the village operated on enlightened principles. Having served on the local school committee, he was thoroughly informed about the unsatisfactory state of public education in Concord, and he was also aware that the town's private school, the Concord Academy, had fallen on hard times. In the past Emerson had corresponded on the subject of setting up a new school with George Bradford, a cousin and classmate at the Harvard Divinity School, and had recently discussed the possibility with Bronson Alcott, whose Temple School in Boston was noted for its progressive teaching methods. Alcott had decided against the proposal, while Bradford continued to vacillate. With the money Henry had borrowed from Emerson he was in a position to make his friend's wish a reality. Within a month after his return from Maine, Henry had opened a school in the village and enrolled four students from Boston who boarded in the Thoreau home. Not long afterward, the Concord Academy closed its doors, and Henry arranged with its trustees to move his school into the academy building and assume its name.

Henry celebrated his twenty-first birthday on July 12, 1838. The fourteen-year gap between his age and Emerson's, which might not have seemed wide if they had met later in life, caused each to see the other at this point in a very specific way. To Emerson, the young schoolmaster was "My good Henry Thoreau," a youth to be enjoyed and guided, not a companion on an equal footing. To Henry, Emerson was a larger-than-life figure to whom he had formed an almost worshipful attachment. Outwardly, Henry's attachment took the form of imitation of Emerson's manner. David Greene Haskins, a college classmate of Henry's and a cousin of Emerson's, encountered him that summer in Emerson's study. "His short figure and general cast of countenance were, of course, unchanged," he observed, "but, in his manner, in the tones and inflections of his voice, in his modes of expression, even in the hesitations and pauses of his speech, he had become the counterpart of Mr. Emerson."[35]

On the surface Henry appeared to have adopted Emerson's philosophical outlook as thoroughly as he had adopted his manner. Already a "striking consonance of perceptions and attitudes" united them. Nevertheless, Henry entered a very important statement in his journal that summer: "Whatever of past or present wisdom has published itself to the world, is palpable falsehood till it come and utter itself by my side." Clearly Henry had accepted Emerson's injunction to think independently and was willing to apply it to Emerson's teachings as rigorously as to those of anyone else. He had no intention of passively accepting the older man's ideas without testing them against his own experience. This streak of independence would play itself out slowly over the years in his intellectual relationship with Emerson in a way that would not always please his mentor.[36]

4

In the autumn of 1838, Emerson suddenly found himself at the center of a controversy that threatened to change the course of his life. On July 15, he had delivered an address to the graduating class at Harvard's Divinity School. The subject he had chosen to explore was the validity of Christian doctrine. Emerson's movement away from the ministry had begun in 1831 after the death of his first wife. It had reached a crisis point the next year when he refused to administer communion to his parishioners and was compelled to resign his pastorate. Although for some time he had preached irregularly in the neighboring village of East Lexington, that arrangement was now drawing to a close. He preferred, he said, to "preach" in the lecture hall, which he called "the new pulpit."[37]

On the day of Emerson's talk, some one hundred people climbed the narrow staircase to the small chapel on the second floor of Divinity Hall. Dean John Gorham Palfrey and the members of his faculty filled the front pews. Behind them sat the seven graduating students and their families. Although such liberal-thinking friends of Emerson's as Elizabeth Peabody, Theodore Parker, George Ripley, and James Freeman Clarke were present, the audience was dominated by members of Boston's conservative establishment, and they were dismayed by what they heard. Emerson entreated his listeners to put their reliance in the moral constitution of man rather than in historical Christianity. Nature, he insisted, must be substituted for revelation "as the ground of faith."[38]

On that occasion, Emerson said nothing he had not already announced in *Nature*. But in addressing his talk directly to the leaders of Unitarian orthodoxy he made it impossible for them to disregard his position. By word of mouth and by letter the shock waves set in motion by his remarks moved quickly through Boston and its neighboring towns. A week later, when the address appeared in pamphlet form, newspapers and periodicals took up the attack. From a scholar whose radical message had agitated a small group of intellectuals, Emerson found himself transformed into a heretic whose opinions were perceived as a threat to the community at large.[39]

"They say the world is somewhat vexed with us," Emerson wrote to his brother William. "I trust it will recover its composure." Although he publicly assumed a good-humored attitude toward his critics, Emerson was disturbed and angered by their reaction. It wounded him to see his talk described in the press as a "great offense" that defiled "God, Religion, Christianity."[40] Nor did he savor being characterized in print as an "infidel and an atheist." In his view, he was "a dispassionate reporter" who should by right be accorded "perfect freedom" to pursue the truth as he saw it. Instead he discovered that his independence of mind could cost him dearly. The social and business leaders who set the tone in Boston were closing their ranks against him. Suddenly he had been thrust into the role of an outsider, a position he would continue to occupy until a decade after the Civil War.[41]

Alone among Emerson's friends, Henry Thoreau discovered an unexpected satisfaction in this new situation. As a child Henry had suffered from the taunts of his schoolmates because, among other things, his parents could not afford to buy him a sled with metal runners. At Harvard he was conspicuous among the black-clad students because of the greenish hue of his homemade suit. Experience had ingrained in him a deep feeling of apartness from those who were well off. Seeing Boston's elite turn their backs on Emerson gave Henry a new sense of identity with his friend. It was as if they now occupied common ground, not simply as intellectuals with sympathetic views but as men facing a hostile world. Emboldened by this shift in their relationship, Henry found himself speaking to Emerson with less restraint about his feelings.

One afternoon in November, as they walked from the village to Walden Pond, Henry was in a rebellious mood. The sight of the fences beside the road particularly angered him. He had not been a "party" to their erection, he declared, and therefore intended to "get over" them whenever he wanted to cross the lands they enclosed. He would not be confined to "a strip of road" when "God's earth" belonged as much to him as to anyone. Emerson's immediate reaction was to defend the institution of private property, not as an ideal system but as the best that had been "hit on" so far. He was, after all, a landowner and a man of independent means; the radicalism expressed in his view of religious questions did not extend itself to the existing economic order. He suggested that to "clear himself" of his frustration Henry "write it out into good poetry." Henry did not like the idea. He responded sharply that "in doing justice to the thought, the man did not always do justice to himself."[42]

While Henry's outspoken manner ordinarily appealed to Emerson, on this occasion it seemed to him that he had expressed himself with "undue and absurd dogmatism." Although Emerson's anger gradually subsided, he found it difficult to understand Henry's behavior. In the next several days as he turned the matter over in his mind, he reached the conclusion that Henry had simply been reacting to the stresses of the society he lived in, just as many other bright young men and women of the period seemed to be doing. Emerson was aware that not all of them railed against private property. Some found fault with social conventions; others, with the unequal distribution of wealth; still others, with the institution of slavery. Regardless of their individual preoccupations, however, Emerson sensed a rancor in these young people that seemed unhealthy to him. He decided to include a lecture in his upcoming series that would explore the effect of their obsessions on their lives.[43]

The lecture, which Emerson called "The Protest," was delivered before a crowded auditorium at Boston's Masonic Temple on January 16, 1839. Fearful that the controversy surrounding his Divinity Hall address would prevent people from attending his annual lecture series, Emerson had not taken a second possibility into account: that for each person who had been offended by his ideas there would be another who was attracted by them. What had changed was the character of the audience. The fashionable conservative crowd had stayed at home, but their seats were filled by "the free, the bold, the seeking" who were avid to hear that there was a better way to live than that pursued by their parents' generation.[44]

In "The Protest" Emerson explored his subject in a general way, but many of his comments were quite specific to Henry Thoreau's situation. The "protestor," as Emerson defined him, was a young person seeking to live a more fulfilling life than the conventional one. In a materialistic society like New England's, obvious difficulties stood in the way of achieving this goal, difficulties that were increased if the "protestor" had the poet's sensibility. Since he had to support himself while developing his genius, his anger was likely to be even greater than that of those who did not have a special gift.

Emerson saw a twofold danger in this situation. If the "protestor" were to allow his anger to dominate him completely, he would live a bitter, unsuccessful life. But to permit his anger to dissipate would lead to his settling for a trade that would provide a living but leave his talent unfulfilled. The difficult task facing Henry—and others like him—was to maintain his vision while supporting himself and continuing to develop his abilities.

Emerson made no secret of the fact that he had quoted Henry indirectly in "The Protest," and it was soon being said in Boston that he considered him "one of the wonders of the age." This created a situation with inherent difficulties for each of the men. Emerson had let it be known that he believed strongly in Henry's abilities, even though in December he had complained in his journal that Henry's poetry was lacking in originality and that he was allowing "mass" to compensate for "quality." Having committed himself publicly, Emerson quite naturally wanted to be proven right in his judgment. This in turn increased the pressure on Henry. Now it became even more important for him to live up to Emerson's expectations.[45]

5

Despite the effort Henry had put into operating a school that was run on enlightened pedagogical principles, his academy had not attracted enough students to be profitable. As the months passed, it became clear that he needed help if the enterprise was not to founder, and once again he turned to his brother, John. Early in February an ad appeared in the *Concord Freeman* announcing that in the future the school would be operated under John's direction with Henry assisting him "in the classical department." John's decision to take over the school not only relieved Henry of considerable responsibility but also strengthened the school's appeal for parents. Three years older than Henry, John was a personable young man and an experienced teacher as well. With John's return imminent, Henry was suddenly "seize[d]" by a creative "frenzy." Emerson, who looked on approvingly, reported that Henry had "broke out into good poetry" and, what would prove more significant in the future, "better prose." Emerson immediately wrote to Margaret Fuller, the friend whose literary judgment he trusted most, to tell her that Henry's poetry was improving and that he wanted her to see for herself when she came to Concord.[46]

Seven years Emerson's junior, Margaret Fuller had determined early in life to dedicate her remarkable energies to the pursuit of fame. Thrown on her own resources at eighteen by the death of her father, a lawyer and former congressman, she had taught school to earn a living while developing her literary skills. Now twenty-six, she had already published several articles and had begun work on a biography of Goethe. Her translation of that writer's conversations with Eckermann would soon go to press in Boston. These efforts had brought her attention, but not contentment. "What have I gained by *my* precocity?" she mused. "I have never been happy."[47]

At the end of March, Margaret journeyed to Concord from Providence, Rhode Island, where she was then living and teaching. When she arrived at the Emersons', the house was crowded with other guests. A month earlier, Lidian Emerson had given birth to a second child. Emerson's brother William and William's wife had traveled from their home in New York City to see the baby girl, and Elizabeth Hoar had moved in to help supervise the servants. While Margaret would have preferred having Emerson to herself, she nevertheless enjoyed the opportunity to shine in a large group. Elizabeth Hoar who shared a bedroom with her on this occasion was awed by "the regal manner in which she takes possession of society wherever she is, and creates her own circumstances."[48] Accused of being "disciplined, artificial" in her conversation, of bringing with her "treasured thoughts to tell," Margaret "pleaded guilty." She was aware that this behavior was a manifestation of a deep insecurity, although she carefully hid the fact. She did not dare "lay aside the armor" of her social manner, she confided to her journal, for without it, "I had lain bleeding in the field long since."[49]

Like Emerson, Margaret could find pleasure in the verse of gifted amateurs. If Henry's work had been presented to her in this light, perhaps she would have greeted it with enthusiasm. But Emerson insisted on taking his young friend's efforts seriously, and she therefore responded in like manner. In her opinion, Henry's poems seemed more like the exercises of a student than the expressions of a poet who possessed a personal vision. While in Concord, Margaret had the opportunity to form a clearer opinion of Henry himself. In his letters to her, Emerson had referred to Henry casually as his "protester," and it was with considerable interest that she listened to Emerson repeat his lecture on that subject before the Concord Lyceum. Her observations of Henry did not support Emerson's picture of a youth struggling to express his genius. On one or two occasions she thought she caught a glimpse of the promise Emerson extolled, but in the main Henry did not seem to her to be markedly different from other shy, sensitive young men she had encountered.[50]

Early in April, Margaret returned home to Providence. If her visit had proved anything to Emerson, it was that he could not expect others, even those he considered the most perceptive among his friends, to share his expansive view of Henry's future. While this did not shake his faith in his young friend, it reinforced the fear, always hovering somewhere in the back of his mind, that Henry might never achieve the level of literary success Emerson believed to be within his reach.

2

A Troubled Dream

On July 20, 1839, a seventeen-year-old girl stepped out of the stagecoach when it drew to a halt in Concord. Although her features were plain, her face beamed with an interior beauty that enchanted all who saw her. Her name was Ellen Sewall, and she had come from Scituate, a coastal town located a few miles south of Boston, to spend two weeks at the Thoreau house where her grandmother, Mrs. Joseph Ward, and her aunt, Miss Prudence Ward, were paying guests.

At that time there was a dearth of eligible young women in Concord. John Thoreau who had returned home the previous winter to preside over Henry's school described the town as a "Sahara" with nothing to offer but "antiquated Spinsters." Ellen Sewall provided a delightful contrast. Since her last visit to Concord when she was fourteen years old, she had blossomed into young womanhood. Her enthusiasm for experience, her bright manner, and her intelligence were like a breath of fresh air for John and Henry. They were determined to see that she enjoyed herself thoroughly while she visited their home.[1]

During the nineteenth century in a small town like Concord the pleasures of life were simple. Walking through the woods, rowing on the river, going berrying, and searching for Indian arrowheads were all considered splendid ways to pass a summer afternoon. Ellen was invited by the brothers to do all these things and many others. They went to parties and picnics and even to see a giraffe then being exhibited in town. As the days passed, the young woman's attraction for the Thoreau brothers grew stronger and stronger. Even the usually reticent Henry made a notation in his journal that was highly suggestive of his state of mind: "There is no remedy for love but to love more."[2]

It didn't take long, however, for John and Henry to discover that they couldn't have Ellen all to themselves. John Shepard Keyes, a Harvard student back in town for the summer, was introduced to her at the home of Captain Moore, whose gardens she was viewing with her Aunt Prudence. That evening Keyes encountered her at a party, sat with her at supper, and even managed to walk her home. Later in her stay he engaged her attention at a second gathering and again accompanied her home. But the Thoreau brothers didn't let that daunt them. They continued to hover around her, filling her remaining days in Concord with a round of enjoyable activities.[3]

There was a great deal of disappointment on all sides when Ellen had to climb back into the stagecoach to return to Scituate at the end of her visit. Ellen, who admitted that she had cried as the town vanished behind her, would miss the excitement of being shepherded from one social event to the other by the two young men. As for Henry and John, they felt as if everything that was bright and charming was suddenly being whisked from the town. Shortly after Ellen's departure it was discovered that she had left behind the Indian relics she had gathered during her walks in the country. In their response to this situation the Thoreau brothers revealed a difference in their makeup that would prove crucial in their relationship to Ellen in the coming months. John, the more socially aggressive of the two, immediately gathered up the relics and sent them to Ellen with a note. Henry, who lived very much within himself, sat by silently and watched.[4]

In his note to Ellen, John mentioned that he and Henry would be leaving in a few weeks on their own vacation. For some time the brothers had been planning to take a sailing trip together on the Concord and Merrimack Rivers. That spring they had decided their old boat was not in good enough condition to sail as far as they wished, and they had gone to work building a worthier vessel that they fashioned to resemble a fisherman's dory. It was fifteen feet long and three and a half feet wide with two sets of oars, slender poles "for shoving in shallow places," and two masts. According to Henry, they painted it "green below, with a border of blue, with reference to the two elements in which it was to spend its existence."[5]

On Saturday, August 31, the brothers packed their new boat with pota-toes, melons, and other stores and set out on their journey. They anchored the boat often as they traveled slowly north so that they could take long walks in the countryside. They fished, picked blueberries, and went sight-seeing. Most afternoons they set up their tent near the shore and cooked their evening meal, but they also checked into an inn on occasion and passed one night at the home of friends. For Henry, especially, the two weeks they spent traveling together was a period of the most intense happiness. It seemed to him that the spiritual union he was experiencing with John was as satisfying in its way as any relationship he could imagine.

The spell was broken as soon as they returned to Concord, however. John immediately packed clean clothes and, leaving Henry behind with his manuscripts, hurried off on a trip that took him to Scituate where he could be with Ellen for two days. John's timing was perfect, for Ellen's parents had left for Niagara Falls, and she was alone in the house with her two younger brothers. John's visit gave Ellen "much pleasure," she informed her Aunt Prudence, and she admitted to being "very lonely indeed for some time after he left."[6]

2

During the autumn Henry and John Thoreau were busily involved in run-ning their school. Luckily the brothers were in complete accord about how to educate young boys. Providing their pupils with a cultural and moral basis for confronting experience seemed more consequential to them than the kind of learning by rote that was practiced in the public schools of the period. Each morning one of the brothers would begin the day by delivering a talk on a general subject he considered important. Years later one former student vividly recalled Henry's talks, which dealt with such varied subjects as the seasons and their beauty, design in the universe, and profanity. The latter subject Henry explored in a "fresh, amusing, and sensible" way by "violently and frequently" interjecting the word "Boot-jack" into an ordi-nary sentence to demonstrate the inanity of street language.[7]

Like good teachers of all eras the brothers approached each child sympa-thetically and as an individual. Toward the end of his life Thomas Hosmer, a student of theirs who had walked four miles from Bedford to Concord each day to attend the school, declared that he would never forget the "kindness and good will" they had shown him. Another student of the school wondered how it had been possible to maintain "military discipline" in the classroom when "there was never a boy flogged or threatened." Under the brothers' tutelage, going to school became a rewarding experience instead of a chore.[8]

John's arrival eight months earlier to take over the administration of the academy had not only reunited the brothers, it had relieved Henry of a burden for which he was not really suited. For the first time since his graduation from college, Henry was able to sit down at his desk in the attic to write without a sense of anxiety about the future hanging over his head. The surge of creative activity that had begun during the winter had culminated in June in a poem Henry called "Sympathy." The "gentle boy" to whom it was addressed was Ellen Sewall's eleven-year-old brother Edmund who had visited the Thoreaus for a week just before her arrival that summer.

Before leaving on his vacation with John, Henry had shown "Sympathy" to Emerson. A "beautiful poem," Emerson had called it, the "purest strain & the loftiest, I think, that has yet pealed from this unpoetic American forest." Although not as great an achievement as Emerson claimed, the poem was markedly more professional than anything Henry had yet written. He was making undeniable progress—not simply with his poems but with the essays he was writing as well—and now had to begin confronting the question of how to find an outlet for his work.[9]

In this, luck was with him. Under Emerson's aegis a group of like-minded intellectuals had come together to form a new magazine, which they called the *Dial*. The need for a journal that would open its pages to progressive writers had been recognized for several years. In 1832 Emerson had seriously considered publishing one with the help of his brothers. In 1835 his friend Henry Hedge had proposed that Emerson, Margaret Fuller, George Ripley, and others join forces to start a journal "devoted to spiritual philosophy." Later, when Hedge settled permanently in Maine, Emerson tried to persuade the English writer Thomas Carlyle to emigrate to the United States to serve as editor of the proposed publication.[10]

Although none of these attempts had succeeded, the idea had never been completely abandoned. In May the subject of establishing a new magazine had come up at a meeting of an informal club of which both Emerson and Margaret Fuller were members. The club came together several times a year to consider matters of importance to their circle. Although most members of the group were Unitarian ministers, literary radicals and others with progressive leanings were welcomed as well. Despite their claim that they were simply a group of the "like-minded" meeting occasionally to discuss issues of interest to themselves, they were known to be proponents of the "new thought," and their group was quickly dubbed the Transcendental Club. Being "like-minded," however, did not mean that the club's members enjoyed a meeting of the mind on all issues. Henry Hedge, one of the originators of the club, made the distinction in this way. The club was made up of individuals who "earnestly seek the truth," he said, while respecting "other men's freedom & other men's opinions." If they did not necessarily "agree in opinion," they did at least "agree in spirit."[11]

The leading topic of discussion at the May meeting of the Transcendental Club had been "the present temper of our journals." While this discussion had not led to a concrete proposal for taking action, a persuasive case had been made for the issuance of a periodical by the group, and when the club had met again in September, it had tackled the subject of a new magazine in earnest. Emerson had said earlier that he knew of enough promising people "who write nowhere else" to launch a periodical. Although he was absent at the September meeting, Margaret Fuller, Bronson Alcott, George Ripley, Henry Hedge, and Theodore Parker joined the others who had gathered in the Boston home of one of the group, where it was decided that the attempt to establish a journal should be made. In succeeding weeks, it was agreed that the journal would be called the *Dial,* that it would be published quarterly, and that Margaret Fuller would edit it.[12]

Emerson wasted no time in taking advantage of the opportunity that the *Dial* presented to Henry Thoreau. In his opinion, "Sympathy," the poem Henry had shown him during the summer, should introduce the young man to the reading public. Without consulting Margaret Fuller, Emerson arranged for Henry to contribute the poem to the first issue of the *Dial,* then wrote to Margaret informing her of his action.

3

With Christmas approaching, Henry and John Thoreau decided to accompany Ellen Sewall's Aunt Prudence to Scituate to spend part of the holiday season at the Sewall home. While there, Henry wrote poetry during solitary walks on the beach and played his flute as Ellen polished the family "brasses." With his grave, courteous demeanor, he was "Dr. Thoreau" to her, while John was a source of endless merriment. She decided later that, without fully realizing it, she had fallen in love with them as a pair, two vital and interesting young men whose differences complemented each other.[13]

In the eyes of Ellen's parents the Thoreau brothers were hardly ideal prospects for their daughter's hand. Ellen's father was a minister who could not have been expected to take kindly to young men from a family that held such liberal views as the Thoreaus. That Henry did not even attend church when he was visiting Scituate did nothing to reassure Reverend Sewall. In addition there was little likelihood that the Concord Academy would ever produce sufficient income to permit either of the brothers to establish a family in comfortable circumstances.

These considerations did not influence Ellen's attitudes, however. After the return of the Thoreau brothers and Aunt Prudence to Concord, Ellen wrote a letter to her aunt that she must have known would be read to the whole Thoreau family. In it, she admitted missing her friends a great deal. "The house seems deserted since you left us," she wrote. "I never was so lonely in my life as the day you went away, and I have not quite recovered my spirits yet." Soon John had put two happy surprises in the mail for her: some opals to be displayed in the cabinet that held her natural history collection and an admonition to her little brother Georgie to give her a kiss for him and wish her a Happy New Year. Characteristically, Henry expressed his appreciation for the hospitality shown him in Scituate by sending a volume of poems by Jones Very, a young Salem writer, to Ellen's father and a group of his own manuscript poems to Ellen. Henry was hurt when Ellen expressed her gratitude for John's offering but did not mention his. When word of this got back to her, she hurriedly penned a letter to Aunt Prudence assuring her that her "neglecting to thank Henry for his original poetry was entirely unintentional," that she regretted it "exceedingly," and that the family was "much pleased at receiving it."[14]

The tenor of Ellen Sewall's letters encouraged Henry and John Thoreau to believe that she was fond of both of them, as of course, she was. Therefore, there seemed to be no reason for either of the brothers to relinquish the hope that *he* would be the one who would ultimately be favored by her affections. The trio had set out on a path that could only lead to difficulties in the future.

4

As Henry and John continued to dream of Ellen, Emerson found himself confronted by a practical problem. The writers who had agreed to contribute to the new transcendental magazine had one by one backed away from their promises. Foremost among these defaulters was Henry Hedge who wrote to Margaret in January 1840 explaining his broken promise by saying he feared he would be labeled "an atheist in disguise" if he openly identified himself with the transcendentalists by publishing in the new journal. For Hedge, who continued to serve as a Unitarian minister, there was, of course, a great deal at stake. To associate himself publicly with transcendental tenets would not be without consequences for a man in his position, and he could not afford to accept them. But the problem ran deeper than that. In his letter he made it clear that he disagreed with Emerson on certain issues. The fact was, as James Freeman Clarke complained, everyone in the Transcendental Club had "a distinct idea, plan, or project" and "no two persons" could be "found to agree in any." While the members continued to be united "in spirit," it was proving difficult to bring them together in support of the new magazine, even though it was being established to promulgate their views. Under the circumstances Margaret Fuller despaired of publishing the first issue of the *Dial* on July 1 as planned. Although Emerson had no official relationship with the magazine, he wrote to Margaret in the tone of a man who had taken charge. He would rely, he said, on a group of young writers of his acquaintance to fill the necessary pages. On the list was Henry Thoreau.[15]

Emerson had recently read a draft of a critical essay Henry had written about the Greek satirist Persius and suggested that he revise it for the magazine. Although this was an excellent opportunity for Henry to see his work in print, he declined. He informed his friend that he had "too mean an opinion of 'Persius' or any of his pieces to care to revise them." He did, however, agree to the publication of the essay if either Emerson or Margaret Fuller would be willing to rework it. Emerson was a remarkably patient man. From his correspondence with Margaret Fuller during the next few days it appears that he undertook the task himself. There was "too much manner" in the essay, he admitted, and "too little method, in any common sense of the word." But he found a value in it that set it apart from conventional criticism. It had, he felt, "always a spiritual meaning even when the literal does not hold."[16]

At times there is a suggestion in Emerson's correspondence that he was more anxious than Henry to see his young friend's work published. Informing Margaret Fuller a few days later that "Persius" had been rewritten he asked, "Can you not put it in Number One?" The next day, as if to underscore the importance of the matter, he repeated the question. After Margaret had agreed, Henry took the manuscript home with him for "recorrection." The word is Emerson's, and it hints at the possibility that the protégé did not altogether approve of the changes his mentor had made.[17]

Soon after the question of the "Persius" essay was settled, Emerson invited Henry to attend a meeting of the Transcendental Club at his home where "the nature of poetry" was to be discussed. While Henry knew most, if not all, of those gathered in Emerson's study, meeting as an equal with a group that included intellectual and literary New Englanders like Bronson Alcott, Margaret Fuller, Henry Hedge, and Jones Very altered his relationship to them. He could no longer be considered, nor need he think of himself, as merely an ambitious young man favored by Emerson. If he hadn't had something to contribute himself, he wouldn't have been invited.[18]

Henry's inclusion in this gathering seems to have marked a turning point in his intellectual life. Not long afterward in a letter to his sister Helen he referred to himself as her "transcendental brother." It was not that his ideas had changed but that his identity with the transcendental movement had solidified. Henry was fortunate that his connection with Emerson had brought him into contact with a group of intellectuals whose philosophical speculations he could endorse, saving him from the arduous task of thinking through many of these questions on his own. As Sherman Paul has noted, Henry "had leaped to liberation over that great distance from Locke to Coleridge that had caused his elders, Emerson, Alcott, Ripley and Parker, so much anguish and doubt." Spared that effort, he could advance more readily to a consideration of questions relating to his own view of transcendental ideas as they were evolving at that time. In the late spring of 1840 Henry's journal abruptly began to deal in depth with the concerns of transcendental thought, as if these questions had assumed a new importance for him. Under Emerson's tutelage he was evolving from a bright college graduate into a serious student slowly working toward an independent view of the world.[19]

Despite Margaret Fuller's fears, she managed to get the first issue of the *Dial* to the printers in time for publication on July 1. Looking over the magazine when he received a copy, Emerson realized that it did not measure up to the expectations that had been raised for it. In commenting to Margaret on the issue he made a suggestion that must have delighted Henry Thoreau, if he knew of it. Emerson referred to Henry's first published poem, "Sympathy," as being "good enough" to save the "whole bad Number" and wondered if it should not have been set in larger type than the rest of the text to indicate its importance.[20]

Immediately after the magazine's appearance a storm of criticism broke out on all sides. The *Dial's* editors were attacked in the press as "zanies" and "Bedlamites."[21] Although irrational, this response sprang from a commonly held belief: that the transcendentalists were "visionaries and enthusiasts, who in pursuit of principles neglected duties."[22] Even Orestes Brownson, an early supporter, became convinced that there was too much "cant" being heard from the transcendentalists about "cultivating one's being." He found it "quite nauseating."[23] In light of this, it was hardly surprising that "men of the world" reacted with growls of anger. Their response, Emerson observed, represented a fear that an adherence to these ideas would "unfit their sons for business and their daughters for society, without fitting them for anything else." In face of this outpouring of scorn one fact stood out more clearly than ever. Emerson and his young friend Henry Thoreau were united at the core of a small band of intellectuals in opposition to a broad range of public opinion.[24]

5

In June, when Ellen Sewall traveled to Concord to spend a few days at the Thoreaus' with Aunt Prudence, the situation was open to misunderstanding on all three points of the triangle that had been formed. As Henry took Ellen rowing on the river in his boat, he dreamed about how pleasant his life would be if he could spend it alone with her. At the same time John found himself wondering if he dare propose to their visitor. Oblivious of the strength of the feelings that were gathering around her, Ellen continued to show openly the affection she felt for both of them.

A few weeks after Ellen's visit, John traveled to Scituate to see her. During a walk with Ellen on the beach, he proposed. Caught up in the emotion of the moment, she found herself accepting him. Later in the day when Ellen's mother learned what had happened, she expressed the fear that Ellen's father, Reverend Sewall, would not be pleased. Ellen had already begun to suspect that she had made a mistake and saw in this a way to back out of her promise. A very unhappy John Thoreau returned to Concord on July 19 with the news of his rejection. On that day Henry expressed his relief in his journal. He had made no entries on the previous two days, apparently upset by the thought that Ellen might accept John. Now he observed rapturously that the night sky was "spangled with fresh stars." The major obstacle in his path had been removed. He was free to propose to Ellen himself.[25]

But instead of bringing Henry peace, the removal of John from the picture merely intensified a struggle that was taking place within him. During Henry's lifetime, the accepted explanation among his friends for Henry's reticence regarding Ellen was that, as the younger brother, Henry had gallantly deferred to John's interest in her. Actually the situation was more complicated than that. Henry's attraction to Ellen had stirred up his forbidden feelings toward his mother. This in turn had associated John in his mind with his father. While drawn strongly to Ellen, Henry found himself in a predicament that generated intense fears within him. He seemed to be reliving the experiences of his early childhood when he had seen himself as his father's rival for his mother's affection. Conceding John's right to pursue Ellen had until this time left him free to indulge his longing for her in his imagination while providing a convenient excuse for inaction.

Since Ellen's visit a year earlier, Henry had been trying to deal with the anxiety aroused in him by "the tournament of love." In his journal he had turned again and again to a complex of ideas surrounding the difficulties that "passion and appetite" awoke in him. He would never be, he admitted, "free from the suspicion of a lower sympathy" where women were concerned, but desire created a conflict in him that he could not easily resolve. Years later as he lay dying he told his sister Sophia that he had always loved Ellen. While there is no reason to doubt his assertion, it is clear from his journal comments that his sexual identity was fragile. The barrier that prevented him from openly pursuing Ellen was not an external one; it lay within himself.[26]

Confronted by internal pressures, Henry found it necessary at times to imagine a different relationship from the one he dreamed of with Ellen, a relationship that would offer him emotional rewards without subjecting him to intolerable tensions. On these occasions he turned in his thoughts to a consideration of ideal friendship. Emerson's sentiment—"I am a worshipper of Friendship, and cannot find any other good equal to it"— undoubtedly encouraged Henry to pursue the inquiry. "Commonly we degrade Love and Friendship by presenting them under the aspect of a trivial dualism," Henry observed. But if love and friendship are really a unitary state, he reasoned, might it not be possible to build a satisfactory life with "some gentle soul" of his own sex instead of with Ellen?[27] His recent vacation with John had provided him with a model of how a relationship of this kind could work in practice. The thought of this caused a cautionary red flag to shoot up in Henry's mind, however. Under these circumstances, the friend would have to "commend virtue to mankind" through his "carriage and conduct." In fact, Henry insisted sternly, he should be "as much better than my-self as my aspiration is beyond my attainment." Even when taking refuge in fantasies about an imaginary friend Henry found it necessary to hedge his feelings with rigid prohibitions.[28]

Without doubt, Henry Thoreau faced a dilemma. He summed it up this way: "Paradise belongs to Adam and Eve. Plato's Republic is governed by Platonic love." What that opposition meant in terms of his own life was clear to him. In his opinion marriage to Ellen would offer him a more rewarding future than he could hope to find through friendship with a member of his own sex. The difficult question confronting him was whether his nature would permit him to enjoy that happier state.[29]

6

Shortly after John's proposal, Ellen Sewall's parents sent her to Watertown, New York, to stay with a cousin with whom she had been at boarding school during her early teen years. From there, far enough away from John Thoreau so that he could not pay her unexpected visits, she continued to correspond with Aunt Prudence. In a letter written toward the end of October, she recalled the "happy times" she had spent in Concord and inquired about both John and Henry. In particular, she asked, "What great work is Henry engaged in now?" This unexpected show of interest on her part infused Henry with courage. He made up his mind to write to Ellen asking her to marry him. Ellen, who was taken completely by surprise by his proposal, felt miserable when she read his letter. She liked Henry very much but could not envision spending her life with him. While she wished that he had not written, she was relieved that at least he had not confronted her "on the *beach* or anywhere else." A second such encounter would have been more than she could have borne. Before answering Henry, Ellen sought her father's advice. He directed her to write in a "*short, explicit* and *cold* manner" and to waste no time in doing so. Composing that letter was one of the hardest tasks of Ellen's young life, but she did it. Henry may not have been surprised by the nature of her reply, but he had to have been deeply wounded by it.[30]

Not long afterward when Emerson wrote that a writer ought neither to be married nor to have a family, he was most likely thinking of how family responsibilities stood in the way of the accomplishment of his own literary aims. Henry would never confront this quandary. With Ellen's refusal, his brief search for a wife ended. If she had consented to marry him, Henry might have achieved a happier balance in his life than he was fated to experience. Instead he faced a future in which his deepest feelings would only find release in the context of friendship. The complication that this created for him lay in the simple reality that others, because of their more varied emotional commitments, would not necessarily be free to reciprocate with the intensity he desired.

Making matters more difficult for Henry at this time was a coolness that had grown up between him and his brother, a coolness that seems clearly related to Henry's proposal to Ellen. Perhaps John had not completely given up all hope in that direction. Henry himself does not specify the cause of their "difference," merely identifying it as a situation in which he had acted in his own "highest interest but completely failed in my hopes." Although he protested that "no innocence can quite stand up under suspicion—if it is conscious of being suspected," an indication that he harbored guilty feelings, he decided that an apology was out of the question.[31]

By February, Henry had begun to find it intolerable to continue living at home given his deteriorating relations with John. He began looking around for a farm to rent in Concord, presumably with the intention of working it himself. And he even discussed the possibility of joining a community such as Brook Farm, although he quickly pushed that idea aside with the comment that he would "rather keep batchelor's hall in hell than go to board in heaven." At the end of March, as the winter term was nearing its end, the brothers abruptly announced that their school was closing. The reason given was that John's health was poor. His weight had fallen to one hundred twelve pounds, and immediately after classes ended he left for the mountains of New Hampshire to recuperate. In the next few days Henry arranged to buy a farm not far from the village, but at the last minute the farmer's wife objected and the sale fell through.[32]

During this period Emerson had been observing a change in Henry's behavior that concerned him. To maintain his psychological balance Henry had withdrawn farther into himself. "I almost shrink from the arduousness of meeting men erectly day by day," he admitted. Although he was naturally reticent, this increase in his propensity to silence was a clear signal that the situation was growing serious. At first Emerson appears merely to have wondered why they saw so little of each other, or when they met, why Henry seemed more silent than usual. But as the days passed he began to sense the depth of Henry's need for help and decided to take matters into his own hands. If Henry would like to, he could move into the little sleeping alcove at the top of the stairs in the Emerson home, he told him. There he would have all the time he needed to devote to his writing and, by tending the garden, he could pay for his room and board.[33]

To Henry the offer seemed to be an ideal solution to his problem. On April 18, with the understanding that he would only stay for a year, he moved in.

3

The Beautiful and the Brave

Emerson derived a deep pleasure from meeting interesting and attractive new people although he often found their company overly stimulating. He was "so born & qualified for solitude," he said, "that as a spoonful of wine makes some people drunk, so a little society . . . turns my head with too much excitement." While Henry Thoreau had been grappling with his attraction to Ellen Sewall and the aftermath of that episode, Emerson had been growing closer to a small circle of Margaret Fuller's intimate friends whose breeding and demeanor proved highly stimulating to his sensibilities. It was an involvement that, in its own way, altered Emerson's attitude toward the practice of friendship as directly as Henry's experience with Ellen influenced the role friendship would play in his own life.[1]

The three friends about whom Margaret Fuller cared most—Caroline Sturgis, Samuel Gray Ward, and Anna Barker—were contemporaries of Henry Thoreau. But they were not at all like him or the other young men Margaret and Emerson knew who yearned to write but lacked a sure means of support. Wealthy, leisured, cultured without being intellectual, Margaret's friends were free to pursue their interests as they pleased. Conversation, which Emerson saw as "the practice and consummation of friendship," was one of their principal pleasures, a circumstance that immediately drew him to them. As he came to know them better, he could barely contain his excitement. They had led him, he believed, into an enchanted world where friendship existed untouched by mundane considerations.[2]

Caroline Sturgis was the sole member of Margaret Fuller's intimate circle Emerson had previously encountered in Boston drawing rooms. Having heard Margaret praise her repeatedly, Emerson suggested in the spring of 1838 that Margaret invite Caroline to accompany her to the Emersons' for a week, an invitation that was accepted. During her first visit there, Caroline sat quietly most of the time while the others conversed, but when she spoke at last, it was to ask the sort of question that "surprised" Emerson into "very pleasant thoughts." After Caroline's departure, Emerson complained that she had permitted him only "glimpses" of her mind, but he invited her back nonetheless. On her return, their walks in the woods together and their quiet moments alone in his study offered greater satisfactions. This time it had been "a sincerely good visit," he announced.[3]

According to a contemporary, Caroline was "plain but with fine eyes." Emerson agreed about her eyes, calling them "a compliment to the human race." They were fit, he said, to inspire a poet to the "task of expressing their genius in verse." One of four daughters of a wealthy merchant, Caroline refused to conform to the pattern of a well-bred young lady of her period. She was described by those who knew her as "picturesque," "gypsy-like," preferring solitary hours with her books to parties and other social activities.[4] Although she frequently jotted down short poems, she had no illusions about being talented. What she lacked was a focus for her life. Caroline did not complain, as Margaret Fuller did, that women were "slaves"; her family's wealth and the indulgence of her parents permitted her to do as she pleased.[5] But she yearned for fulfillment without knowing where to turn to seek it. Her growing acquaintance with Emerson promised her entry into a world of the mind where she believed she would find greater satisfaction than in her usual occupations.

Not long after Caroline Sturgis's first visit to the Emerson home, Margaret Fuller's friend Samuel Gray Ward also accepted an invitation to call.[6] Sam had recently returned from a lengthy stay in Europe and had brought with him several hundred engravings and sketches of the works of Renaissance masters that he had acquired while abroad. On two occasions during the summer of 1838 Margaret arrived in Concord carrying a portfolio that contained selections from these works. "Saw beautiful pictures yesterday," Emerson noted in his journal after her second visit, singling out a chalk sketch of Raphael's Sibyls for special notice. Although he had encountered many of the great works of Western art while touring Europe ten years earlier, Emerson realized that he knew very little about art and artists. He decided to send a note to Sam asking him to "come and spend a day" in Concord so they could discuss the subject.[7]

Emerson discovered in Margaret's friend "a beautiful & noble youth of a most subtle & magnetic nature." Like Caroline Sturgis, Sam Ward had been born into a rich Boston family. His father, an investment banker and partner in the Baring Brothers firm, wanted him to become a businessman, but Sam had other ideas about his future. Like most of the young men and women Emerson found attractive, Sam wrote poetry, but he did not consider this to be his true vocation. He was a student of art and literature who planned to live "a scholar's life."[8]

Sam Ward aroused an intense curiosity in Emerson who saw in him a young man with "tastes" similar to his own. But Emerson also recognized that Sam possessed "tastes and powers and corresponding circumstances" that were completely foreign to him. Sam's choice of painting as his central concern combined with his equally real interest in poetry and literary matters intrigued Emerson. In addition, Emerson was awed by the freedom Sam enjoyed to engage in these activities due to the wealth his father had accumulated. Sam's unusual combination of interests and the power he possessed to pursue them exerted a strong pull on Emerson's imagination. More than with any other young man of his acquaintance except Henry Thoreau, Emerson actively sought Sam Ward out. Nevertheless, Emerson found it difficult to establish the sort of intimacy with him that he desired, despite his repeated attempts to arrange to meet him. Fifteen months after their first encounter, Emerson was still seeking an "opportunity of being better friends."[9]

Anna Barker, the third member of Margaret Fuller's small circle, did not appear on Emerson's horizon until three years after Margaret had begun telling him about her. Although Anna came from a New England family, her father's business activities had taken her parents first to New York, then to New Orleans, where they were still living. The Barkers often spent part of the year in Newport, Rhode Island, however, and while there Anna could be depended upon to journey north to see Margaret. When Anna visited in October 1839, Emerson passed several hours on two successive days at Margaret's home in Jamaica Plain, then a suburb not yet incorporated into Boston, getting to know Margaret's guest.

Unlike Caroline Sturgis and Sam Ward, Anna Barker had made no attempt to set herself apart from the privileged society into which she had been born. "So lovely, so fortunate & so remote from my own experiences," Emerson observed after meeting her. He would comment later that the "predominating character of her nature" was not "thought but emotion." Nevertheless, the frankness and sincerity of her manner made a strong impression on Emerson, as did her beauty. Even though Anna did not resemble the women he "most admired & loved," Emerson found that she didn't "distance" him, as women whose interests centered on the social world usually did. Since Anna trusted him instinctively, a warm sympathy quickly arose between them.[10]

Emerson's relative isolation in Concord made it somewhat difficult for him to pursue his developing relationship with the members of Margaret Fuller's intimate circle. Since he could not simply walk down the road and call on these young people as he did with Henry Thoreau, he chiefly corresponded with them. To keep in touch, they exchanged letters, poems, even their journals. But Emerson also made it his business to see them in Boston as often as possible. They met in galleries, went to concerts, and gathered in the homes of mutual friends. Considering himself lucky to have become acquainted with them, Emerson invested a great deal of energy in their pursuit.

Over time Emerson became convinced that in getting to know Margaret's most intimate friends, he had discovered a world from which the temptations of ordinary experience had been banished. Since Margaret's friends derived deep enjoyment from being together and exchanging their thoughts, he happily concluded that theirs was a union of the mind, divorced from earthly considerations. To him they seemed to be living proof that platonic friendships could be maintained on the highest level—at least by "fine people," as he put it. The truth, of course, was somewhat different, as he would learn eventually to his regret.[11]

2

Shortly after Emerson's initial meetings with Anna Barker at Margaret Fuller's house, Margaret visited Emerson in Concord. While there, she told him that during Anna's stay in Jamaica Plain she had learned that Anna and Sam Ward had fallen in love. Although to Emerson the story Margaret recounted might seem to be "a chronicle of sweet romance, of love & nobleness," for Margaret it had an entirely different significance. In subsequent weeks she confided her dilemma to Emerson in great detail and lent him letters and pages from her journal that further clarified her predicament.[12]

Margaret had been living and teaching in Providence, Rhode Island, in the summer of 1838 when Sam had returned to Boston from New York City, where he had been working in a mercantile firm since his return from Europe.[13] While the distance between Providence and Boston did not permit them to see each other with any frequency, their separation made it easier for her to weave romantic fantasies about Sam and for him to ignore what was happening. Margaret knew that Sam was unhappy about the pressure he was under to give up his intention of living a scholar's life in order to commit himself fully to a business career, and she offered him the sympathy and understanding that he was not getting from his father. Although brief, their interlude of emotional closeness lasted long enough for Margaret to allow herself to fall in love with him, even though, as she admitted, "age, position, and pursuits being so different," the difficulties facing a union between them were almost insurmountable.[14]

That autumn Sam Ward set out on a long journey that would lead him first through the Midwest, then south to New Orleans. Although his ostensible purpose for traveling to Louisiana was to assess the cotton market for his father's firm, another of his motives for going seems to have been to see Anna Barker. They had met while he was a student at Harvard, and he had most recently encountered her while she was traveling with friends of his in Switzerland where he had spent two months in her company. On that occasion she had made a profound impression on him, which was reinforced when he saw her in her own home.[15]

The following spring, when Sam returned from New Orleans to Boston, he found that Margaret had given up her teaching job in Providence and moved to the house she was now occupying in Jamaica Plain. Although they were living a short distance from each other, Sam avoided seeing Margaret, and she realized quickly that there had been a change in his attitude. Her letters to him expressed her surprise and concern. Although she hoped desperately for a "second Spring" in their relationship, those hopes were crushed when Anna visited her early in October full of her own happy news and unaware of Margaret's feelings. What had followed were "nights of talk and days of agitation." The "tides of feeling which have been poured upon and from my soul have been too much for my strength of body or mind," Margaret had exclaimed. Although she had forgiven her friends, she had crept into her bed and stayed there for several days.[16]

Emerson's reaction to Margaret's story was complicated. On the one hand, reading and rereading the material she sent him plunged Emerson into a confrontation with raw experience that he found exhilarating; it made him wish "to live a little while with people who love & hate, who have Muses & Furies." But at the same time he realized that the tale Margaret had told him conflicted with the view he had formed of relationships within her circle, and this he found disturbing. He made this feeling clear when he remarked in a letter to Caroline Sturgis that "the facts" of friendship "are never quite beautiful," an admission that obviously upset Emerson. In the next sentence he retracted the statement, labeling it "low & libelous." He had had "no such experience as my caution would seem to imply," he claimed falsely. Despite what Emerson had learned from Margaret Fuller, he continued to insist upon the validity of his original view of the nature of her friends' involvements.[17]

3

The winter months were traditionally the busiest of the year for Emerson because of his annual lecture series in Boston. In 1839–40, the receipts from these lectures fell considerably short of his earnings from the previous two years. Faced by the need for more income to support his growing family, he agreed to lecture outside New England for the first time. In March he traveled to New York City where he made several appearances at the Mercantile Library. He then extended his New England tour to include three lectures in Providence, Rhode Island. Not until the last day of the month could he begin to settle back into his normal pattern of life.

During the winter and early spring Emerson had corresponded regularly with Margaret Fuller and had exchanged letters with Sam Ward and Caroline Sturgis. The subject of friendship, which Emerson had described in a letter to Sam as "the most attractive of all topics," had been very much on his mind. In that letter he had also been quite open about his feelings toward the young man. "I wish you to like me," he had said. The "mutual sympathy" that Emerson recognized as existing between them did not express itself easily, however. Because their encounters never seemed to live up to the intensity of his expectations, Emerson felt thwarted in his dealings with Sam, a concern that he expressed obliquely in the same letter: "Because the subject is so high and sacred, we cannot walk straight up to it; we must saunter if we would find the secret."[18]

The previous summer Emerson had begun to write an essay on friendship that explored its complexities. Now as he sat down to complete it, he recalled his earlier exchanges with Margaret, Sam, and Caroline on the question and openly wove them into his text. Emerson's decision to use material from his correspondence with his young friends in the writing of his essay indicates just how important his growing involvement with them had become to him. His need to respond to his attraction to them, and to the facts of their complicated relationships with each other, was undoubtedly a major reason for his returning to the subject at this time.[19]

But there was another force at work on Emerson as he picked up his pen. He shared a concern held by a broad spectrum of bright and sensitive people, like Margaret and her friends, who were interested in the issues raised by transcendentalism. As a group, they found that the practice of friendship did not live up to the hopes they had invested in it. They sought to understand why the kind of relationships they lived out in their imagination seemed so much more fulfilling than those they encountered in the real world. In an attempt to elevate the actual experience of friendship to the level of their expectations, they recast their thoughts about it, projecting them onto a higher plane. Emerson followed the same pattern in his essay, moving his argument from everyday matters to the metaphysical level as he grappled with the question.[20]

Emerson had no doubt about the practical benefits of having friends, and he stated them succinctly. "The end of friendship," he wrote, is "for aid and comfort through all the relations and passages of life and death." By forming friendships over time we "weave social threads of our own," thereby creating "a new web of relations." We benefit greatly from this "new world of our own creation" that sustains us in our passage through the seasons of life. We are "no longer strangers and pilgrims" as we make our way through the society into which we were born.[21] But if Emerson saw the rewards to be gained from forming friendships like these that were struck to offer us practical benefits, he also saw the dangers. For in Emerson's opinion this kind of friendship "quite loses sight" of "the delicacies and nobility of the relation," essential qualities in his view.[22]

In light of this consideration Emerson turned his attention to an aspect of friendship that was of far greater importance to him than "commodity," as he called it. To him, emotional involvement and mutual understanding were the true rewards friendship offers. What is "so delicious," he asked, "as a just and firm encounter of two, in a thought, in a feeling?" When these are at the core of an attraction, the result is transformative for the friends. "The moment we indulge our affections," he said, "the world is metamorphosed." Under these circumstances friendship assumes the qualities usually associated with love. The new friend's "goodness seems better than our goodness, his nature finer, his temptations less. Everything that is his,—his name, his form, his dress, books and instruments,—fancy enhances."[23] A union is created that lasts forever. "Who hears me, who understands me, becomes mine,—a possession for all time." It is in the hope of attaining *this* state that "every man passes his life in the search after friendship."[24]

Before going on, Emerson paused to make his intentions clear. It was not his purpose to approach his subject "daintily," but rather "with the roughest courage," he said, and he proceeded to live up to his word. The feelings of intense attraction and desire he had been describing, Emerson observed, do not hold up well in the face of reality. "Friendship may be said to require natures so rare and costly, each so well tempered and so happily adapted, and withal so circumstanced . . . that its satisfaction can very seldom be assured." To support this statement Emerson presented an unflinching view of the difficulties inherent in maintaining satisfactory relations between friends. He repeated the admonition he had included in a letter to Margaret Fuller a year earlier. "We are armed all over with subtle antagonisms, which, as soon as we meet, begin to play, and translate all poetry into stale prose. Almost all people descend to meet. All association must be a compromise."[25] Even "in the heyday of friendship," he warned, we can expect to be "tormented . . . by baffled blows, by sudden, unseasonable apathies, by epilepsies of wit and of animal spirits." There was a simple reason for this, Emerson explained with chilling finality: "I cannot make your consciousness tantamount to mine."[26]

Nevertheless, Emerson could conceive of a realm of friendship that would offer him greater rewards than the mundane relationships life had so far brought his way. He was referring to "that select and sacred relation which is a kind of absolute" and which can only exist "on a higher platform." "Shall we fear to cool our love by mining for the metaphysical foundation of this Elysian temple?" he asked, indicating his awareness that "the vast shadow of the Phenomenal" can be an enemy to the actual. "He who offers himself a candidate for that covenant comes up, like an Olympian, to the great games where the firstborn of the world are the competitors." He "demands a religious treatment."[27] Compared with him "all else is shadow." The friend has become the only reality. "I who alone am, I who see nothing in nature whose existence I can affirm with equal evidence to my own, behold now the semblance of my being."[28]

Emerson's journals and letters make it clear that he poured a great deal of effort into the composition of "Friendship." As his major statement on the subject, his words deserve to be considered carefully to see what light they throw on his relations with his friends and on his expectations of them. In the text Emerson focused considerable attention on a conception of friendship as it might be if the realities of day-to-day life played no role in it. "Should not the society of my friend be to me poetic, pure, universal and great as nature itself?" he asked. Inevitably there is a cost associated with this kind of thinking, as Emerson admitted. "It would indeed give me a certain household joy to quit this lofty seeking, this spiritual astronomy or search of stars, and come down to warm sympathies . . . ; but then I know well I shall mourn always the vanishing of my mighty gods," he confessed.[29]

Emerson was perfectly willing to discuss the day-to-day demands and disappointments associated with having and being a friend as long as he was free to avoid probing the deeper feelings he associated with the process. He was calling for friendships that would provide him with rewards he could deal with safely but that would not confront him with demands he shied away from embracing. Unfortunately, this orientation made it more, rather than less, difficult for him to experience satisfactory relationships with others.

Emerson was too insightful to fool himself about what he was doing. "The higher the style we demand of friendship, of course, the less easy to establish it with flesh and blood," he admitted. At several points in the essay he confessed that friends such as he described were "dreams and fables." But these asides did not alter the major thrust of his argument, which is one that, if adhered to in practice, could only lead sooner or later to the kind of conflicts with his friends that he wished to avoid.[30]

By favoring the ideal over the real, not only in the essay but also in his demands on his friends, Emerson formed expectations of others that they often found difficult, if not impossible, to live up to. In order to achieve the balance Emerson sought from them, it was necessary for his friends to control their feelings as tightly as he attempted to control his. Given the strong appeal that Emerson's powerful personality exerted on young people, this was very difficult for them to do. They were often confused by the conflicting signals they received from him, sensing his intense interest in having them draw closer to him while at the same time insisting that they not make great demands on him in return.

Since the turn of the year, nevertheless, events had seemed to support Emerson's view that it was possible to separate the actual practice of friendship from emotional involvement. Margaret Fuller had been devoting most of her energies to editing the first issue of the *Dial*. Caroline Sturgis had continued to pursue her interests in her own quiet way. Even the relationship between Anna Barker and Samuel Gray Ward had seemed to shift its focus. Although Anna and Sam remained friends, the talk of marriage had receded. Emerson was delighted by the news. He favored a spiritual union between them rather than a marital one; it fit in perfectly with his belief that platonic relationships should be striven for above all others. Actually, the differences between Anna and Sam that had prevented them from formalizing their engagement were soon resolved. While Emerson was congratulating them in his mind for preferring a spiritual union, they were moving ahead quietly with their plans to be married.

Emerson was equally in the dark about the emotional stresses that were continuing to buffet Margaret Fuller. He admired her ability to maintain friendly relations with Anna and Sam after her disappointment but did not sense that this had been made possible by a major shift in her feelings, a shift away from her emotional commitment to Sam toward an increased attachment to Emerson himself. Margaret had initially sought Emerson's friendship and had never hidden its importance to her. In the months after learning about Sam's love for Anna, her dependence on Emerson had grown steadily, to the point where she had begun to yearn for a closer relationship with him than he realized. At the time she did nothing to enlighten him.[31]

In reality, Emerson's friends were hiding their feelings from him. And, as it turned out, he was guilty of playing the same game with himself, at least as far as Caroline Sturgis was concerned. Emerson employed two distinct styles in writing letters. Most of the time he wrote in a straightforward, business-like manner, but when he was corresponding with someone he wanted to impress, he used an elevated tone, often drafting the letters first, then copying them. Toward the end of 1839, he had begun writing to Caroline in the latter manner. Her innocence and charm had slowly worked its magic on him, and without his realizing it, she had become more important to him than he wanted to admit to himself. In an attempt to fit these feelings into an acceptable mold, he tried to impose a fraternal pattern on their relationship, calling her "my dear sister" and demanding, "am I not your brother?"[32]

This period of apparent calm for Emerson, which lasted into the summer, reached a climax when Anna Barker visited Boston in August. Emerson decided to invite Margaret, Caroline, and Anna to Concord for a long weekend. After a hurried exchange of notes concerning such questions as whether Emerson should escort them to Concord in "the stage" or hire a horse and come for them "in a carryall," the details were agreed upon. From dinner time on Saturday until Monday afternoon, the Emerson home in Concord became, for its owner, a "house of heaven." How could it have been otherwise, surrounded as he was by his wife, his mother, Margaret Fuller, Caroline Sturgis, and Anna Barker—all adoring him?[33]

These "three golden days" left Emerson in a state that bordered on exhilaration. In a letter to Thomas Carlyle he announced that he had been "drawing nearer" to a few chosen people "whose love gives me in these days more happiness than I can write of." He was "greatly struck," he commented to Caroline Sturgis, by the fact that friends "understand each other so fast, so surely & so dearly," to which he added, "yet passionless withal," an afterthought that, under the circumstances, could only be termed a romantic illusion.[34]

4

There had been one bleak moment during Anna Barker's recent stay in the Boston area, however, that Emerson could not ignore. Riding back to Jamaica Plain with Margaret Fuller after visiting Anna one day at the home of a relative in Cambridge, Emerson had found himself the focus of an angry attack. Margaret had "taxed" him "with inhospitality of soul," saying that both she and Caroline felt that he did not treat them as true friends. He was cold and aloof, she had insisted. No matter how often they met, they met "as strangers." Instead of giving them emotional support and approval, he "catechized & criticized" them.[35]

Ever quick to accept blame, Emerson "confess[ed] to this charge with humility unfeigned." He was aware of the distance that separated him from others and had often castigated himself for it. What immediately concerned him, however, was not Margaret's reproaches but the possibility of Caroline's displeasure. On his arrival home he wrote Caroline an emotional letter and then decided not to send it. In the letter he said, "I cannot tell you how warm & glad the naming of your name makes my solitude. You give me more joy than I could trust my tongue to tell." A gulf separated them, he admitted, but whose fault was that? "With all my heart I would live in your society," he insisted.[36]

Emerson explained to Caroline that he would like her to establish a home near his so that he could spend "the remainder of [his] days" in her "holy society." Although he was consciously seeking what he thought of as a spiritual union with her, the coloration of his comments in the series of letters he wrote to her at this time suggests that his feelings ran deeper than that. In fact, in one of these letters he confessed his fear that if he allowed her to become "necessary" to him, he would be opening himself up to rejection. He might learn any day, he told her, that she had found "[her] mate" in "some heaven foreign to me," and then the "beautiful castle" of his dreams would be "exploded."[37]

As it happened, Emerson's fantasy about the viability of spiritual unions was about to receive a crushing blow. In Cambridge at the end of August he encountered Anna Barker, who admitted to him in "tremulous tones" that she and Sam had decided to marry in October. To Caroline he wrote that the news "affected me at first with a certain terror." He remarked in surprise that Anna, despite having chosen "vulgar" happiness over "ideal" friendship, "does not feel any fall." Nor, in fact, did Sam, for there was "no compunction written on either of their brows." Emerson immediately proceeded to wish the pair every happiness, but their decision disturbed him.[38]

Although having a family and home of his own was important to Emerson, he did not respond positively to the idea of Margaret Fuller and the members of her circle being encumbered by similar ties. His fears that Caroline would shatter his dreams by finding a mate and his response to the impending marriage of Anna to Sam Ward are evidence of how deeply embedded this feeling was. As long as his young friends remained single, he was free to enjoy his dream of spiritual union, but in their deciding to marry they made a mockery of the scenario he had so carefully constructed and that appeared to be so necessary to his emotional needs.

Within a few weeks Emerson had to face yet another unexpected revelation. At a meeting with Margaret Fuller toward the end of September, she let him know how deep her attachment for him had grown. In a letter written to her a few days later he attempted to clarify his attitude toward her. "You must always awaken my wonder: our understanding is never perfect: so was it in this last interview, so is it ever," he told her. In the letter Emerson confined his remarks to playful chatter about their relationship and a few shrewd remarks about her character. Despite the blandness of these comments, there is other evidence that Emerson saw to the core of the situation. In his journal on that day he wrote: "You would have me love you. What shall I love? Your body? The supposition disgusts you. What you have thought & said? Well, whilst you were thinking & saying them, but not now. I see no possibility of loving any thing but what now is, & is becoming; your courage, your enterprize, your budding affection, your opening thought, your prayer, I can love,—but what else?" Another fissure had been opened in Emerson's theory that platonic relationships could be maintained with ease between men and women.[39]

As these events unfolded, Emerson entered into what has been called an "electrically charged period of correspondence" on friendship with Margaret and the members of her circle. Through a torrent of letters Emerson was striving to make sense of the skein of emotions in which he found himself entangled, while holding on to his belief in the supremacy of platonic relations. Under the circumstances, this was an impossible task. No matter how he twisted and turned he could not bring the two sides of the equation together. He stated and restated in glowing terms his views of the sort of rarified intercourse that he had extolled in his essay, but could not escape the fact that his behavior and that of the others was grounded thoroughly in their emotions.[40]

Sam Ward and Anna Barker were married on October 3 and moved off into the world of their new life together. Caroline wondered why Emerson paid her "so many pretty compliments," suggesting that his manner toward her had begun to raise questions in her mind. Margaret prodded him to come to grips with the actuality of their relationship, instead of dallying endlessly with theories about it. Angry and frustrated, Emerson cut off the correspondence on friendship. On October 24 he announced his decision in a letter to Margaret. He "ought never to have suffered" her to have engaged him in this subject, he said, and warned her, "Do not expect it of me again for a very long time."[41]

Although Emerson's experience with Margaret and her circle did not prevent him from continuing to yearn for relationships with young people, it altered the manner in which he chose to deal with the opportunities for friendship with them that life brought his way. Recognizing the possibilities that opened up when he grew too close to young women, he no longer sought them out. And even with the ambitious young men that his mounting fame attracted, he showed an increased wariness. While welcoming their interest, he tried to encourage relationships with young men whose circumstances, unlike Sam Ward's, clearly placed them in a position subordinate to his. And he carefully avoided any exploration of the deeper feelings that might be aroused by their association, such as those he had experienced with Sam Ward.

If there was a beneficiary of this new concern for limitations, it was Henry Thoreau who was already an established figure in Emerson's life and whose undemanding adulation seemed, at the moment, to offer no threat of complications. Emerson clearly saw himself as Henry's mentor. In his eyes, inviting Henry to live in his home not only promised him the continuing companionship he required outside of his marriage, it did so without appearing to raise the question of his being drawn into any sort of emotional entanglement that he would find uncomfortable.

4

The Womb of Zeus

Emerson's home—"a square, comely mansion, after the pattern often seen on the main street of the older New England villages"—stood in a meadow not far from the main road connecting Concord with Boston. When one entered the center hall, Emerson's study lay to the right; on the left was the guest room that he called "the Pilgrim's chamber." Beyond these rooms were Lidian's parlor, the dining room, and an extension at the back containing a kitchen with servants quarters above. Upstairs in the main house were four bedrooms and a small room that had not been completely partitioned off and that served as a passageway. It was here that Henry Thoreau settled down.[1]

When Henry wrote to a friend that he was "living with Mr. Emerson in very dangerous prosperity," he was probably referring not only to the comparative luxury of his surroundings but to the freedom of choice provided by adequate private means. Relieved of household responsibilities by three servants, the Emersons structured their days around their interests. They were free to read, write, entertain, or travel as they chose. During Henry's early months in the house Lidian Emerson twice went off on extended visits, first to New York, then to Plymouth, and Emerson vacationed alone for a fortnight in a hotel at Nantasket Beach. In a letter to Lidian during one of her absences Emerson provided a glimpse of life in the Emerson home that summer. "We all remain as busy, as idle & as languidly happy as the last week knew us," he said, adding that on Sunday, "your sinful household were for the most part worshipping each in his or her separate oratory in the woodlands—what is droll, Henry Thoreau was the one at church."[2]

Visitors to the Emerson home often commented on the exceptional courtesy that prevailed there. Although ten people including children and servants lived in the house during Henry's first summer as a resident, along with frequent guests in the Pilgrim's chamber, each family member and guest had ample space to pursue his or her preferred activities behind closed doors. When writing, Emerson closeted himself in his study from six in the morning until one o'clock in the afternoon. Lidian often passed the day in her room as did Emerson's mother in the "quiet sanctuary" that was hers. In fact, members of the household frequently communicated with each other by notes carried from room to room by a servant. One such note that Emerson sent that summer from his study to Henry in his small room on the second floor read: "My dear Henry, We have G. P. Bradford, R. Bartlett[,] Lippitt[,] C[.]S[.] Wheeler and Mr. Alcott. Will you not come down & spend an hour? Yours, RWE."[3]

Although the maids noticed that Henry never passed through the kitchen "without colouring," he quickly established a pattern of daily activity that suited his particular needs. When his work in the garden was completed, he had the rest of the day to read and write. Among the books in Emerson's library, he discovered a rich collection of oriental literature that fascinated him. True to his regular practice, he collected notes on the subject throughout the summer, a study that would strongly influence his writing in later years.[4]

Having Henry in his home was important to Emerson. Shortly after his arrival, Emerson had fallen ill and his recovery had been slow. With Henry there to work with him outdoors he was able to report, "I have quite deserted my books, & do hoe corn & wheel a wheelbarrow whole days together." He found Henry "a great benefactor & physician to me for he is an indefatigable & very skillful laborer & I work with him as I should not without him and expect now to be suddenly well & strong."[5] Henry was "a noble manly youth full of melodies & inventions"; he was "a scholar & a poet & as full of buds of promise as a young apple tree."[6]

In moving to the Emersons', Henry had brought with him the boat he and John had built for their vacation in 1839. It was moored on the river about two hundred yards from the house, and he often took it out on the water late in the day when the air had cooled down. One evening Emerson joined him and afterward recorded the event:

> The good river-god has taken the form of my valiant Henry Thoreau here & introduced me to the riches of his shadowy, starlit[,] moonlit stream, a lovely new world lying as close & yet as unknown to this vulgar trite one of streets & shops as death to life or poetry to prose. Through one field only we went to the boat & then left all time, all science, all history behind us and entered into Nature with one stroke of a paddle. Take care, good friend! I said, as I looked west into the sunset overhead & underneath, & he with his face toward me rowed towards it,—take care; you know not what you do, dipping your wooden oar into this enchanted liquid, painted with all reds & purples and yellows which glows under & behind you.[7]

2

Despite Lidian Emerson's reclusiveness, her presence dominated the house. While gentle in manner, she was a woman of strong views and distinct character. "*Very refined,*" Elizabeth Peabody said, "but neither beautiful or elegant." Instead she "had the rare characteristic of genius—inexhaustible originality." A deeply religious woman, Lidian had a saintly quality about her that was one of the things that had attracted Emerson to her. He nicknamed her Asia, claiming that he could not remember having met a New Englander who "possessed such a depth of feeling," an inexhaustible resource that she could dip into on any occasion, large or small, to offer understanding and support to those around her.[8]

During the early years of their marriage, Lidian had attempted to accommodate herself to Emerson's world. In matters of the mind Emerson was attracted to a miscellaneous group of visionaries and radical intellectuals who were popularly categorized as transcendentalists. To please her husband Lidian had welcomed these people into her home and had tried to be sympathetic to them and their cause. Now, pregnant for the third time, Lidian turned her full attention to raising her children and making a home for them. Two-year-old Ellen and six-year-old Waldo were a source of endless delight to her. Waldo was unusually mature in outlook for such a young child. Henry Thoreau said that "his questions did not admit of an answer; they were the same which you would ask yourself." Nevertheless, like all children he could at times behave mischievously, or "unphilosophically," as Lidian preferred to characterize his behavior on these occasions.[9]

Henry and Waldo immediately became good friends. Henry treated the boy with "gentle firmness," which quickly earned his respect. But what cemented the relationship was Henry's skill with his hands. Unlike Emerson, who was all thumbs, Henry found it easy to make whistles and boats for Waldo to play with and had no trouble dealing with a popgun that needed repair.[10]

In June, Mary Russell, a young cousin of Lidian's from Plymouth, arrived to spend three and a half months, bringing youth and vitality into the Emerson household. She had come to reopen a "little school" that she had established in their barn the previous summer. The original purpose of the school had been to provide activity and instruction for Waldo, but it had quickly attracted children from other families. In its enlarged state, the school had moved into a vacant shed then standing between two neighboring houses.[11]

Henry had met Mary during her stay in Concord the previous summer and, in the company of John, had made a point of spending time with her when they attended neighborhood parties. Living under the same roof gave them the opportunity to get to know each other better. They discovered that they had a great deal in common, and a friendship blossomed that endured long after Mary had married and settled down.

During the summer months, it was a pleasant trip by stagecoach from Boston to Concord, and a steady stream of visitors took advantage of the good weather to visit. Margaret Fuller came for a fortnight. Caroline Sturgis came also, and stayed with Emerson while Lidian journeyed to Staten Island to visit the family of her brother-in-law William Emerson, who practiced law in New York City. And Lucy Brown, Lidian's sister, made the trip from Plymouth to pay an extended visit. Emerson conversed with his guests for long hours in his study, and when they were ready to move outdoors, Henry was always there to take them on the river in his boat. These visitors made the Emerson home an even more stimulating place for Henry Thoreau to live. "I do not know what right I have to so much happiness," he said.[12]

3

A year earlier, in a book on one of the shelves in Emerson's library, Henry had found an orphic hymn in Greek that caught his attention. Having had a strong interest in classical languages since his college days, he had set himself the task of translating the hymn into English. In these verses the womb of Zeus was depicted as the locus of creation, a function that the Emerson home would in its own way perform for him. Since Henry's arrival at the Emersons', the pages of his journal had begun to provide dramatic evidence of the "maturing of his thought and the sharpening of his talent for expression." Emerson had been right, it appears, when he had said that "living with any great master in one's proper art" was better for a young man than going to college.[13]

For Emerson each day offered a fresh opportunity to expand his understanding of human experience. In the morning he went immediately to his study to await the emergence of new insights. "All thoughts are holy when they come floating up to us in magical newness from the hidden Life," he said in commenting on this process. Emerson had recently published his first collection of essays bringing together under one cover the ideas he had been discussing in his lectures since 1836. Although the book's appearance had added considerably to his renown, he did not intend it to represent a final statement of his positions, and he was pursuing his intellectual explorations as actively as ever. The opportunity to be an intimate associate of Emerson's as this process continued contributed greatly to Henry Thoreau's intellectual development.[14]

During the fortnight in July that Emerson spent alone at Nantasket Beach, Lidian sent a packet to him that included several of Henry's recent poems. In the peaceful solitude of his vacation retreat he read the poems "thrice over with increasing pleasure" and pronounced them "very good." Henry was now in his most productive period as a poet, but he had had only two poems published in the four lengthy issues of the *Dial* that had appeared since the initial one. When Emerson returned to Concord, he began to press Margaret Fuller to accept one or more for the October 1841 issue, only to see her respond with a variety of strategies that allowed her to forestall any definite decision regarding them.[15]

Ultimately Emerson was to accuse Margaret of accepting work inferior to Henry's while consistently rejecting the material Henry submitted. In her defense she claimed to expect more of Emerson's protégé than of others. The statement was not without irony, for she clearly resented Emerson's partiality to the young man. In describing Henry to her brother in a letter written during her visit that summer, she said, "H.T. is three and twenty, has been through college and kept a school, is very fond of classical studies, and an earnest thinker yet intends being a farmer. He has a great deal of practical sense, and as he has bodily strength to boot, he may look to be a successful and happy man." By ignoring his literary ambitions—the attribute that particularly attracted Emerson to him—she appeared to be denying that he was worthy of her friend's regard.[16]

Aware of Margaret's growing antagonism toward Henry, Emerson decided to seek another outlet for his work. On September 25, he wrote to Rufus W. Griswold, editor of *Poets and Poetry of America,* calling attention to Henry's poems that had already appeared in the *Dial* and suggesting that one or more of them might be included in the next edition of Griswold's anthology. Apparently Henry was enthusiastic about this opportunity for he wrote to Griswold asking him to correct several textural errors if he saw fit to reprint the poems. While Griswold seems to have considered them, they were not included in the anthology when it was published.

Although Emerson devoted a great deal of energy to promoting Henry's work and recognized the improvement in it, he was not satisfied with Henry's development as a poet. Emerson had grown tired of verse in which "the rhythm is given, & the sense is adapted to it." In its place he yearned for a poetry in which "the sense dictates the rhythm." Henry's poems did not approach Emerson's vision of what the new poetry should be. That year Emerson had set down a comparison of genius and talent. The difference between them, he concluded, "is in the direction of the current; in genius, it is from within outward; in talent, from without inward. Talent finds its models & methods & ends in society and goes to the soul only for power to work; genius is its own end and derives its means & the style of its architecture from within." Henry had proven that he had talent, but did he possess genius? To Emerson, for whom his young friend's literary ambitions had grown so important, this had become a central question.[17]

It was no more apparent to Emerson than to Henry that the growth in Henry's power as a writer was taking place slowly in his journal, not in the poems that he produced so rapidly. Unfortunately, the poems, along with a few labored essays, were the works that were completed, read, and discussed, for Henry hadn't yet learned how to take the journal passages and successfully fuse them into longer pieces. Several months after Henry moved in with Emerson and his family, Emerson set down on paper some thoughts about Henry's progress. His comments have a brutal ring, suggesting the depth of his disappointment. Henry had "not yet told what that is which he had been created to say," Emerson stated bluntly. He was "very familiar with all his thoughts" because, although "quite originally drest," they were Emerson's "own." Henry might be a person "of unerring perception, & equal expression," but these qualities did not yet "flow through his pen."[18]

Emerson, it seems, was being unnecessarily impatient. Recently in conversation with Theodore Parker he had referred to Henry as "but a boy," yet he was expressing disappointment in him because he was not producing the work of a mature man.[19] "Imitation cannot go above its model," Emerson complained. "The imitator dooms himself to mediocrity." Henry himself was aware of the problem that confronted him. "It is easy to repeat, but hard to originate," he observed. Although, as he noted on August 13, "Men are constantly dinging in my ears their fair theories and plausible solutions of the universe," he was not yet sure of his direction. "I return again to my shoreless—islandless ocean, and fathom unceasingly for a bottom that will hold an anchor, that it may not drag," he said.[20]

4

Adding to the pressure of Emerson's displeasure was Henry's knowledge that a young poet had come along whose work Emerson regarded more highly than Henry's. Recently Sam Ward had brought the verse of his friend William Ellery Channing to Emerson's attention. Ellery, nephew and namesake of Boston's celebrated preacher, had gone off to Illinois to try his hand at farming before Emerson had had a chance to meet him, but that hadn't prevented Emerson from using eleven of his poems to illustrate an article on "the new poetry" that he had written for the *Dial*.

During the first decade of Henry's friendship with Emerson, there were always other talented young men like Ellery Channing in the picture, sometimes several of them at one time. A few years earlier Emerson had taken up the cause of Jones Very who had graduated from Harvard a year before Henry. At his own expense Emerson had edited and published a collection of Jones's poems and essays. Subsequently Emerson had discovered two other young men for whom he foresaw a future in literature. They were Charles King Newcomb, a friend of Margaret Fuller, and Christopher Pearce

Cranch, a recent divinity school graduate. Emerson invested considerable time and interest in their literary activities, corresponding with them, inviting them to his home, and encouraging them to develop their talents.[21]

Each of these relationships began with a period of intense interest on Emerson's part that dissipated as it became apparent that the young man in question, while bright and eager, was not going to live up to Emerson's expectations. In the long run, none of these involvements rivaled Emerson's attachment for Henry Thoreau in its depth or duration. However, this was not apparent until much later. At the time, Henry was merely aware that he always seemed to be vying for Emerson's approval with one or the other of them.

To further complicate matters, the situation had grown tense in the Emerson home with the arrival of autumn weather. Lidian Emerson, undergoing a difficult pregnancy, had not been well. And Emerson, with his responsibilities increasing, found his unearned income falling through the repeated failure of his bank stocks to pay dividends. Once again he was forced to set aside work on the essays that engaged his deepest interest to prepare lectures to earn money. "I am awkward, sour, saturnine, lumpish, pedantic, & thoroughly disagreeable & oppressive to the people around me," he confessed.[22]

The happy, carefree days of Henry's first few months at the Emersons' had faded, presenting him with an unavoidable reality of his own. After spending four years at Harvard and conducting his own school for two years, Henry, at twenty-three, was living in a state greatly resembling adolescence. He had been residing in Emerson's home as a guest for six months, eating the food provided by him, doing chores around the place, and sleeping like a boy in the little passageway room at the top of the stairs. Although he and Emerson continued to think and speak of each other as friends, Henry's situation as a dependent had created a new dynamic between them.

It was not surprising, then, that there was a great deal of the adolescent in Henry's behavior. He would pass silently through the house without joining in with the activities of others. He did not always do his chores.[23] He would disappear into the woods to spend the entire day by himself. He was often sullen and even at times rude. Without doubt he was the "young friend" who told Emerson in a thoughtless moment that "it destroyed his reverence for a great man to come near him." This remark hurt Emerson who accepted it in silence but brooded about it later.[24]

On November 22, Lidian gave birth to her third child, a daughter who was named Edith. Shortly after Edith's appearance in the household, Henry went to Emerson to borrow fifteen dollars in order to go Cambridge for a week or two. In making the loan, Emerson noted that he was advancing the money for the trip so that Henry could work on "his book."[25] The book Henry was planning appears to have been a study of English poetry "from Gower down."[26] Henry's friend and classmate Stearns Wheeler was then living in a dormitory at Harvard while pursuing a degree at the Divinity School. Henry apparently shared his room with him for eleven days, spending his free time in the Harvard Library. During his stay he amassed nearly three hundred pages of notes on English poets and of extracts of their work.[27]

Henry's decision to embark on a critical study of this magnitude appears to have been related to Emerson's attitude toward the poems he had been producing. Since Emerson did not think that Henry's future lay in writing poetry, this seems to have been an effort to focus his attention on a prose work. Although Henry pursued the task of gathering notes energetically, he wasn't happy with the experience. The "dry and dusty volumes" through which he thumbed did not house the "fresh and fair creations" he had expected to find there. He decided to put the project aside.[28]

After his taste of independence in Cambridge, Henry found it difficult to settle down again in Concord. Although the original plan had been that he would remain at the Emersons' for twelve months, it seemed to him that although only eight of them had passed, the time had come to end his "sojourn" with his friends. He felt that he ought to strike out on his own, to "begin to live" in earnest. For him that meant something quite specific. "I want to go soon and live away by the pond," he said, "where I shall hear only the wind whispering among the reeds."[29]

5

Before Henry could make arrangements to retreat to "the pond," a pair of tragic events intervened. Shortly after the start of the new year John Thoreau cut a sliver of skin from the end of a finger while stropping his razor. He replaced the skin, covered the cut with a rag and paid no attention to it until three days later when it began to pain him. That evening after visiting the doctor, he became ill as he walked home. When he woke up the next morning, he complained of stiffness, and toward sundown was seized with the violent spasms typical of lockjaw.

Henry, the "most untiring and watchful of nurses," returned home immediately to help care for him.[30] From the first, John knew that his cause was hopeless but he accepted the situation serenely, saying "that God had always been good to him and he could trust Him now." The next day he said goodbye to his family, then when he was once again alone with Henry, he asked him to sit down near him and talk "of Nature and Poetry." Later, he turned to Henry with "a transcendent smile full of Heaven," which Henry returned. That exchange of smiles was "the last communication that passed between them."[31] Henry was holding John in his arms when he died.[32]

After the funeral Henry remained at his parents' home in a state of shock. Apart from his tie to his mother, his attachment to John had been the strongest he had formed in his life. It seemed "as if part of himself had been torn away," a family friend reported. Completely in control of his emotions during John's short illness, Henry now withdrew into an inner world, sitting passively in the house and refusing to speak, although he occasionally listened to the music box he loved so much. When his sisters led him outdoors hoping his interest in nature would rouse him, the attempt failed.[33]

Later in the month while Emerson was in Boston delivering the last lecture of his winter series, Henry suddenly began to experience the same symptoms John had suffered. Returning to Concord on Saturday, Emerson discovered that Henry had been put to bed under the doctor's care. Although the situation continued to grow worse, it was obvious that he did not have lockjaw. To Emerson, this reaction on Henry's part to his brother's death was "strange—unaccountable," but he did not have long to reflect on its implications.[34] On Monday the Emersons' son, Waldo, became ill with what at first seemed to be a cold but was soon identified as scarlet fever. He was kept in bed and given castor oil with every expectation of a prompt recovery. Then on Thursday he became delirious. Lidian who had left the room briefly to take a much-needed rest was brought back to his side. Doctor Bartlett, who had been caring for him, was in the room when she returned. When she asked if he would be better soon, the doctor replied, "I had hoped to be spared this." There was nothing he could do to save the child.[35]

Emerson was despondent. The boy had been his constant companion, often sitting for hours in his study beside him, quietly occupied in his own activities, never saying a word. So sharp was Emerson's sense of loss that he wondered if he would "ever dare to love" again. For the next week and a half the Emersons remained secluded in their home, attempting to deal with the reality of their loss. Unlike Henry, Emerson could not permit himself to withdraw into his sorrow for an extended period. Despite his hope that the income from his lecture series in Boston would make up for the failure of his bank stocks to pay dividends, he had seen his audiences fall off drastically. In order to pay his debts he now found it necessary to travel to Providence to repeat five of his new lectures, leaving his distraught wife alone for ten days with their two young daughters and his aged mother.[36]

Despite assurances from friends in Providence that he would find a large audience there, Emerson attracted only "a small company and a trivial reward." Under the circumstances, he was forced to extend his tour to New York City, allowing only a week at home with Lidian between engagements. By this time Henry's health had improved sufficiently for him to consider returning to the Emersons' to keep Lidian company during her husband's absence. Shortly before Emerson left on his tour, Henry moved back to the little room on the second floor that he had occupied since the previous spring.[37]

The effort involved in returning to the Emersons' apparently caused a setback in Henry's recovery. Responding from New York to a letter from Lidian, Emerson mentioned, "You speak of Henry as if he had been more ill than I know. Do tell him with my love to favor himself." Emerson's concern was not misplaced. The collapse of Henry's health following John's death reflected an emotional disturbance of a serious order. Henry himself characterized his mental state in these words: "I am like a feather floating in the atmosphere, on every side is depth unfathomable."[38]

Although Henry's health improved as the weeks passed, he continued to feel anchorless in a hostile world until Emerson's arrival home in the middle of March. After two days in his company, he abruptly turned in his journal from morbid thoughts about the "phenomenon of death" to a consideration of the importance of friendship. He began by observing that Emerson often seemed "cold and reserved" in his manner toward him but construed this as the behavior of an essentially shy man who was embarrassed by his growing affection for Henry.[39] As he continued to explore his feelings toward Emerson and his expectations of their relationship, his musings were suddenly illuminated by a thought that signaled a shift in his outlook from despair to hope. "My friend is my real brother," he noted simply.[40]

A view of the center of Concord village a few years after Thoreau met Emerson. *Photograph courtesy of the Concord Free Public Library.*

The shopping center of Concord in the 1860s about the time that Thoreau died. *Photograph courtesy of the Concord Free Public Library.*

The crayon drawing of Emerson by Samuel Worcester Rowse, a frequent visitor to Concord. *Photograph courtesy of the Concord Free Public Library.*

The crayon portrait of Thoreau made by Samuel Worcester Rowse while he was boarding with the Thoreau family. *Photograph courtesy of the Concord Free Public Library.*

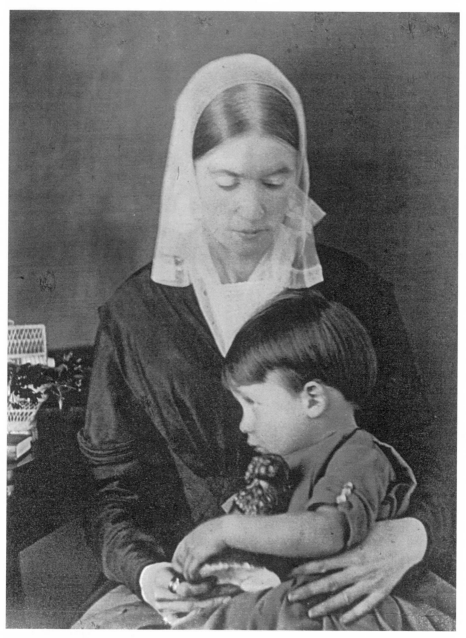

Lidian Emerson with the Emersons' first child, Waldo, 1838 or 1839. *Photograph courtesy of the Concord Free Public Library.*

The Emerson home on Lexington Road where Thoreau lived from April 1841 until May 1843 and again from September 1847 until July 1848. *Photograph courtesy of the Concord Free Public Library.*

Ellen Sewell about 1840, the year she refused Thoreau's proposal of marriage.

Caroline Sturgis, who, through her friendship with Margaret Fuller, became an intimate member of Emerson's circle. *Photograph courtesy of George Eastman House.*

Samuel Gray Ward, another friend of Margaret Fuller's, who came to enjoy a close relationship with Emerson. *Photograph courtesy of Boston Athenaeum.*

Margaret Fuller, the brilliant conversationalist and editor of the *Dial*, played a central role in the development of Emerson's views on friendship. *Reproduced by permission of the Houghton Library, Harvard University [bMS Am 1086].*

Waldo Emerson, whose tragic death when he was five years old permanently altered Emerson's conception of experience. *Reproduced by permission of the Houghton Library, Harvard University [bMS Am 1280.235 (706)].*

John Thoreau Jr., Henry Thoreau's elder brother, who died in his arms at the age of twenty-seven. *Photograph courtesy of the Concord Museum, Concord, Mass.*

5

One of the Family

"Life is a train of moods like a string of beads, and, as we pass through them, they prove to be many-colored lenses which paint the world with their own hue, and each shows only what lies in its focus," Emerson wrote in his essay "Experience." That spring when he entered the opening sentences of the essay in his journal his mood was heavily influenced by the loss of his son. Determined to describe life with absolute "honesty" in the essay, he presented a picture starkly different from that which emerges from his previous writings. The inner strength provided by faith in the power of the individual mind had given way to a vision of the world in which there is no certitude. "Sleep lingers all our lifetime about our eyes, as night hovers all day in the boughs of the fir-tree. All things swim and glimmer." Bitterly he concluded that satisfaction in life is reserved for those who can accept whatever comes to them without questioning it.[1]

The impact of little Waldo's death on Lidian Emerson was equally as great. "An incarnation of Christianity," in Emerson's words, Lidian had since childhood possessed a feeling of "blessed nearness to God." However, as Emerson's beliefs had grown progressively more radical during the early years of their marriage, hers, she realized, had become "unconsciously warped" by his. Although religion had remained "the foundation of her life," she had discovered that "its fulness was gone."[2] Now when she most needed its consolation, it was in part denied her. Brooding over "unanswerable questions," she became more rigid in her orthodoxy in a futile attempt to assuage her sorrow.[3]

Like his friends, Henry was weighted down with grief. But instead of turning to philosophy or religion for solace, he turned to them. Emerson had already declared him "one of the family." If Henry had found a brother in his friend, then he had found a sister in Lidian. Sympathetic, perceptive, concerned, they gave him the understanding and the emotional support he needed at this time. But even more important, the strengthening of his bond with the Emersons provided him with a new sense of identity. When in his early twenties he had written, "I am a parcel of vain strivings tied / By a chance bond together, / Dangling this way and that," he had described a life without a center. His acceptance as a member of the Emerson family not only offered him a place in the world more congenial to his temperament than that into which he had been born but also, by increasing his importance in his own eyes, provided him with a desperately needed source of self-esteem for use in integrating the conflicting elements of his personality.[4]

2

A circumstance that arose immediately after Emerson returned from his lecture tour helped to draw him—and Henry—away from this period of intense grieving. Due partly to ill health and partly to the fact that she could not afford to continue working without pay, Margaret Fuller resigned the editorship of the *Dial*. Although reluctant to take over the reins of leadership from her, Emerson decided within a week to "make the trial of one or two numbers at least" and a few days later extended his commitment to a year. He immediately asked Henry to be his "private secretary" and began soliciting contributions for the next issue from Theodore Parker, Henry Hedge, Bronson Alcott, Stearns Wheeler, Charles King Newcomb, and Margaret herself. Henry, of course, would also be expected to write for the journal.[5]

One of the "charms" of the *Dial* for Emerson was that it offered talented young people an opportunity to reach a sympathetic audience. That Henry's efforts had not struck a chord with its readers was a matter of concern to him. He had sought "in vain," he confessed, for some positive reaction to Henry's poems during his travels on the lecture circuit. Moreover, in considering what writing assignment to give Henry for the next issue of the *Dial*, he could not have helped recalling Theodore Parker's biting comment about "Persius," Henry's only prose contribution to the magazine. In response to Emerson's remark that "Persius" was "full of life," Parker had quipped that the life was "Emerson's, not Thoreau's."[6]

Anxious that Henry find his own voice, Emerson decided to suggest a change of direction for his work that turned out to have great significance for his future as a writer. Early in April Emerson obtained copies of a series of scientific surveys of Massachusetts recently issued by the state legislature. The series included Thaddeus W. Harris's *Insects,* Chester Dewey's *Flowering Plants,* David H. Storer's *Fishes, Reptiles, and Birds,* Augustus A. Gould's *Invertebrata,* and Ebenezer Emmons's *Quadrupeds.* Emerson suggested that Henry review them, pointing out "the felicity of the subject for him as it admit[ted] of the narrative of all his woodcraft, boatcraft, fishcraft." Until then Henry had kept his intense personal involvement with nature separate from his formal attempts at writing. The lecture he had delivered at the Concord Lyceum in the spring of 1838 had discussed "Society"; his essay on Persius had been an attempt to write literary criticism; and his only other completed prose work had been a short piece entitled "Service," which Margaret Fuller had rejected. When Emerson informed Margaret, after he had assigned the review to Henry, that he had "set" him on a "good track," he was not mistaken. Henry approached the task with such enthusiasm that within a month he had "fifty or sixty pages of MS in a state approaching completion."[7]

Henry Thoreau's essay, called the "Natural History of Massachusetts," was his first original piece of writing. Although the prose of the introductory paragraphs imitates the method Emerson used so well—the thoughts expressed in forceful sentences leaping from one to another without connectives—Henry quickly proclaimed his intention to "draw a little nearer to [his] promised topics," and when he did, the style and subject matter foreshadowed the method he would employ for the rest of his life. Instead of discussing the surveys themselves—dry reports that were scientific in method—Henry used the review as an occasion to string together "a lengthy mosaic of choice excerpts from the best nature writing in his journal." In turning to his journal as a source he was merely following the pattern Emerson had established.[8]

When the "Natural History of Massachusetts" appeared in the July *Dial,* its merit was widely perceived and commented upon. In face of this reception it may seem surprising that Emerson, as he quickly confided to Margaret Fuller, did not "like [his] piece very well." It is true that the character of the writing displayed "a significant move away" from "the Emersonian manner."[9] Where Emerson discussed nature as an abstraction without reference to specific natural phenomena, Henry employed direct observation as the foundation of his style. But it is unlikely that this was the reason Emerson disliked it. Having developed a distinctive style of his own, Emerson approved of the steps Henry was taking in this direction. What surprised Emerson was that the essay contained hints that their intellectual paths had begun to diverge. There are passages in "The Natural History of Massachusetts" indicating that Henry's attitude had changed toward one of the principal views expressed in *Nature*. He had become convinced that the physical universe was intrinsically more important than Emerson had been willing to admit. His belief that there is "nothing in the intellect which was not previously in the experience of the senses" was "anathema to Emerson and his followers." Emerson, who had been calling for Henry to allow his own thoughts to "flow through his pen," was not prepared to have him contest so fundamental a concept of his own. And, as if this dereliction were not enough, Henry had also lashed out against the "din of religion, literature and philosophy, which is heard in pulpits, lyceums and parlors." Such words could easily be read as critical of his friend.[10]

The writing of the "Natural History of Massachusetts" had a liberating influence on Henry Thoreau. Shortly after it appeared in the *Dial*, he spent four days in the company of Richard Fuller, Margaret's younger brother, hiking to Wachusett Mountain and back, a fifty-mile round-trip. The detailed record that he kept of this excursion formed the basis of his next essay, aptly titled "A Walk to Wachusett." In it he established the pattern he would use so successfully in all his major writings, that of venturing out into the world, using his observations as an occasion for moralizing, and returning a wiser man to Concord.

3

In August the calm that had reigned in the Emerson home since the spring was interrupted with the arrival of two guests. The first was Ellery Channing. In the two years since Emerson had used Ellery's poems to illustrate his essay on the new poetry in the *Dial,* Ellery had given up his attempt to earn a living as a farmer, married Margaret Fuller's sister, Ellen, and decided to devote himself to writing. Learning that Ellery planned to spend a few weeks in Concord to look for living quarters there for himself and his wife, Emerson immediately invited him to stay at his house while in the village.[11]

Ellery, Emerson quickly noted, was "very good company, with his taste & his cool, hard, sensible behavior, yet with the capacity of melting to emotion or of wakening to the most genial mirth." All the attention that Emerson had for so many months directed toward Henry, he now focused on his new guest. He encouraged him to talk freely about his ideas, to accompany him on his walks through the neighboring woods, and even to read his poetry aloud to the others assembled in the house—a mark of special favor. Although Henry had become accustomed to Emerson's enthusiasms for other young writers, this was the first time he had to live with the situation from day to day.[12]

As it turned out, Henry was not the only member of the Emerson household who had reason to feel rejected. Margaret Fuller's arrival, shortly after Ellery's, diverted Emerson's attention from his wife just as surely as Ellery Channing's presence had thrust Henry into the shade. Lidian, often in poor health, was suffering from an intermittent fever when Margaret reached Concord. Happily occupied with Emerson, Margaret paid little attention to her hostess, who was confined to her room much of the time. When she looked in to see her after neglecting this duty for a "day or two," an unhappy scene ensued. Lidian was unable to hide her jealousy of the attention Emerson lavished on the visitor. Although Margaret attempted to soothe her, she later remarked in her journal: "As to my being more his companion, that cannot be helped. His life is in the intellect not the affections."[13]

Seven years earlier, immediately after proposing to Lidian, Emerson had made the nature of his feelings for her quite clear. "In this new sentiment that you awaken in me, my Lydian Queen, what might scare others[,] pleases me, its quietness, which I accept as a pledge of permanence." What he admired in her was "her air of lofty abstraction, like Dante." How different was the memory he carried of his first wife, Ellen Tucker Emerson. Reminiscing about Ellen in 1839, Emerson had written, "She taught the eye that beheld her, why Beauty was ever painted with loves & graces attending her steps."[14]

Contending with her husband's impassioned memory of his first wife could not at any time have been easy for Lidian, but she believed that her marriage to him had increased in happiness in their early years together only to reach a point of estrangement when Emerson became more deeply involved with the participants in the transcendental movement. As for Emerson himself, he was acutely aware of the distance that now separated them. Where three years after their marriage he had happily signed a letter as her "desiring husband," he now complained in his journal of "this bachelor life I lead."[15]

While it is doubtful that Henry knew the details of the Emersons' private life, his growing affection for Lidian would have made him sensitive to her feelings. With Margaret Fuller's distaste for Henry now out in the open—Emerson having recently informed her that he was sorry she did not "like [my] brave Henry any better"—he had every reason to sympathize with Lidian's situation. Moreover, the fact that Emerson continued to keep Ellery Channing "before him as an object of smiling contemplation" did not make the days pass any more pleasantly for Henry.

On August 31, Henry escaped the hothouse atmosphere of the Emerson home to have dinner with a neighbor, but the relief was temporary. On the following day, Emerson's enchantment with Ellery openly reached a new height. Permitting Ellery to work beside him in his study Emerson enthused: "It is much to know that poetry has been written this very day, under this very roof, by your side. What[!] that wonderful spirit has not ceased! these stony moments are still sparkling and animated! I had fancied that Nature had intermitted her finer influences, and no oracle spoke: & behold all day from every pore these auroras have been streaming."[16]

For three weeks Emerson had been indulging his personal predilections without concern for the feelings of the others in the house. That afternoon Lidian shattered the composure of the little group surrounding him when her pent-up emotions erupted unexpectedly at the dinner table. The incident began innocently when she asked Margaret Fuller to take a walk with her after the meal was concluded. What happened next is described in Margaret's journal:

> I said, ["]I am engaged to walk with Mr. E. but["]—(I was going to say, "I will walk with you first,") when L. burst into tears. The family were all present, they looked at their plates. Waldo looked on the ground, but soft & serene as ever. I said, "My dearest Lidian, certainly I will go with you." "No!" she said,

"I do not want you to make any sacrifice, but I do feel perfectly desolate, and forlorn, and I thought if I once got out, the fresh air would do me good, and that with you, I should have courage, but go with Mr. E. I will not go."

I hardly knew what to say, but I insisted on going with her, & then she insisted on going so that I might return in time for my other walk. Waldo said not a word: he retained his sweetness of look, but never offered to do the least thing.[17]

During that afternoon walk and a ride they took together the next morning Lidian bared her heart to Margaret. More and more she had begun to feel excluded from the mainstream of Emerson's life. The "intimate union" she longed for seemed to be beyond her grasp although she continued to hope that her husband's character would alter in a way to make it possible. For her part Margaret was convinced that things between them would not improve. As Emerson's confidante, she knew that "he was sorely troubled by imperfections in the tie" and did not "believe in anything better."[18]

Predictably, the altered mood in the Emerson home following Lidian's public display of tears had its effect on Emerson's humor. Ellery Channing, who had so recently delighted him, bore the brunt of his displeasure. Emerson began by objecting to the "sudden crystallization" of Ellery's poetic imagination. "A pleasing poem, but here is a rude expression, a feeble line, a wrong word. 'I am sorry,' returns the poet, 'but it stands so written.' 'But you can alter it,' I say. 'Not one letter,' replies the hardened bard." This lack of willingness to work at the craft of poetry irritated Emerson despite his earlier protestation that "poetry of the portfolio" pleased him. Ellery, he concluded abruptly, was "much of the time a very common & unedifying sort of person."[19]

Not long afterward the gathering at the Emersons' was brought to a dramatic conclusion in a way that served to reinforce Emerson's opinion. Shortly before Ellery's young wife was expected to join him in Concord, he impulsively responded to an invitation from Caroline Sturgis to visit her in New Bedford. Since Ellery had once been in love with Caroline, hurrying off to spend a few days with her was hardly prudent. When he had not returned to Concord at the time of his wife's arrival at the Emersons', everyone was quite naturally upset: Ellen to find Ellery gone, Margaret attempting to conceal where he was, and the Emersons because of Margaret's discomposure. Upon Ellery's belated return, the Channings quickly concluded that Concord did not offer the accommodations they sought, and the party broke up.

With the house suddenly quiet again, Henry Thoreau was left to ponder the events of the last three weeks. One fact that clearly emerged from the rest was how similar his dependence on Emerson had become to Lidian's. Both had placed Emerson at the center of their emotional lives; both could readily be ignored when the opportunity for a new or more compelling experience presented itself to him. For the young man this could only have been a sobering realization and one that quickened his sympathy for Lidian.

4

One fine day in late September Emerson set out to walk to a Shaker community twenty-three miles away. With him was his new neighbor, Nathaniel Hawthorne, who had settled in Concord with his bride two months earlier. Sophia Peabody had long been a friend of Elizabeth Hoar's, and it was she who had arranged for the couple to rent the Old Manse, a house built by Emerson's grandfather.

Emerson had suggested the two-day excursion on foot to give the men a chance to get to know each other better. Shortly after the Hawthornes' arrival in the village, Emerson, with Henry by his side, had paid a call on them, but the visit had turned out to be uncomfortably formal. Their trip together succeeded in making them more at ease with each other, but in the long run Hawthorne's shyness prevented them from achieving any form of intimacy. That fall Sophia Hawthorne observed that her husband seemed "to fascinate" Emerson, who "talks to him all the time," she said, while "Mr. Hawthorne looks answers." Elizabeth Hoar explained Emerson's interest by saying that people around him "so generally echo him, that it is refreshing to him to find this perfect individual, all himself and nobody else."[20]

Hawthorne's independence of Emerson made it easier for Henry Thoreau to establish a separate relationship with him. Hawthorne found Henry to be "a singular character—a young man with much of wild original nature still remaining in him." He considered him to be "uncouth and somewhat rustic," although noting his "courteous manners." But like Emerson, Hawthorne saw beyond these surface characteristics to Henry's essential being, which impressed him. He "is a keen and delicate observer of nature—a genuine observer, which, I suspect, is almost as rare a character as even an original poet; and nature, in return for his love, seems to adopt him as her especial child, and shows him secrets which few others are allowed to witness."[21]

Considering Henry to be a good writer on the basis of the article he had recently published in the *Dial*, he determined to help him find a home for "A Walk to Wachusett" on which Henry had been working hard. Having recently been offered five dollars a page to contribute to a new Boston magazine, Hawthorne wrote to the editor, Epes Sargent, describing Henry as "capable of becoming a very valuable contributor." A series of nature articles by him would be a new feature in the magazines then being published and "perhaps a popular one," he added. Speculating that Henry should be able to write with a wider appeal than had been necessary for the *Dial*, he declared, "The man has stuff in him to make a reputation of; and I wish that you might find it consistent with your interest to aid him in attaining that object."[22]

Although Epes Sargent did not publish Henry's work, the young man quickly found a place for his new essay in the January issue of the *Boston Miscellany*, a magazine that nine months earlier had printed a piece by Hawthorne. Later in the month, Henry's possibilities began to look even brighter. At the Concord Athenaeum he was introduced to John O'Sullivan, editor of the *Democratic Review*, and afterward invited by Hawthorne to join them at his house for tea. O'Sullivan made a point of asking Henry to write for his magazine, which Henry would be "glad to do" he reported to Emerson. After five years of apprenticeship he had at last reached the point where he could begin to think of himself as a professional writer.[23]

5

With attendance having dwindled substantially the previous year at Emerson's annual Boston lecture series, he decided to forgo lecturing in Boston during this winter season and instead seek new audiences in New York, Philadelphia, Baltimore, and neighboring cities. Although he expected to be away for six to eight weeks on his lecture tour, Emerson felt secure in the knowledge that Henry would be living at home with his family.

On his journey south Emerson carried with him a group of five newly written lectures on the general subject of New England. In them he discussed not only literary influences, religion, and spiritual history, as might have been expected, but also trade, manners, and customs. In comparison to the material he had been presenting in his lectures until then, Emerson had clearly scaled down the demands he placed on his listeners. This may have been a conscious attempt to broaden his appeal and therefore bring in a larger paying audience. However, it was also a reflection of a change that had begun to take place in his view of the role that perceived reality plays in understanding human experience.

Although in *Nature* Emerson had produced one of the great manifestos of American transcendentalism, he had recently begun to separate himself from some of the ideas he had expressed in that book. Only ten months earlier he had declared himself to be "wholly guiltless" of transcendentalism. It irked him that transcendentalism was "spoken of as a known & fixed element like salt or meal." This was simply not true, he insisted. He himself, in referring to the writing then appearing in the *Dial,* spoke of "the direction of these speculations" to characterize their content. Why, he wondered, did his auditors not understand that his thought, like that of his colleagues, moved in a flow; no final statements had been made, or intended.[24]

Within this flux, however, there had recently been a clearly marked turning point. The death of Emerson's son, Waldo, is generally agreed to have marked a watershed in Emerson's intellectual life. It had taught him that there are situations where idealism simply proves inadequate. In the year that had passed since his son's fatal illness he had come to concede that it did not suffice to live in "the world of pure thought"; that "experience" counted for a great deal more in the order of things than he had earlier supposed. Through an "acceptance of limitations" he was slowly achieving a "basic adjustment of belief." While he continued to stress the importance of the soul in establishing man's relationship to the world, his change in attitude was having an eroding effect on his fidelity to transcendental thought.[25]

For many of its adherents, Emerson now believed, transcendentalism had become a "Saturnalia of faith."[26] Perhaps for that reason he felt the need to take note of the popular response to the *Dial*'s editorial content. He had "no defense to set up," Emerson said, for "The Dial and its sins." Speaking for himself as well as for the magazine's other contributors, he said simply, "We write as we can." But having made this admission, he quickly added that if the ideas explored in the magazine seemed to encourage its youthful readers to commit excesses, it should nevertheless be recognized that "all the bright boys & girls in New England, quite ignorant of each other, take the world so." Once having made this assertion, however, he went on to confess to a concern: "They are all religious, but hate the churches: they reject all the ways of living of other men, but have none to offer in their stead." Apparently he could not bring himself to stand completely apart from the condemnation directed by conservative critics toward the effect that transcendental ideas were having on young people in that part of the country.[27]

The change in Emerson's views had begun to move him intellectually in a different direction from Henry Thoreau. For Henry, transcendentalism was also a saturnalia, as Joel Porte has pointed out, but in his case it was "a Saturnalia of sense experience" not of "faith." Transcendentalism revealed itself to him through mystic states that occurred under certain circumstances when he confronted nature. Unlike Margaret Fuller who, upon entering the woods, did not "*think*," but found "herself expressed," Henry could on rare occasions attain to a loftier level of unity with nature. These events took the form of ecstatic states during which his being opened to "a higher light" that allowed him to "escape" from himself and to "travel totally new paths." Although Emerson agreed that it was necessary to "transcend" ordinary sensory experience if one was to attain the highest level of understanding, he did not enter into these mystical states himself.[28]

From the beginning Henry had understood Emerson to be sympathetic to his epiphanies despite his inability to share them. Still, the fact that the act of transcendence was an experience for Henry while remaining merely a concept for Emerson describes an important difference between them, one that meant they approached many questions from different angles. Now that Emerson had adopted a greater practicality into his worldview, the sense of solidarity in their outlook was less clear. In some ways Emerson seemed to be retracting the advice he had given five years earlier when Henry had sat in the Emerson parlor listening as he delivered the "Human Culture" lecture series for Lidian's benefit.

In the middle of February, with Emerson still away on his speaking tour, Henry once again found himself seated in the Emerson parlor, this time in the midst of a heated discussion. The occasion was a "Conversation" conducted by Bronson Alcott for Concord residents who were interested in exchanging ideas on various topics, among them "the love of nature." Lidian described the scene in a letter to Emerson written the next day:

> Mr. Lane decided, as for all time and the race, that this same love of nature—of which Henry was the champion . . . —that this love was the most subtle and dangerous of sins; a refined idolatry, much more to be dreaded than gross wickednesses, because the gross sinner would be alarmed by the depth of his degradation, and come up from it in terror, but the unhappy idolaters of Nature were deceived by the refined quality of their sin, and would be the last to enter the kingdom. Henry frankly affirmed to both of the wise men that they were wholly deficient in the faculty in question, and therefore could not judge of it. And Mr. Alcott as frankly answered that it was because they went beyond the mere material objects, and were filled with spiritual love and perception (as Mr. T. was not), that they seemed to Mr. Thoreau not to appreciate outward nature.[29]

Lidian thought the scene "ineffably comic." If Emerson had been at home that evening he would undoubtedly have been equally amused and would almost as certainly have found himself on Henry Thoreau's side of the question. But that apparent agreement would have masked a fissure developing between them on a more fundamental question concerning man's relationship with nature, one that went directly to the roots of moral behavior.[30]

Emerson had made clear his belief that "the moral law lies at the centre of nature"; in fact, that things "hint or thunder to man the laws of right and wrong, and echo the Ten Commandments." Given his adherence to these opinions, he would have been unpleasantly surprised if he had happened upon certain observations Henry had tucked away recently in his journal. "The moral aspect of nature is a disease caught of man—a jaundice imported into her," his young friend had written in 1841, adding a year later, "Man's moral nature is a riddle which only eternity can solve."[31] He had come to dismiss "'certain divine laws'—the moral sentiment—onto which Emerson fell back."[32] "What offends me most in my compositions is the moral element in them," he confided.

Clearly events were taking place in the intellectual lives of the two men—overtly and covertly—that created a field of tension between them. When the cement of a friendship is intellectual discourse, the sense that there is not a complete concordance of thought, even when its cause cannot easily be pinpointed, can mark the beginning of a rift.

6

Despite Emerson's continued fondness for and trust in Henry, an element of friction had become increasingly apparent in their relationship in the months preceding his tour. Referring to Henry's "perennial threatening attitude," he said wryly that he admired it "just as we like to go under an overhanging precipice." More and more Henry's presence in his house had begun to get on the older man's nerves in small but unmistakable ways. Shortly before he left on tour he lashed out at Henry because he was dissatisfied with a book review he had written. This incident left him feeling guilty but did not relieve his pent-up anger.

Not long after his departure in January 1843, Emerson wrote to Lidian making it clear that it had become a point of pride with him that Henry write to him first. He insisted that someone—he could not recall whether it had been Lidian or Elizabeth Hoar—had informed him that Henry in fact planned to do so. Emerson would look for the letter every day, he declared, and when he received it, would reply to Henry directly. The importance of the matter to him was underscored when, a week later, he demanded impatiently, "Where is Henry's letter that I heard of?"[33]

Actually, on the day before Emerson composed his final query, Henry had sat down to set the matter straight. "The best way to correct a mistake is to make it right," he began mildly. "I had not spoken of writing to you, but as you say you are about to write to me when you get my letter, I make haste on my part to get yours the sooner." To a great extent Henry blamed himself for the situation that had recently developed between them. He knew that his sudden shifts from silent withdrawal to belligerence were difficult for Emerson to accept and apologized for having "molested" him with his "mean acceptance" of his hospitality. Although he found it difficult to speak openly about his feelings, Henry took this occasion to thank the Emersons in writing for their "long kindness." He had been, he said with marked emotion, their "pensioner for nearly two years, and still left free as under the sky."[34]

The news soon reached Concord that Emerson had read Henry's letter "with great contentment." A week later, however, not having received the reply Emerson had promised, Henry decided to take the initiative and write to him again. At Lidian's suggestion he confined his comments to "domestic affairs." They had just finished supper, he explained, and two-year-old Edith had been brought into the room. The scene he described—with little Edith racing across the carpet, Lidian speculating about her husband, "Uncle" Henry writing his letter, and Emerson's aged mother smiling "over all"— gave graphic evidence of how important his place in the Emerson home had become to him.[35]

Meanwhile, Lidian's interest in Henry had been deepening, as her constant references to him in her letters revealed. When Henry received a music box from Richard Fuller as a New Year's gift, she wrote to Emerson: "I never saw anyone made so happy by a new possession. He said nothing could have been so acceptable. After we had heard its performance he said he must hasten to exhibit it to his sisters & mother—My heart really warmed with sympathy, and admiration at his whole demeanour on the occasion—and I like human nature better than I did." When Henry danced with little Edith, played the flute for her, or carried her about on his shoulders, Lidian reported it with fond approval. And when he made a comment she thought particularly amusing, she repeated it. After a lecture given by her brother Charles T. Jackson at the Lyceum, she noted: "Henry liked the lecture well enough, but declareth—that the more obtuse a discourse is 'the more popular will it be,' which proposition I submit to you as 'Henry's law.'"[36] Soon she was referring to his conduct as "brave and noble" and confiding, "Well as I have always liked him, he still grows up on me."[37]

But as her affection for him increased, her concern did also. Bradbury and Soden, the publishers of the *Boston Miscellany*, had just informed him that they intended to cut his promised fee for "A Walk to Wachusett" by "one third certainly." Realizing how large the question of earning money loomed for him, she petitioned Emerson for help: "Henry ought to be known as a man who can give a Lecture. You must advertise him to the extent of your power. A few Lyceum fees would satisfy his moderate wants— to say nothing of the improvement and happiness it would give both him & his fellow creatures if he could utter what is 'most within him'—and be heard."[38]

Five weeks after Emerson's departure, when Henry had not yet heard from him, Lidian felt obliged to prod her husband. "I think you have made Henry wait a reasonable—or *un*reasonable time for an answer to his letter," she asserted. On the same day, discovering that the packet including his second letter to Emerson had not yet been posted, Henry added a long note on the subject of friendship. Although he assumed an impersonal tone, the import of his message was clear. "How mean are our relations to one another!" he began. Reflecting on this unhappy thought, he concluded that it was "only essential to friendship that some vital trust should have been reposed by one in the other." That this confidence be "reciprocal" was, of course, necessary. "Other chains may be broken, but in the darkest night, in the remotest place, I trail this thread," he informed Emerson. Given his almost unnatural reticence, only a compelling need could have driven him to expose his feelings in this way. He clearly wanted reassurance that the tie between them remained as strong as ever.[39]

On successive days in the middle of the month two letters arrived from Emerson to Henry, each written before he received Henry's expression of concern about the path their relationship was taking. The first—commenced on February 4 and completed a week later—contained news about his lecture tour; the second, dated February 12, discussed details of the April *Dial*, which Henry was editing in Emerson's absence. Only in a parenthesis in the second letter did Emerson refer to a personal matter, taking the opportunity to apologize for his "rude and snappish speech" regarding Henry's attempt to write a book review. Henry sat down immediately to reply. He could recall no "rude and snappish speech," he claimed, and was "quite happy" to receive Emerson's letters. Five days later, perhaps embarrassed by how openly he had displayed his feelings in his note on friendship, Henry wrote to Emerson yet again. No "special answers" to individual letters of his were necessary, he told his friend.[40]

Regardless of Henry's protestation, his letter about friendship had clearly required an answer. When day followed day and no reassuring word reached him, the signal was unmistakable. The time had come for him to move on.

7

On March 1, with Emerson scheduled to return to Concord within a week, Henry once more took up his pen. He was "meditating some other method of paying debts than by lectures and writing," he said. Would Emerson look around in the New York area to see if he could find work for him there? Perhaps to Henry's surprise, Emerson returned to Concord with an offer in hand. Emerson's brother William wanted to hire a companion for his son Willie who would "put the boy and not his grammar and geography under a good and active influence." Among Henry's duties, if he accepted the job, would be to accompany his young charge from the family's home on Staten Island "to the woods" on the island and "to the city" across the bay. He would be paid one hundred dollars a year and provided a room of his own to study in "with fire when the season requires."[41]

Although Lidian quickly declared that she could not "spare" Henry, even she could recognize the advantages of the offer and was pleased for him. Hawthorne saw clearly that moving to New York was "one step towards a circumstantial position in the world" for Henry. And Emerson shared Henry's hope that once established in the metropolitan area he would "procure for himself literary labor from some quarter."[42]

Concerned about the welfare of the "solitary youth" in New York, Emerson wrote to a recent acquaintance, Giles Waldo.[43] By a stroke of good luck, Giles, a young man Emerson had met that winter while giving several unscheduled lectures in Washington, D.C., had recently moved to Brooklyn and now shared a room there in a boarding house with William A. Tappan. Giles, "a faithful subscriber to the Dial," had impressed Emerson with the "kindest & gentlest manners." William Tappan, whom Emerson had also met during his tour, he considered "tranquil and wise." Such "noble youths," he concluded, would be ideal companions for Henry Thoreau.[44]

In his letter, Emerson proposed that Giles meet Henry when he reached New York. Always cautious when bringing people together, Emerson considered it prudent to prepare Giles and his friend William for Thoreau's unorthodox appearance and manners. After all, Giles, like Emerson, was a direct descendant of Deacon Cornelius Waldo who had settled in Massachusetts in 1654, and William was the son of a leading antislavery advocate and successful businessman, Lewis Tappan. Giles responded to Emerson's comments with enthusiasm: "Henry Thoreau we shall be glad to see.—he is a wild man of the woods you say,—and we shall take no pains to conceal from him that we are as wild men of the city. I hope we may have some pleasant Sundays together." There was no need for formality, Giles insisted; let Henry "bring no 'letters of introduction' but only such messages as you may have to send,—and he shall be received and cherished." Having arranged for Henry to meet his young acquaintances, Emerson lent him twenty dollars to use in outfitting himself for his new situation. Emerson seems to have been at once gratified for Henry that his life was taking a new turn and relieved for himself at the prospect of having him out of the house. As he admitted to Hawthorne, he had "suffered some inconveniency" from having Henry "as a permanent guest at table and fireside." Sensing this, Henry, despite his appreciation for all Emerson had done for him, felt at the deepest level of his being like a rejected child.[45]

6

Into the World

On Saturday, May 6, 1843, Henry began the overnight journey to Staten Island in the company of his new employer, Mrs. William Emerson, who had been visiting her brother- and sister-in-law in Concord. In his pocket he carried seven dollars that Emerson had advanced him to pay for his traveling expenses and a letter to deliver to Giles Waldo as a means of meeting him. Sailing from Boston later that day, the traveling companions enjoyed a good passage until their ship ran aground in the mouth of the Thames River near New London where they were detained until the tide came in. When they reached New York City at ten o'clock the next morning, Henry and Mrs. Emerson hurriedly transferred to the Staten Island ferry for the final leg of their journey to the William Emerson home.

Dubbed the "Snuggery" by Emerson, it was a "long, low brown house, standing with its end to the road, with grapevines on the piazza and box plants in the garden." Henry quickly discovered that he could climb the hill directly behind it and see the city, its suburbs, and the bodies of water separating them, although the house was seven and a half miles from Manhattan. Within a few days he had "run over no small part of the island" and even "some way along the shore."[1]

Although the countryside delighted him, he appeared less certain about his situation. "Give me time enough, and I may like it," he said ominously after he had been there a few days. His employers were kind and attentive, but he soon discovered that their interests, their tastes, and their attitudes were poles apart from those of their Concord relatives. While he might respect and even like them, he didn't feel at home with them. They were not, he informed his parents, of his "kith and kin."[2]

A week after his arrival, Henry set off on the ferry to deliver Emerson's packet to Giles Waldo. From the Battery at the tip of Manhattan Island it was only a short walk to Lewis Tappan's office at the corner of Hanover Street and Exchange Place where Giles and his friend William Tappan worked. A few years earlier the elder Tappan had established the firm to "obtain and record . . . the standing of merchants throughout the country, for the use of those who might sell to them on credit," and the enterprise had proved successful enough for him to employ a growing number of clerks to collect and interpret the intelligence he sold.[3]

Delighted by Henry's appearance at the office, Giles and William led him to an alehouse in the neighborhood. Since they could stay away from their desks only a short time, Henry did not have an opportunity to observe them closely on this occasion. But the next day Giles traveled to Staten Island to return the visit, and Henry had the chance to talk to him uninterruptedly for two hours as they walked through the woods near the William Emerson house.

Like so many of the young men and women whose company Emerson enjoyed, Giles Waldo hoped to become a writer. Early in his correspondence with Emerson, Giles had sent him several of his verses and had been delighted to learn that he "intended printing" them in the *Dial*. Now even more exciting news had arrived in the packet Henry had brought from Concord. The "letters & fragments of journal" Giles had recently submitted for publication were also "acceptable," Emerson said, and he went on to encourage Giles to consider making a career of writing.[4]

Henry was not so supportive, however. As he and Giles walked through the woods together, it became uncomfortably apparent to him that a wide gulf stretched between them intellectually. To the bewildered Giles Waldo "all the fine things" Henry told him "of the signification of words, & letters" were "so new as never to have been dreamed of before." In a letter he wrote to Emerson that evening he explained: "My interview with Thoreau has shown me how desperately ignorant I have been content to remain of books. He found that on this subject, in regard to 'this scholar stuff' there could be but little sympathy between us,—at least that he had nothing to learn of me, while I must owe everything to him." Henry could not suppress his feelings of superiority with William Tappan either. Not long afterward Henry spent a few hours with William during which he grilled him zealously to measure the depth of his learning. Later William confessed to Emerson that Henry had "left many questions sticking in my shield," which he had felt inadequate to deal with. He had tried to bluff his way through the conversation, he admitted, and was rather ashamed of himself for having done so.[5]

Although Henry's treatment of the two young men was heavy-handed, his displeasure was directed not at them but at Emerson for having exaggerated their abilities. Henry liked the pair, he admitted. In fact, there was "a certain youthfulness and generosity" about them that he found "very attractive." But when he wrote to Emerson, he emphasized the disappointment he'd felt in meeting them. "They are so much better than the great herd," he conceded, "and yet the heavens are not shivered into diamonds over their heads." Furthermore, Henry implied, to have praised them equally had been a mistake. William's "more reserved and solitary thought commands respect," he asserted. But there was something about Giles Waldo that made Henry hesitate. Perhaps he had already sensed the weaknesses in his character that would later become apparent.[6]

From Emerson's point of view Henry had behaved badly. Secure in the knowledge of his own capabilities, Emerson treated everyone he met with courtesy. He would never have flaunted his intellectual superiority as Henry had. Furthermore, when Emerson was in the heat of one of his enthusiasms, he did not like to see its subject or subjects deprecated. This incident only served to intensify his feeling that Henry was unnecessarily difficult to deal with at times.

2

Still, Emerson's concern about whether Henry would be able to "make his pen useful to him" in New York remained as strong as ever.[7] Although experience had taught Emerson the difficulty of making books pay, he had recently learned from Horace Greeley of the explosive growth in the readership of general interest magazines. The aims of the *Dial*—which had been established to "further the best culture of New England"—were fundamentally different from those of the popular periodicals.[8] Nevertheless, he was convinced that Henry had the ability to write "very valuable papers" on "many subjects" and could succeed in their pages if he made a serious effort to do so.[9]

The interest that John O'Sullivan had shown in Henry's writing earlier in the year presented Henry with a capital opportunity. In March, O'Sullivan's magazine, the *Democratic Review*, had been described as "the most valuable journal of the day" if it "were not for its ultraism on politics" by Edgar Allan Poe in an article discussing the state of the nation's periodicals. Among its regular contributors, as Poe pointed out, were Orestes Brownson, George Bancroft, John Greenleaf Whittier, William Cullen Bryant, Nathaniel Hawthorne, and Catherine M. Sedgewick. If Henry's "valuable papers" were to begin appearing regularly along with theirs in the *Democratic Review*, he would have established an excellent base from which to launch himself into the turbulent world of magazine journalism.[10]

In his first letter to Henry after his departure for Staten Island Emerson made no attempt to hide his interest in how this aspect of his venture was progressing. He wanted to hear all about Henry's "experiences especially in the city," he told him. Henry's reply reflected his desire to ward off the pressure Emerson was putting on him to get on with the business of making a career. "You must not count much on what I can do or learn in New York," he warned. Two weeks later when he again wrote to Emerson, he had crossed the bay to the metropolis several times. During these visits his apprehensions had hardened into aversion. "I don't like the city better, the more I see it, but worse. It is a thousand times meaner than I could have imagined," he complained.[11]

In subsequent letters Henry avoided any mention of the steps he was taking to find "literary employment" in New York.[12] To his mother, however, he admitted that he was "getting the bait ready," and not long afterward he submitted an article to John O'Sullivan on J. A. Etzler's *Paradise within the Reach of All Men*. While in England the previous year, Bronson Alcott had sent a copy of the book to Emerson who had suggested that Henry review it. The article, which Henry had begun in the spring, discussed with intelligence and humor Etzler's conception of a utopian community powered by sunlight, wind, and the changing tides. While revealing none of Henry's special qualities as a writer, the article nevertheless was evidence that, as Emerson had predicted, Henry could write competently about subjects of general interest.[13]

As Henry waited to hear from John O'Sullivan about his essay, he was beset by a mysterious and unremitting sleepiness that left him listless and unable to work. Although he attributed his condition to a "demon" that traditionally afflicted his mother's family, the more likely explanation is that his system was responding to the stress of his situation as he confronted the demands of producing material for the New York literary market. Although he was free from his tutoring chores by two in the afternoon, he found himself unable to work on the kind of article Emerson expected him to produce. Instead he mused over anthologies of English poetry or struggled with a scholarly translation of Aeschylus's *Seven against Thebes.* In many ways he was still behaving like an adolescent who resisted doing what was expected of him.[14]

3

Before leaving Concord, Henry had learned that Ellery and Ellen Channing were still considering settling in the town and, at Emerson's request, had arranged for them to rent a little red farmhouse that stood on a lot adjacent to his garden. Shortly after Henry left for Staten Island the Channings moved into their new home. Very much in love, the young pair lived a simple, quiet life. Ellen was a fragile young woman with blue eyes and blonde hair who placed her young husband's interests before her own. By July she had opened a school for children in their house to bring in some income. Ellery tended the garden, cut wood for Emerson, and pursued his interest in writing.

Emerson was delighted to have Ellery as a neighbor and found him to be "excellent company."[15] The mannerisms that had bothered him when Ellery was visiting in his home no longer seemed important now that the young man had a place of his own. Ellery loved to talk and had an amusing and individual way of seeing things that Emerson enjoyed. He told Emerson, for instance, that he hoped "there would be no cows in heaven" although he could see their value on earth. It was to keep farmers busy during the summer, he said, thereby reducing "Intemperance" and "Crime." Emerson immediately adopted him as his walking companion in Henry's absence.[16]

Not long after the Channings arrived in Concord a small volume of Ellery's poems appeared on booksellers' shelves. Sam Ward had paid to have the book printed and Emerson had edited it. Emerson had undertaken the project with complex motives. He knew its audience would be limited to "a hundred or so" readers who knew Ellery or had already encountered his poems in the *Dial*.[17] Emerson was aware of the limitations of Ellery's verse, yet he had "persuaded" himself that Ellery was "a true poet" and deserved to be encouraged. When the book appeared, Ellery's supporters rallied round. Henry Thoreau reported that he had read the poems "two or three times over . . . with new and increased interest." Elizabeth Hoar admitted that she had carried the book to bed with her and had been unable to fall asleep until she had finished it.[18]

Four years earlier when Emerson had brought out a volume of Jones Very's poems and essays, he had done nothing to promote the book. His relationship with Ellery Channing was different, however. Where Jones Very, an odd but interesting person, had remained on the periphery of Emerson's life, Ellery had been accepted into his circle of young friends. Despite his private reservations about the quality of Ellery's output, Emerson decided to publicize it in an attempt to help Ellery establish himself as a writer. He included a notice of the poems in the July *Dial* in which he commented approvingly on the individuality of Ellery's talent. He also wrote a favorable notice that he submitted to the *Democratic Review*.[19]

Within a few weeks Emerson was to learn about the risks inherent in publicly taking a position in this way. Before Emerson's review was printed by John O'Sullivan, one by Edgar Allan Poe was published in *Graham's Magazine* that made it appear foolish. Poe ridiculed Ellery's verse. The poems were "full of all kinds of mistakes, of which the most important is that of their having been written at all," he said. The language Ellery chose to employ was "not precisely English," he continued, and his sense of meter and rhyme was faulty, to say the least. Poe's position was reinforced by the English poet John Sterling, who wrote to Emerson after receiving a copy of the volume from Ellery as a gift. Sterling found the poems too derivative and thought that if Ellery would read the correspondence of Schiller and Goethe, he "would either cease to be a poet or become a good one."[20]

Poe's review hit Ellery hard. He took long walks alone, wrestling with questions of esthetics in an attempt to deal with the chill that Poe's words had cast over him. But in doing this he was avoiding the real problem. It was his inability to pursue an effort to a successful conclusion that had laid him open to ridicule. As Emerson had pointed out a year earlier in his journal, Ellery simply could not make himself do the work necessary to take the verse that flowed so easily from his pen and polish it until it shone.

4

The longer Henry remained on Staten Island, the more anchorless he felt. Consequently, it had become very important to him to receive reassurance from Concord that Emerson and Lidian continued to think of him as "one of the family." Still stung by the conviction that Emerson had unfeelingly thrust him into the world, he couldn't bring himself to write to him seeking emotional support. Instead he fixed his attention on Lidian, who in her kind way had insisted that she could not "spare" him.[21]

During his years in the Emerson home Henry had undeniably become very attached to her, but now his affection for her assumed an even greater importance. Addressing her as his "elder sister," he told her that she had become "a lunar influence" in his life. His adoration took an almost mystical form. She often seemed to be looking down at him "from some elevation," he confessed, and he "was better for having to look up." He made no attempt to hide the fact that he worshiped her.[22]

Lidian was touched by the depth of Henry's regard. Encountering his mother in the village one day she told her of his praise, exclaiming, "I don't deserve it[;] he sets me higher than I am." (Mrs. Thoreau's reply—"Well, Henry was always tolerant"—continued to amuse the Emerson family for years to come.)[23] Although Lidian's answer to Henry's letter hasn't survived, Henry's response leaves no doubt that it was affectionate and encouraging. "I have only read a page of your letter," he began, "and have come out to the hill at sunset where I can see the ocean to prepare to read the rest. It is fitter that it should hear it than the walls of my chamber."

In his reply Henry allowed the emotion that had been building up within him for months to erupt. "Your voice seems not a voice, but comes as much from the blue heavens, as from the paper," he told her. "The thought of you will constantly elevate my life; it will be something always above the horizon to behold, as when I look up at the evening star. I think I know your thoughts without seeing you, as well here as in Concord." As he returned to her words again and again, his excitement grew: "I could hardly believe after the lapse of one night that I had such a noble letter still at hand to read—that it was not some fine dream. I looked at midnight to be sure that it was real. I feel that I am unworthy to know you, and yet they will not permit it wrongfully." The last phrase—"they will not permit it wrongfully"—suggests that he was wrestling with feelings that he only dimly perceived. He seemed to be claiming a special relationship with her that she could not in good conscience accord him. And he had done so in a letter that she would certainly show to Emerson, who in turn could not be expected to be pleased. In his loneliness Henry's affection for Lidian had almost crossed the line into a danger zone.[24]

Henry waited a month for a reply during which time he did not hear from either of the Emersons. When the reply came, it was from Emerson, not from Lidian herself. Emerson's note was cool, correct, impersonal. Lidian had not been well and had gone to Plymouth where she hoped "to recruit her wasted strength," he wrote. Before her departure she had asked him "to acknowledge and heartily thank" Henry for his last letter to her.[25]

In the spring when Henry had written to Emerson of his friendship, there had been no answer; now when he had opened his heart to Lidian she had relayed her thanks with devastating politeness through her husband. There was clearly a lesson to be learned from this experience, and Henry did not ignore it. Never again would he permit himself to lay bare his feelings before his "brother" and "sister." In his dealings with them he would contain himself as rigidly as he did with others.

5

For some time Emerson had hoped that Giles Waldo would visit him in Concord. At first the young man found a trip of this length impossible to make due to his financial situation. "I have so hedged up my paths in life with embarrassment of debt," he wrote, "that I am now constrained for a time to give up the freedom I love." But in July he decided to disregard his personal situation and venture northward. He arrived on July 15, at a time when Emerson was ready for company. Lidian had not yet returned from Plymouth, and he had no pressing affairs to attend to. Before long he discovered that Giles's presence engrossed him so completely that he was neglecting his writing.[26]

Since their initial meeting, Giles Waldo had been assiduous in his pursuit of Emerson. At the time of their introduction by a mutual acquaintance in Washington, D.C., Giles had told Emerson that for some time he had wanted to meet him "more than any other person in the country."[27] At his suggestion Emerson had moved from Gadsby's Hotel into the boarding house where Giles was staying. Four days later, when Emerson had continued on his lecture tour, Giles had written him the first of many flattering letters: "—how full of joy I am at having seen you—and how more than full, at having been able to know you so well. You have already done me much good—more than you can think." At first Emerson had tried to hold Giles at "arms length," sending him "warnings" that his "company was made up." But Giles's unflagging enthusiasm for Emerson disarmed the older man. Before long Giles could write, "You have received me! It is more blessed than I thought."[28]

In reading these letters, and others of the period, it is necessary to remember that the exchange of language that expressed heightened feelings was a convention at the time practiced by educated people. Thoreau, Emerson, and their friends were not alone in adopting this manner when corresponding with each other. Their constant references to "love" and their regular use of other elaborate phrases to express their feelings for each other should not be understood to mean precisely what those words and phrases would be understood to mean today. This is not to say, however, that they were without emotional content. They expressed real feelings, but through a practice that regularly employed exaggeration.[29]

During the "calm sunny hours" Emerson and Giles spent together in Concord, Emerson was once again struck by his young friend's "fine, gentle spirit" and "great intelligence."[30] But his enthusiasm for his poetry was already cooling, and he decided not to include any of it in the July issue of the *Dial.* The manner of Henry's criticism of Giles may have irritated Emerson, but by now he had come to see the justness of his remarks. If Giles really intended to be a writer, he would have to "learn English," Emerson advised him, "namely, by reading a multitude of books."[31] However, no hint of this shift in attitude appeared in the letter Emerson asked him to carry to Henry when he returned to New York. Instead Emerson wrote sharply,

"Giles Waldo has established himself with me by his good sense. I fancy from your notices that he is more than you have seen. I think that neither he nor W. A. T[appan] will be exhausted in one interview."[32]

It was not entirely Henry's fault that "for some weeks" the three had "strangely dodged one another." Giles had been forced to cancel a meeting on June 2, and soon after that went to his family home in Scotland, Connecticut, to attend his dying father. William, for his part, was a shy, elusive figure, difficult to know. Nevertheless, Henry, to whom Emerson's good will was important, could not ignore his displeasure and immediately took steps to improve the situation. Two weeks later Henry informed his Concord friend that he had "spent some pleasant hours" with them at their "intelligence office."[33]

6

The summer of 1843 continued to be a difficult time for Henry Thoreau. Early in August he belatedly told Emerson about the article he had submitted to the *Democratic Review,* but only to inform him that it did not suit its editor: "I sent a long article on Etzler's book to the Dem Rev six weeks ago, which at length they have determined not to accept as they could not subscribe to all the opinions, but asked for other matter—purely literary I suppose." In this report Henry suppressed as much as he revealed. To begin with, John O'Sullivan's rejection of the article had not been unconditional: "If . . . you would not object I think it very likely that some addition & modification made with your concurrence would put your review of it into the shape to suit my peculiar notion on the subject," he had written. In addition O'Sullivan had been quite specific about the kind of submissions he would like to receive from Henry in the future. "Especially should I like some of those extracts from your Journal, reporting some of your private interviews with nature, with which I have before been so much pleased."[34]

As it happened, Henry had recently sent Emerson the manuscript of a new article, "A Winter Walk," which was based on the nature writing from Henry's journal. Since Emerson hadn't received it in time to include it in the July *Dial,* he had informed Henry, "I shall then keep it for

October, subject however to your order if you find a better disposition for it." Clearly that occasion had arrived, yet Henry made no move to retrieve the essay.[35]

Henry's reply to O'Sullivan, which had been posted several days before he relayed the news to Emerson, provides additional evidence of his conflicted attitudes toward the effort he was engaged in. About the Etzler article he was conciliatory, if vague, and O'Sullivan at length decided to publish it. But his response to O'Sullivan's request for more material showed neither a willingness to please nor an understanding of the *Democratic Review*'s editorial policy. "If I should find any notes on nature in my Journal which I think will suit you I will send them—" he wrote. He then proceeded to inquire if his translation of *Seven against Thebes* would "be suited to your review." Obviously it would not, as he should have realized. And no "notes on nature" were culled and forwarded to O'Sullivan.[36]

By now Henry, who had been away from Concord for three months, had at last begun growing "more wakeful." Convinced that he might "yet accomplish something in the literary way," he completed a short piece called "The Landlord," written expressly to sell, and offered it to John O'Sullivan, who accepted it. He also mustered up his courage and called on "every bookseller's or publisher's house" in the city to which he could gain admittance. How he approached them, we do not know, but this experience—which he described as "very valuable" and "the best introduction I could have"—opened his eyes to the realities he was facing. Harper's told him bluntly that their business brought in fifty thousand dollars a year and they intended "to let well alone," while other booksellers, unidentified in his correspondence, suggested that he do "what an honest man cannot." Nor were his visits with magazine publishers any more encouraging. The *New Mirror*, the *New World*, and *Brother Jonathan*, he learned, were "overwhelmed with contributions which cost nothing, and are worth no more," while the *Knickerbocker*, an older and more prestigious publication, was "too poor" to compensate its contributors for their work. Only the *Ladies' Companion*, it seemed, could be depended upon to pay.[37]

Discouraged, Henry decided to try to supplement his earnings as a tutor by selling subscriptions to the *American Agriculturalist*. One day in the middle of August, Henry took the ferry to Manhattan and began knocking on doors. His effort was interrupted by a tremendous rainstorm that suddenly swept over the city, making the streets impassable. Giles Waldo gladly sheltered Henry in his boarding house room until "the Great Storm," as the *New-York Daily Tribune* described it, passed. According to that newspaper: "It is not too much to say that so great a quantity never fell in this city in any previous twelve hours during the memory of the present generation. An immense amount of damage was done by the overflowing of sidewalks, flooding of cellars and basements, washing in of yards, sidewalks, etc." The next day Henry returned to Staten Island. Peddling magazine subscriptions, he had decided, was not the solution to his problem.[38]

Not long afterward, when Emerson learned the surprising news from Giles Waldo that Henry had been forced to go "a-peddling," he broke a silence that had once again lasted a month. He had reread "A Winter Walk" carefully and had noted in his journal that "it makes me nervous & wretched to read it, with all its merits." Although Emerson focused his complaint on Henry's "trick" of "substituting for the obvious word & thought its diametrical antagonist," that objection alone does not explain a reaction as strong as his. Perhaps the tone of the piece clashed with the mood of deep pessimism that had enshrouded Emerson since his young son's death eighteen months earlier. Having lost the power to generate the ebullient sense of optimism that had characterized his public statements before the tragedy occurred, Emerson may have found it difficult to respond positively to the buoyancy of Henry's narrative.[39]

At any rate, a basic difference in attitude between the two men had begun to emerge. Within months Emerson would note that "the absence of any appearance of reconciliation between the theory & practice of life" had become a matter of serious concern to him. In August, while waiting to hear from Emerson regarding "A Winter Walk," Henry had commented in a letter to his mother, "This life we live is a strange dream, and I don't believe at all any account men give of it." Both men were confronting an inability to find absolutes in human experience, but each was doing so in a way that was peculiarly his own. Emerson's comment was based on the belief that the development of a viable theory of life is a reasonable expectation; Henry's, on the rejection of this supposition. Moreover, Henry, although disappointed that no acceptable explanation of human behavior had yet presented itself to him, possessed the capacity to plunge into the natural world for emotional and intellectual refreshment. Emerson did not share that ability. Where Henry found his stimulus as a thinker and writer in immersion in nature, Emerson found his in introspection coupled with observation of social activity.[40]

Although Emerson had been disturbed by the "mannerism" of "A Winter Walk," he informed Henry, he had by "pretty free omissions" removed his "principal objections" and would print the piece in the October *Dial*. Henry was particularly gratified to learn of this decision, since, as he admitted in his reply, things were not turning out for him in New York as either of them had hoped. "Literature comes to a poor market here," he said bluntly, "and even the little I write is more than will sell." When "The Landlord" appeared in the *Democratic Review,* it dissatisfied him so thoroughly that he refused to buy a copy of the magazine to send to his family. He did not consider it "worth fifty cents," he informed his sister. But if he found writing for a superior publication like the *Democratic Review* unsatisfactory, the prospect of writing blatantly commercial pieces for magazines like the *Ladies' Companion* appalled him. Poe had categorized this type of periodical scathingly in his essay on the state of popular journalism: "Instead of instructing the youthful mind, they 'please with a rattle, tickle with a straw'—instead of instilling a sound morality, they inculcate a neglect of everything that is valuable—instead of making the poor contented with their condition, they descant upon the luxury of fashion and wealth, causing a thousand hearts bitterly to ache for an imaginary want." Emerson could not have expected, indeed would not have wanted, Henry to be a party to this.[41]

By the end of summer several things about Henry's situation had become clear. Producing the kind of writing that commercial outlets demanded went completely against his grain. Writing to satisfy their demands was extremely difficult for him, and when he did do this successfully, he was ashamed of the product. Therefore, he could not make a living for himself in New York through his literary efforts alone. But as he was learning this, he was also hesitating to confront a real opportunity by ignoring John O'Sullivan's interest in his nature writing. If he had been willing to respond to his request for material based on entries in his journal he would have been introduced to a broader audience than the *Dial* would ever reach. It appears that he was not ready yet to take the steps necessary to establish his independence as a writer. Emotionally, he needed to continue to develop under the sheltering mantle of Emerson's interest.

7

The relationship that had briefly flourished between Henry Thoreau and Emerson's "noble youths" began to subside as the summer ended. Unhappy with teaching school in Washington, D.C., at the time that Emerson met him there, Giles Waldo had initially liked the idea of working in the Mercantile Agency in New York. But now, with several months of experience behind him, he was as dissatisfied as ever. William Tappan swore he would be "caged no longer" in his father's office. For some time the pair had been flirting with the idea of studying Italian and now William threatened to run off "to Italy by the first conveyance." Giles, who had apparently borrowed money from Emerson while visiting in Concord, was still too deeply in debt to consider the venture. Instead, he moved into an Italian boarding house where he hoped to find the surroundings more congenial.[42]

One day, while visiting a little church on Thames Street a few blocks from the Mercantile Agency, Henry "held forth" to the young men "after a creed somewhat heterodox."[43] His vision of what life could be, freed from "commerce, & degrading trades," seems to have had a powerful effect on his companions. In mid-September Giles and William suddenly left New York together to try an experiment. They had decided to see if they could "avoid the mere mercenary ways of living" that they found themselves "obliged to use in the city." Traveling to the forests of Hamilton County, New York, they "lived like Indians for a few weeks," even getting their food by hunting deer.[44]

After their return, Henry saw little of them. William left shortly afterward to vacation with his mother at Hopkinton Springs, then journeyed to nearby Concord to visit Emerson who had just printed one of his poems in the *Dial.* Meanwhile, Giles had moved again, this time taking a room in a tavern in Brooklyn. Henry continued to perform his duties as tutor to Willie Emerson and in his free time returned to the study of English poetry that he had begun in 1842. Having been given members' privileges at the New York Society Library and the Mercantile Library, he visited them frequently to withdraw the books he needed to pursue his interest. In addition he worked on a series of translations of Pindar's odes, which Emerson had asked him to undertake for the *Dial.*

Life in New York seemed purposeless to Henry now that he no longer hoped to earn a living there through his writing. He was considering going home for a visit at Thanksgiving when a letter arrived from Emerson mentioning that possibility. Emerson had once again been elected a curator of the Concord Lyceum, and he asked Henry to lecture there if he should decide to return for the holiday. Perhaps influenced by this appeal, Henry made up his mind to go, arriving in Concord sometime before November 23, 1843.

The town had changed in his absence. The railroad that was being built between Boston and Fitchburg had reached Concord as it pushed slowly westward. In doing so it had brought with it a new population, the immigrants from Ireland who were doing the backbreaking work of clearing the way and laying the track. They worked from dawn to dusk for fifty cents a day and housed their families in dismal shacks that rose near the tracks and also along the river. Their presence gave the quiet village the appearance of a frontier town.[45]

But this didn't matter to Henry; for him the important thing was to be home again with his friends and family. In his previous encounters with Ellery Channing he had found that they got along very well, and he was happy to find him comfortably settled in Concord with Ellen. He was also pleased to be able to renew his acquaintanceship with Nathaniel Hawthorne. And by this time Bronson Alcott had found a house in the village for himself and his family. Emerson who had dreamed for many years of surrounding himself with a community of literary people had to some extent been successful in achieving that goal, a circumstance that promised a great benefit to Henry Thoreau as well if he should come home permanently.

For some time Henry had not felt "especially serviceable" to the William Emersons. As for his charge, Willie Emerson, he was "not attracted toward him but as to youth generally." There seemed to be no impediment in the way of his resigning his post, and he quickly made up his mind to do so. After a hurried trip to Staten Island to retrieve his belongings, he settled down with his parents in their rented house on Main Street. The question of his returning to live with the Emersons does not seem to have been discussed.[46]

7

A Beautiful Asylum

I

Aware that he had "awakened a great hope" in Henry Thoreau, Emerson felt a strong sense of responsibility toward him. A year earlier he had noted in his journal that Henry's verse was "poetry of the second degree," and nothing had happened since then to change his opinion. In fact, when Henry had submitted a group of poems to him for the *Dial* the previous summer, Emerson had neither commented on them in his letters nor published them in the magazine. Emerson was convinced that at twenty-six Henry should face certain realities about his ability as a poet and decided that it was time to have a frank talk with him on the subject.[1]

Shortly before his death, Henry told his neighbor Franklin Sanborn that during the early 1840s he had destroyed much of his poetry at Emerson's prompting.[2] The exact date of this episode hasn't been established but the evidence points to its having occurred not long after his return to Concord from Staten Island. For Henry, destroying the bulk of his manuscript poems was a traumatic experience. They did not just represent years of effort; they established his importance as a person in his own eyes. That Emerson was right in his judgment didn't make the task any easier. Whether Henry burned the manuscripts or tore them up and threw them away, no one knows. But once the deed was done, he had to view himself as doubly a failure. He had been unable to succeed as a magazine writer in New York, and now his ability to write poetry had been condemned by the man whose critical opinion he valued most. In addition, Emerson had decided that the

April issue of the *Dial* would be the last. Henry would not even have that outlet for the prose works he might produce.

As the New England winter set in, Emerson secluded himself in his study to complete his second collection of essays. His first collection, which had appeared in 1841, had carried his reputation far beyond the small group of intellectuals who had responded so strongly to *Nature*. Now he was again gathering together material that he hoped would "interest all men permanently." His practice was to write "a good deal," he said, but "for the most part without connection, on a thousand topics." From this mass he was striving to "get a few chapters ripened into some symmetry and wholeness." This volume, when published, would not only solidify his standing as America's leading thinker, but would enlarge his audience in Europe as well.[3]

Emerson's immersion in the task at hand led him to avoid even those contacts that would have occurred in the normal course of events. Henry was forced to pick up his life in Concord without Emerson's support at a time when he needed it badly. He dealt with the situation by putting aside his literary pursuits and committing himself fully to the family pencil-making business.

Although Henry's father had established it in 1823, it had never provided more than a meager income for the Thoreaus, primarily because of the low quality of the product. In their workshop, as in all American workshops at the time, wood was cut, split, and grooved to receive a lead paste, then the two sides of the pencil were glued together. Aware that these pencils made a gritty mark, Henry determined to improve the Thoreaus' product as well as their production methods.

Henry became so engrossed in improving the Thoreaus' manufacturing procedures, he admitted, that he even began dreaming about it at night. Though taxing, this intense involvement began to pay off quickly. It was possible, he had learned in an encyclopedia in the Harvard Library, to mix the lead with Bavarian clay that could be baked and cut into pencil leads to replace the gritty paste the Thoreaus had been using. In time he discovered that by varying the amount of clay in his mixture, he could produce leads of differing degrees of hardness or softness, permitting the Thoreaus to advertise graded pencils. And he also developed a machine to drill holes in the solid pencil woods into which the lead could be inserted, eliminating the need to split the woods and glue them together.[4]

Although it hadn't taken Henry long to demonstrate that he could manu-facture pencils more effectively than his father, he had no interest in spend-ing his time running a business. For him writing was as much a necessity as eating and sleeping. Maintaining his journal in his free hours or continuing to pursue his study of the history of English poetry did not suffice to satisfy this need. He had to find a more gratifying way to fulfill himself.

Three years earlier, after Henry's return with his brother, John, from their trip along the Concord and Merrimack Rivers, he had begun entering his recollections of their journey in a notebook. The entries in this "long book," as he named it because it was twice as wide as it was high, had grown to considerable length. The record of his excursion with John, it seemed to him, would provide an effective framework for a volume of reflections on life and literature. What he needed was the leisure to write it.[5]

2

Ellery Channing's presence in Concord during these months proved to be a boon for Henry. With Ellery, who was also twenty-six years old, he did not need to be on his intellectual mettle all the time, as he felt compelled to be with Emerson. Henry could be as natural and spontaneous with Ellery as he had been with his brother, John. This was particularly helpful during the period of reappraisal that Henry was going through. It was healthy for him to have a companion who laughed easily, who enjoyed roaming the woods in his company, yet whose life had a different focus than his own.

Ellery's world was centered around his marriage to Ellen Fuller, which had brought him the stability he formerly lacked. He had left Harvard without completing his first term, had moved west where his attempts to succeed at farming and journalism had failed, and had settled down in Concord with his young wife without a dependable means of support. But the "indescrib-able happiness" of his marriage had begun to generate a new sense of self-worth in him. "It is my experience," he wrote to his sister Mary, "that each day of married life adds a new charm to the relation, deepens the faith of the husband and of the wife in each other, fortifies them against trial, suffer-ing and misfortune, & increases, instead of diminishing their love." If Hen-ry's life had stalled, Ellery's seemed to be moving forward in a positive way. Ellen had become pregnant for the first time and, while there may have been frightening aspects for Ellery in the prospect of becoming a father, there was also pride in the thought of starting a family of his own.[6]

During the winter and spring of 1844 a strong bond developed between Henry Thoreau and Ellery Channing. In his lifetime Henry formed only three lasting attachments of major consequence to men—with his brother, John, with Emerson, and with Ellery. Each of these relationships played itself out within the context of a family situation. In the case of John, the family was, of course, Henry's own, and he was functioning within a predetermined framework. But in the other two instances he chose to experience friendship as an integral part of a larger series of interconnected relationships. His role in these constellations shifted from friend, to brother, to son, to rival, to "uncle" for the children, depending upon the circumstances he was responding to at the moment. The sole constant was that the friendship existed in an arena large enough for him to act out a variety of needs in the safety of a situation that circumscribed his action. The pattern of Henry's relationship with Ellery and Ellen Channing that began to emerge that summer was very different from the one Henry had established with the Emersons. The fact that Ellery and Ellen were contemporaries while the Emersons were older certainly had something to do with this. In his relationship with the Emersons, Henry had tended to side with Lidian and in turn expect her protection. With the Channings, he behaved as he might have if John Thoreau had married Ellen Sewall. He was very considerate of Ellen Channing but did not place her on a pedestal as he did Lidian. Instead he tended to act as her protector, shielding her from contention by providing Ellery with companionship at times when the stresses of family life seemed to overwhelm him.

The earliest evidence of this developing pattern surfaced in July, a few months after the birth of the Channings' first child, Margaret Fuller Channing. Her presence altered the balance in the Channing home. While proud of his newborn daughter, Ellery was irritated beyond reason by the sound of her crying, and he disliked the Miss Prescott who had come to care for her during Ellen's recovery. After Ellery had retreated to the White Mountains on his own for a short time to escape the situation, Henry arranged to meet him in the Berkshires in northwestern Massachusetts. By keeping Ellery peacefully occupied for several days as they traveled down the Hudson River and took a walking tour in the Catskills, Henry gave Ellen time to regain her strength.[7]

During the next few months, when the pressures at home were more than Ellery could stand, he would slip away to join Henry in the woods. Ellen, who understood Ellery's emotional makeup, was glad to have his attention diverted at tense moments like these. She was aware, however, that there was more than momentary annoyance weighing on him. Like Henry he was trying to come to grips with his future. Although Emerson considered him "a person of the finest wit and of very extensive information," he had concluded that "his writing is unworthy of him." For Ellery to continue to devote himself to the pursuit of a literary career seemed foolhardy now that he had a family to care for.[8]

Since resigning from the editorship of the *Dial,* Margaret Fuller had published two books. The most recent, *Women in the Nineteenth Century,* had enhanced her reputation as a writer and she had accepted a position working for Horace Greeley on his newspaper, the *New-York Tribune.* As Ellen's sister, Margaret had found her concern about the future of the Channing family growing as Ellen and Ellery "stumbled along" during the summer. Apparently through her good offices, Ellery was offered a job at the *Tribune,* which he accepted.[9]

At the end of November, Ellery moved to New York City, leaving his wife and child in Boston to spend the winter with his father. Ellery's departure to work at the *Tribune* sharply underscored Henry's failure a year earlier to establish himself in New York. Henry could not escape the fact that his friends were proceeding with their lives, while he seemed endlessly locked into a conflict with himself. Ellery, who saw that this knowledge was eating away at Henry with a disturbing intensity, knew that something had to be done.

3

One day in September 1844, before Ellery's departure for New York, Emerson had set out to walk alone to Walden Pond. On his arrival there he had encountered "two or three men" who were discussing the sale of a field "on the shore of the pond." They asked Emerson to bid on it and he did, feeling that for many years he had had "a sort of daily occupancy in it." For $89.10 he purchased eleven acres. The following day he invited several friends— Henry and Ellery most certainly among them—to see his purchase, and they persuaded him that to protect it he should also buy Heartwell Bigelow's adjacent pine grove. Thus without planning to do so, he became the owner of about fourteen acres of fine waterfront property on Walden Pond.[10]

It was Ellery Channing who saw in Emerson's new landholding the solution to Henry Thoreau's problem. A few years earlier while walking with Emerson and Margaret Fuller beside the pond, Ellery had heard Emerson say he would like to build himself a study there where he would be free to compose "verses from eight in the morning until four in the afternoon." Apparently recalling this, Channing wrote to Henry from New York in February advising him to construct some sort of shelter for himself out there and settle down in it to write. "I see no alternative, no other hope for you," he said.[11]

Emerson agreed readily to the proposition that Henry build a one-room house on his land in which to write the book that would become *A Week on the Concord and Merrimack Rivers.* The site that Henry chose lay on a rise two hundred feet from a small cove on the north side of the pond. Toward the end of March before the ice had melted, Henry began to cut down slim white pines for timber in the nearby woods. Although there were occasional snow flurries as he worked, the spring sun shone most of the time. By the middle of April he had finished hewing timber, studs, and rafters, and the frame of the house was ready to be raised. Early in May Emerson joined a group of neighbors to help him set it in place. When that was done, Henry "carefully feather-edged and lapped" sun-bleached boards to make his house "impervious to rain" and carried stones from the shore of the pond to lay the foundation of his brick chimney.[12]

On Independence Day, Henry settled down beside the pond. His removal there was more than a retreat from the world; it was a retreat into the past. Day after day he sat at his desk re-creating from his notes the events of the weeks he had spent exploring the Concord and Merrimack Rivers with his brother. Every word he set down evoked John's presence. He wrote and re-wrote passages chronicling the details of their voyage together. He described their meals and their hikes, the people they encountered, and the wildlife they observed. The conflicts that had driven the brothers apart toward the end of John's short life were shunted aside by Henry in hurried allusions buried within the text of the manuscript; only the happy times remained. In spirit, if not in fact, John was there at Walden with him. His presence sustained Henry during four months of intense work. In that time Henry assembled a manuscript of approximately forty thousand words from his notes in the "long book."

Embracing the past so intensely may have been crucial in enabling Henry to produce his first book, but the experience had a darker side also. In the ordinary course of events it was difficult enough for him to relate satisfactorily to people. By locking his deepest feelings into the world of memory he was accentuating the sense of separateness that plagued him during his lifetime. During Henry's stay at Walden, this feeling of separation persisted despite the fact that he continued to enjoy the companionship of his friends and family. He walked to the Thoreau house regularly, often staying for a meal, and he made a practice of dining every Sunday with the Emersons. As Emerson commented later, Henry would call on him and Lidian "without ceremony" whenever it suited him. In fact, he felt so much at home with the Emersons, his friend added dryly, that he would "help himself to any axe or spade or bucket that he found," considering it his right to "keep it until he was through with it."[13]

Emerson in turn stopped in frequently to see Henry in the course of his walks, as did others including Bronson Alcott, George Ripley, Edmund Hosmer, and Ellery Channing who had come back to Concord with Ellen and their baby when his attempt to earn a living as a writer for the *New-York Tribune* had faltered due to his inability to discipline himself. However, this activity did not alter the reality that John was the central fact of his existence there. Henry's encounters with family, friends, and neighbors were momentary diversions; John was with him during the bulk of the day when his mind was occupied with the task of taking his first draft and turning it into a finished book, an effort that grew more difficult as his ambitions for the book increased. He had come to the conclusion that it is "harder to write great prose than to write verse" and had set himself the task of creating a book in the classical tradition of the "whole man" whose everyday life is "pervaded with the grandeur of his thought."[14]

4

In Emerson's mind there appears to have been little doubt about the wisdom of Henry's decision to free himself from the "trouble and anxiety" of earning a living by conventional means. Not long after Henry moved to Walden,

Emerson amended his will to establish him as heir to the land on which his "solitary house" stood.[15] In addition he supported the venture by paying Henry for a variety of tasks. Years later when Henry recalled that at the time he had done "various jobs—about the town—some fence building, painting, gardening, carpentering, etc., etc.," he neglected to mention that much of this work had been commissioned by Emerson. Actually, of the $13.34 Henry proudly claimed was all he needed to earn through manual labor to support himself during his first eight months beside the pond, $10.00 was paid him by his friend.[16]

While outwardly supportive, Emerson seems at another level to have been challenged by Henry's newfound sense of purpose. Although the publication of his second collection of essays in 1844 had brought Emerson a more solid fame than he had previously enjoyed, he still hoped to earn a place among the world's truly great writers by proving himself to be the "genuine poet of [his] time." In recent months he had been considering bringing together his published poems into a single volume. Now, with Henry hard at work on a book, Emerson was suddenly beset by a "rhyming mania." He quickly announced that he would collect the best of his published work in a single volume and add a group of new poems to it. By the end of the month his sense of urgency had become so pronounced that he informed Thomas Carlyle he hoped to print his volume before New Year's Day. It was as if he felt compelled to have it ready before Henry finished his book. For the first time, an overt element of competition appears to have entered into Emerson's attitude toward his young friend.[17]

It should be noted that Emerson was no easier on himself as a poet than he had been on Henry. He was not at all satisfied with what he had accomplished so far. Unhappy with poetry that was derived from the ideas of other countries and earlier times, his goal was "to refashion the objects of nature, with which he [had] long been familiar, into symbols of his own thought."[18] In an attempt to write poetry that was truly American, he was investigating irregular stanzas, occasional rhymes, feminine endings, and the dimeter usually associated with nursery rhymes. Today the work he was doing would be labeled "experimental," a category of effort unknown at the time. Although his best verse, it would later be observed, gives "the notion of inspiration," he had to struggle to achieve this effect.[19] "No wonder a writer is rare," he concluded. "It requires one inspiration or transmutation of nature into thought to yield him the truth; another inspiration to write it."[20]

A continuing distraction for Emerson was that he was chronically short of money to maintain the standard of living that he and Lidian found desirable. Therefore, although reluctant to do so, he made the decision to interrupt work on his volume of verse to "read a new course of lectures in Boston early in the season," and by the middle of October he had put his poems aside for the winter to concentrate on this lecture series. He had not lectured in Boston since his financially unsuccessful appearances in the winter of 1841–42, and it was important to him that the new series attract a larger audience. The subject he chose—"representative men"—was a concession to audience tastes. Unlike his recent courses in Boston, which had dealt with more abstruse questions demanding his listeners's strict attention, this one would be anecdotal and therefore easier to follow. His subjects would include Plato, Shakespeare, Napoleon, Swedenborg, Montaigne, and Goethe.[21]

Meanwhile, Lidian had become pregnant again. Her health had never been good, and she found herself "too weak, too miserable, to keep house at all." Even directing the daily activities of her maids had become too demanding for her. That spring, after Emerson completed his lecture series, it was decided that the Emersons would turn their home over to Mrs. Marston Goodwin to run as a boarding house. The family kept four rooms for their own use—Emerson's study, his mother's room, and two other bedrooms—and emptied the rest of the house for Mrs. Goodwin, her family, and a group of boarders. Not long after Mrs. Goodwin took over the management of the house, Lidian gave birth to a son who was named Edward. When boarders were added to the Emerson family with its three small children and to Mrs. Goodwin's brood of four, there might be as many as eighteen people living there at any time.[22]

Under intense internal pressure to finish his collection of poems once his lecture series was completed, Emerson could not help looking with envy on the freedom Henry enjoyed at Walden. In December Emerson had purchased—with Henry witnessing the deed—forty additional acres across from the site where Henry's house stood. It seemed to him that it might be a good idea to follow Henry's example and construct a small study of his own there in which he could enjoy "uninterrupted seclusion for writing."[23] This new land rose to a commanding height that, seen through the mist, looked to Henry "like a dark, heavy, frowning N Hampshire Mt."[24] Henry immediately began to design a small house for Emerson to be erected "on the peak of his woodlot." From its windows there would be a sweeping view that took in Mount Monadnoc, Mount Wachusett, the church spires of Groton and Sudbury, and the Concord River. Pleased by Henry's design, Emerson decided to go ahead with the project, although he wasn't yet ready to choose a date for construction to start.[25]

When Emerson had finally turned his attention to his volume of poetry after being away from it for several months, he hadn't found it easy to pick up the thread of his work. Not until the second week in April did an incident occur that set him on the right path. Browsing in Elizabeth Peabody's bookstore one day while visiting Boston, he happened upon a German translation of the Persian poet Hafiz. Emerson had once commented that he found it "sufficient to set me in the mood of writing verses at any time, to read any original poetry." In Hafiz, Emerson discovered not only the stimulus he needed to return to his own book of poems but also an approach to experience different from that of his New England neighbors, one that took joy in the physical aspects of daily life. The previous summer Emerson had confined himself to experimenting with form; now he concluded that to accomplish his aim he had to place his thoughts in a new context as well. Although reading Hafiz had a liberating effect on Emerson's imagination, the work itself did not go easily. The ideas came, but the poems did not often realize themselves in the form he was seeking. He began to doubt his ability to achieve the ambitious goal he had set for himself.[26]

5

In July, Henry celebrated the first anniversary of his new life at Walden Pond. He had worked hard on *A Week on the Concord and Merrimack Rivers* and was anxious to learn what Emerson thought of it. One afternoon in the middle of the month they settled down together "under an oak on the river bank" where Emerson listened as Henry read selections from the manuscript. Emerson's response was enthusiastic. "Invigorated" by Henry's prose, he announced that he found the book not only "spicy as flagroot" but also "broad and deep."[27] In the composition of *A Week* Henry had incorporated considerable material unrelated to his voyage with John, much of which he had developed earlier under Emerson's tutelage. That *A Week* was thus heavily influenced by "the pull of Emerson's thought" may in part account for Emerson's characterization of Henry's reflections in its pages as "profound."[28]

After nine years of effort, it appeared that Henry had finally proven to Emerson's satisfaction that he had what it took to fulfill the promise he had shown as a college senior. In fact, Emerson insisted that the book was ready for publication. Henry's response to Emerson's recognition of his achievement was as surprising as it was unexpected. He became embroiled with the law.

A week after meeting with Emerson beside the river, Henry walked into the village to pick up a shoe he had left for repair. While there, he was approached by Concord's tax collector, constable, and jailer, Sam Staples. For several years Henry had refused to pay the Massachusetts poll tax in protest against the government's support of slavery. Staples, who had already given him several warnings, insisted that something had to be done about the situation. He offered to lend him the money if he was "hard-up," but the young man refused his help. "Henry, if you don't pay, I shall have to lock you up pretty soon," Staples informed him. Henry's reply—"As well now as any time, Sam"—led to his being jailed immediately.[29]

Henry's eagerness to be arrested was trivial in comparison with his anger the next morning when he discovered that his back taxes had been paid— probably by his Aunt Maria—and that he was to be released. "Mad as the devil," he insisted to Staples that, not having paid the taxes himself, he had the right to stay in jail.[30] Never having encountered a prisoner who was not happy to leave at the earliest opportunity, the incredulous Staples told him, "Henry if you will not go of your own accord I shall put you out, for you cannot stay here any longer." Although Henry claimed—and undoubtedly believed—that he was taking this stand on principle, his enthusiastic embrace of a symbolic punishment immediately after having won Emerson's endorsement of his book strongly suggests that he was reacting unconsciously to that circumstance.[31]

Although Henry had strenuously sought Emerson's approval, it's not surprising that receiving it aroused anxiety in him. By applauding Henry's book, Emerson had in effect recognized him as an equal. But this hardwon acknowledgement placed Henry in his own mind in a highly exposed position. For close to a decade his dependence on Emerson had been a central fact of his life. Would his newly achieved independence be construed by his friend as a challenge? If so, what form would the inevitable retribution take? Complex and deeply buried fears had engulfed him that afternoon as he was approached by Sam Staples. Seeing an opportunity to escape from these fears, he had impulsively courted arrest. After all, to be jailed was to be removed from the contention that caused the anxiety.

Emerson's response to the situation was no more obvious in its motivation than his young friend's. In regard to the principle on which Henry claimed to have acted, he commented simply that "refusing payment of the state tax does not reach the evil so nearly" as withholding other taxes would, since it was the federal government and not the Commonwealth of Massachusetts that was supporting slavery. This cool judgment masked a deep annoyance, however. To Bronson Alcott he confided that he considered Henry's behavior "mean and skulking, and in bad taste."[32] For some time a dichotomy had been growing in his attitude toward Henry. While he continued to praise Henry's abilities in his letters, he had begun to present quite another picture of his feelings in his journal. When Henry insisted—tactlessly— "that philosophers are broken down poets," Emerson seemed merely hurt and defensive. But on other occasions the aggressiveness of Henry's manner clearly irritated Emerson: "H.'s conversation consisted of a continual coining of the present moment into a sentence & offering it to me. I compared it to a boy who from the universal snow lying on the earth gathers up a little in his hand, rolls it into a ball, and flings it at me."[33] Emerson had clearly been affronted by Henry's refusal to pay his tax; his friend had behaved as no gentleman should. But behind Emerson's judgment lay a mounting anger with Henry for his growing independence, a reaction that suggests that Henry's perception of the situation was not without foundation. For Emerson, fulfilling the role of mentor was undoubtedly more important than he himself realized. Relinquishing that role would have been hard for him at any time but was particularly difficult when doubts of his own ability to achieve his highest ambitions were never far from his thoughts. While outwardly pleased with Henry's accomplishment, inwardly he resented the necessity of giving up his superior position in the relationship. Withholding his approval, and his affection, was his way of punishing Henry for asserting his independence.[34]

Not long after Henry's release from jail, the men sat down to discuss his actions. Emerson had conceded earlier that Henry's position was more defensible than that of the abolitionists who continued to pay all their taxes while objecting to the government's position on slavery. But this papering over of the issue did not affect the emotion that underlay the disagreement. Henry's anxiety had not vanished, nor had Emerson's growing discontent with him.[35]

6

During this period Emerson's poems—twenty-eight new ones and thirty-two that had been published previously—had finally gone to press. Still haunted by misgivings as he waited to see them in print, he could not help recalling how few English poets had produced verse that to contemporary eyes seemed "still glowing and effective." In his journal he carefully listed them: Milton, Shakespeare, Pope, Burns, Young, Cowper, Wordsworth, Herbert, Jonson, Donne. The hope that his name would be added to this distinguished body seemed more remote than ever. On December 29, a few days after his *Poems* reached the bookstores, a review appeared in the *Boston Courier* describing it as "one of the most peculiar and original volumes of poetry ever published in the United States." While there was "exceeding refinement" in the sentiments expressed as well as "piercing subtlety" in the imagination displayed by the poet, the reviewer continued, the diction often seemed harsh and the thought obscure. This summed up the comments that began appearing in other publications. The originality of the poetry was recognized, as was the special Emersonian sensibility, but the praise was muted.[36]

Henry's response to Emerson's "peculiar and original" volume was recorded by Bronson Alcott after they had discussed the *Poems* at some length. It seemed to him that his friend's work lacked "merits of the highest order." His concrete remarks about the poetry suggest that he was unaware of, or perhaps did not understand, Emerson's aesthetic goals. To him, "continuity and flow were wanting, as we find them in some of the older poets."[37] Two years earlier he had expressed his reservations about one of the poems in the collection more explicitly. While living with the William Emersons on Staten Island, he had read Emerson's "Ode to Beauty" with considerable dissatisfaction. Specifically he had objected to aspects of Emerson's technique. The verses seemed "chopped off . . . some short and some long," making the setting of the poem "altogether unworthy of the thoughts." This earlier attempt of Emerson's to find new rhythms suitable to the new world clearly hadn't pleased him. "Yet," he had concluded, "I love your poetry as I do little else that is near and recent."[38]

At this time Emerson was flirting with the idea of going abroad. The previous summer Margaret Fuller had left New York to travel in Europe with friends. While in England, she had mentioned Emerson's success as a lecturer to Alexander Ireland, who had written to Emerson inviting him to lecture there, an opportunity that appealed to him. At forty-two, he found, as many people do in their middle years, that life was not turning out as he had expected it to. He sympathized with Lidian's difficulties, but boarding at home was a most unsatisfactory way to live. He was not happy as things were, and to make matters worse, he seemed to sense that his powers as a writer were waning.

Although Emerson's second collection of essays had been more popular than his first, he was aware that it had lacked the intellectual force of the earlier volume. And now his poems had failed to meet his expectations. "I reckon myself a good beginning of a poet, very urgent & decided in my bent and in some coming millennium I shall yet sing," he remarked. While he was candid enough with himself to admit that "literary power would be consulted" not by traveling "the public road" but by following Henry Thoreau's example and seeking solitude in which to work, he was finding it difficult to resist the opportunity offered by a trip to London to escape the pressures at home.[39]

Despite his unsettled state of mind, Emerson responded immediately when Henry told him that *A Week* would soon be ready for publication. In fact, he seemed more anxious than Henry to have the matter settled quickly. On March 12, 1847, Emerson wrote to Evert Duyckinck, literary adviser to Wiley and Putnam in New York City, informing him that Henry had "just completed a book of extraordinary merit." He wondered if it would be an appropriate title for the publisher's American Library series that was featuring new writers like Edgar Allan Poe and Herman Melville. Duyckinck responded that he would be glad to read the manuscript and offer his advice. But unlike Emerson who had rushed his poems into print, Henry hesitated. Continuing to labor over his manuscript, he put off sending it to Duyckinck from day to day.[40]

In recent months Emerson's displeasure with Henry's brashness of manner had continued to grow. By the summer of 1847 he had concluded that Henry lacked "that power to cheer & establish, which makes the value of a friend." The only outward sign Emerson gave that his feelings had cooled to this extent, however, was his decision not to build a study opposite Henry's house at Walden. His proposed trip to London provided an obvious pretext for this reversal, but later he hinted to a friend that Henry's behavior had also influenced him. Instead of building at Walden, Emerson resolved to "ornament" his grounds at home. Bronson Alcott, not Henry, was asked to design a summer house for him and to supervise its construction, with Henry contributing manual labor.[41]

While it was impossible for Henry to avoid the realization that Emerson had come to consider him a "very poor companion," it's unlikely that he understood the sharpness of the split that had developed in the older man's feelings toward him.[42] Although Henry's attitudes toward Emerson were also in flux, they did not parallel his friend's. He still insisted that there was "no such trustworthy and faithful man," that there was "more of the divine realized in him than in any." But he had begun to question the clarity of Emerson's vision. It seemed to him that Emerson did not "consider things in respect to their essential utility," seeing instead only a "partial & relative" aspect of their nature. His "probes pass one side of their centre of gravity," he complained. "His exaggeration is of a part, not of the whole." Reading Emerson's works had begun to leave Henry vaguely dissatisfied.[43]

Henry, of course, was looking at Emerson's writings from his own perspective, which was a highly personal one. The fact that he and Emerson approached experience differently, and for that reason perceived reality differently, did not seem to occur to him. To begin with, Henry believed he was "favored by the gods." Convinced that he had "a solid warrant and surety at their hands, which my fellows do not," he felt himself to be "especially guided and guarded." Emerson's view of his own relationship to the world was very different from that. He certainly did not believe he was "especially guided and guarded." His consciousness of the demands imposed on the individual by his responsibilities to himself and to others led him to an entirely different appreciation of the consequences that flow from making choices. This basic cleavage between the outlook of the two men could—and with increasing frequency did—lead to significant differences in perception, even when they were confronting similar situations.[44]

In addition, when Henry took a position on an issue, his view was often influenced by a healthy dose of self-justification, which did not seem to be the case with Emerson. When Henry told his friend that "the man that shoots a buffalo, lives better than he who boards at the Graham House," he may have made his point neatly, but in doing so he exposed a bias that was linked to his need to define issues in a manner that offered no threat to his way of life. This stance, which informed Henry's thinking on a broad range of subjects, contributed to his growing sense that Emerson's writings did not connect with the "centre of gravity" of things. To some extent it was his own peculiar angle of vision that made this seem to be the case.[45]

During these weeks, as Emerson edged toward a decision to lecture abroad, Henry was growing restless in his house in the woods. He wanted to travel, too, he told his friend, but "to Oregon[,] not to London." Afterward Emerson commented impatiently, "Yes, surely; but what seeks he but the most energetic nature? & seeking that, he will find Oregon indifferently in all places; for it snows & blows & melts & adheres & repels all the world over."[46] Nevertheless, he once again sat down at his desk to see what he could do to help. As it happened, Lidian's brother, Charles T. Jackson, had undertaken a geological survey of the federal mineral lands in Michigan. While at the time he had adequate assistance, he seemed to hold out hope that Henry might be able to join the group at some point in the future.

As Henry waited to hear from Jackson—fruitlessly, as it turned out—he was also nervously watching the mail for a reply from Duyckinck to whom he had at last posted his manuscript of *A Week*. What Henry apparently did not know was that holding back the manuscript had been costly for him. In May Duyckinck had lost his position as editor of the *Literary World*, a publication principally backed by Wiley and Putnam, and was presently at odds with them. When Emerson learned that Wiley and Putnam had turned the volume down, he had already committed himself to lecturing abroad and was busy preparing for his trip. Nevertheless, he immediately proceeded to solicit the interest of other publishers in New York and Philadelphia. Henry's was "a book of wonderful merit, which is to go far and last long," he announced, supporting his friend's wish to have it "printed in a cheap form for a large circulation." Toward the end of August, James Monroe and Company, which had brought out Emerson's poems, expressed interest on the condition that the author contribute to the cost of the edition. By now Emerson was deeply involved in the details of his tour and therefore withdrew from the negotiations, turning them over to Henry to conduct.[47]

As Emerson completed his preparations to leave the country, he found himself in an unexpected position in relation to Henry Thoreau. During Henry's stay at Walden Pond each had produced a book for which he had set lofty goals. In literary terms Emerson's volume of poetry was probably of more lasting interest than *A Week on the Concord and Merrimack Rivers.* But to the friends at the time, that likelihood was not apparent. Instead it seemed as if Emerson had failed to achieve his aims while Henry had succeeded in attaining his. In the consciousness of the two men, if not in the eyes of the world, the effort had leveled the playing field on which they contended. They were no longer Emerson and his "Henry young and brave." They were Emerson and Thoreau, two adult men, who in striving to fulfill high personal ambitions, could not avoid the fact that they had become competitors.

That sense of competition was underscored for Emerson by the general interest that Thoreau's stay at Walden Pond had aroused in the community. In response to the questions people had begun asking Thoreau—"What's it like there?" "What do you eat?" "Aren't you lonesome?"—he had prepared a lecture on his life at Walden that he had delivered before the Concord Lyceum in February. Not long before reading the lecture he had begun working on a draft of a book on the subject. While Emerson was busily pinning down the details of a lecture tour that would keep him away from his writing for a year, Thoreau had embarked on *Walden,* the volume that would secure his place in American literary history. It would take him seven years to complete it.[48]

8

At Home with Lidian

As the time for Emerson's departure drew near, he and Lidian decided that the experiment of boarding in their own home should come to an end. Unhappy at the prospect of spending nine months without her husband in a household comprised exclusively of women and children, Lidian Emerson invited Henry Thoreau to live with her while Emerson was away. Without hesitation Thoreau accepted the invitation and began making plans to abandon the house he had built beside Walden Pond. Later he wrote in defense of this choice: "I left the woods for as good a reason as I went there. Perhaps it seemed to me that I had several more lives to live, and could not spare any more time for that one." The life he was about to assume as man of the house while his friend traveled was not so much his own, however, as Emerson's. And that more than anything else defined the meaning of the experience for him. Taking Emerson's place, even in the limited sense that the circumstances permitted, released powerful and complex emotions that he was ill-equipped to handle.[1]

To facilitate Thoreau's return from Walden Pond Emerson offered to buy his house.[2] An agreement was reached quickly, and on September 6, a month before Emerson was scheduled to sail for Liverpool, Thoreau settled down to work at the "green desk, in the chamber at the head of the stairs." He had moved in "with Mrs. Emerson, whose house is an old home of mine," he announced, "for company during Mr. Emerson's absence" and would be free to pursue his literary interests as he had been during his earlier two-year stay under their roof.[3]

During the coming weeks the Emerson house was enveloped in continuous activity. Arrangements had to be made for Emerson's mother to journey to Staten Island to stay with her eldest son during Emerson's absence; for Lidian's sister, Mrs. Lucy Brown, to move from the little house Emerson had built for her across the road into the big house for the winter; and for providing adequate household help under the new conditions. At first it was hoped that only one servant, Abby, would suffice, but at last it was decided that Abigail would be needed as well. Then there was the question of how Emerson should travel. Would it be better to book aboard one of the new steam-driven liners that crossed the Atlantic in twelve days or on a sailing ship that would take twice as long? Passage on the sailing ship would cost less, and Emerson decided on that.

To finance the trip Emerson had already arranged for a bank loan. Now he issued oral and written instructions about how he wished his property maintained and hurriedly began preparing himself for his lecture tour. A week and a half before his departure he wrote to his brother that he ought to be ready by now but wasn't. He needed to finish editing a second edition of his first series of essays and had promised a contribution to the newly established *Massachusetts Quarterly Review.* "All my life is a sort of College Examination," he complained. "I shall never graduate. I have always some tormentors ahead." Although he would have found it "a great pleasure" to prepare a new series of lectures, he was reduced to pulling together a group of old ones to deliver before his British audiences.[4]

On October 5, a small band set out by train from Concord to accompany Emerson to the dock. In addition to Lidian Emerson and Henry Thoreau the group included Bronson Alcott and his wife, Abigail. Thoreau found his friend's cabin on the *Washington Irving,* a 155-foot-long packet, depressingly small. It reminded him of "a carpeted dark closet, about six feet square, with a large keyhole for a window." As the party said goodbye to Emerson, Mrs. Alcott wept convulsively, but Lidian Emerson did not shed a tear. Conscious of the irony of this, Lidian wondered what her friend thought of her. Nevertheless, she kept her emotions carefully hidden from the others, including her husband.[5]

Back in Concord, Henry Thoreau and Lidian Emerson settled into a comfortable routine. The days were long enough for Thoreau to work steadily on a lecture describing his visit to Mount Katahdin in Maine and to deal with the household responsibilities he had inherited from his friend. He "banked up the young trees against the winter and the mice," kept an eye on the fence "to see when a pale is loose or a nail drops out of its place," made sure there was "good mortar" for the chimney of "the airtight stove," paid the gardener, and even arranged for the purchase of railroad stock for Emerson's portfolio.[6]

Since Lidian's health was "so feeble and [her] leisure hours so few," Thoreau devoted a good deal of his time to the Emerson children, eight-year-old Ellen, six-year-old Edith, and little Edward, who was now three.[7] He made it a practice to breakfast with them before the rest of the household had come down. He roughhoused with Eddy and discussed "the pictures in the portfolio and the Turkish book" with Ellen. He sat patiently with all three youngsters going through "the Penny Magazine, first from beginning to end, and then from end to beginning." He even entertained them with his favorite song, "Tom Bowline."[8]

The "tragedy and comedy and tragic-comedy of life" continued "as usual" in the Emerson home, Thoreau assured his friend when he wrote to him on November 14 for the first time since his departure. In his letter Thoreau chatted familiarly about the activities of the Emerson family during the previous six weeks and the responsibilities he had assumed as Emerson's surrogate. The life he was leading in his friend's absence was clearly a deeply satisfying one for him. "Lidian and I are very good housekeepers," he informed Emerson, and he was spending much time with the children. In fact, he continued, little Eddy had asked him "very seriously" a short time before, "Mr. Thoreau, will you be my father?" Therefore, Thoreau quipped, "you must come back soon, or you will be superseded."[9]

That autumn the rhythm of Thoreau's days was almost identical to Emerson's when he was in Concord. The critical difference, of course, lay in Thoreau's dealings with Lidian. As Robert Sattelmeyer has indicated, "Thoreau's chivalric idealization of Lidian" was a central factor in "his emotional life." Thoreau's manner toward her made it abundantly clear that she occupied a significant place in his affections. The deepest stratum of his feelings for Lidian, however, those that lay carefully concealed from the world, could only reveal themselves in subtler ways. She was his "very dear sister," not his wife, and this circumstance structured their daily encounters.[10] Although Thoreau's manner toward her was always circumspect, it concealed attitudes no less intense than those he had expressed in his initial letters to her written four years earlier when he was acting as tutor to Emerson's nephew on Staten Island. Later, in a lengthy journal entry similar in content and tone to his effusive letter of June 20, 1843, he would develop these feelings in detail, apparently assuming that his words would be read by no one else.[11] "A sister," he wrote, is "One in whom you have—unbounded faith—whom you can—purely love. A sweet presence and companion making the world populous. Whose heart answers to your heart. Whose presence can fill all space." As he continued down the page, the internal guards that checked his feelings seemed to relax. He imagined "the stream of [her] being" uniting with his "without a ripple or a murmur" and slowly spreading "into a sea." Addressing her directly, he admitted, "When I love you I feel as if I were annexing another world to mine. We splice the heavens." She was, he proclaimed, one "into whom I flow." As he rambled on in this manner, his thoughts became increasingly confused, however. Suddenly he addressed her as "my young mother" and called himself her "eldest son." Surprised by the emergence of this idea from his unconscious mind he paused over it. "Whether art thou my mother or my sister—whether am I thy son or thy brother," he pondered. He had touched on a subject that had to be repressed immediately; she was "a sister," he decided, although one who had "recreated" him. But in the process of allowing his thoughts to flow without restraint he had revealed a crucial fact concerning the nature of his attachment to his friends's wife, a fact that explains a great deal about his behavior to both of them.[12]

Despite the many real gratifications Thoreau derived from living with Lidian Emerson, there were inevitable moments when the conflicting feelings she aroused in him erupted in a spasm of guilt. The most vivid picture we have of how he felt at these times appears in a long poem, hastily set down during this period, which begins with these lines:

> If love fails in strife with love
> Then it boldly looks above
> And appeals to higher Love.
> Sweet Friend, Sweet Friend,
> I ask not for Love but Hate without end[.]
> Erect me, restore me, hearten me then
> With so dear severity fatal to men.
> Sear my humanity,

Cure my insanity.
O wrack me, grind me, crush without end,
Let me taste of the worst,
Sweet Friend—sweet friend.[13]

The walls that separated Thoreau from Lidian were not merely those on the second floor of the Emerson home that divided his bedroom from hers. Nor were they those that convention erects between a man and his friend's wife. They had sprung up within him when he had associated her too closely in his emotions with the mother he had adored as a child and to whom he was still strongly attached.

Although these forbidden associations were never far from Thoreau's consciousness, to maintain his emotional balance he necessarily had to dwell in his thoughts on the more acceptable, if hardly commendable, fact of his having allowed himself to become too closely attached to the wife of his best friend. All the guilt he felt could conveniently be transferred to that situation. Under the circumstances it isn't surprising that Emerson's warm reply to his letter intensified Thoreau's sense of shame. "Very welcome in the parcel was your letter," Emerson began, "very precious your thoughts & tidings. It is one of the best things connected with my coming hither that you could & would keep the homestead, that fireplace shines all the brighter,— and has a certain permanent glimmer therefor." In his answer Thoreau subtly attempted to warn Emerson that he did not deserve this praise. From the long poem in which he had attempted to deal with the twisted knot of his feelings he had selected fourteen lines to include in his answer, beginning with these words: "The good how can we trust?" That he should have alluded to these verses in writing to his friend in itself suggests a strong compulsion to rid himself of his secret. But he had gone even further. He had intimated to Emerson that even his "good Henry Thoreau" was capable of betraying him—in his thoughts, if not in his actions.[14]

2

In his letters to Emerson, Thoreau had kept him informed about his efforts to find a publisher for *A Week on the Concord and Merrimack Rivers*. His negotiations with James Monroe and Company had not been successful. Like Wiley and Putnam, Crosby and Nichols, and Harper Brothers, they would bring it out, but only at his expense. "If I liked the book well enough, I should not delay," he explained, "but for the present I am indifferent. I believe this is, after all, the course you advised,—to let it lie." That, however, was not Emerson's position. "I am not of opinion that your book should be delayed a month," he replied. "I should print it at once, nor do I think that you would incur any risk in doing so that you cannot well afford. It is very certain to have readers & debtors here as well as there."[15]

If in Thoreau's mind a vision of Lidian Emerson as a loving mother hovered behind his view of her as his "sister," it's not surprising that his perception of Emerson as his "real brother" was at times overshadowed by the looming figure of a father who was not so benign in his attitudes. From the beginning Emerson's manner of expressing his expectations of his young friend had displayed unmistakable elements of paternal presumptuousness. When he insisted that Thoreau would not "incur any risk" by publishing *A Week,* he was behaving like a father who sees only one side of a situation, the side that is important to him. For Thoreau, publication of *A Week* clearly entailed risks, but they were psychological as well as financial. What he perceived these risks to be is evident in the passages from Ovid's *Metamorphoses* that he chose to translate that year. From "The Story of Phaethon" he selected two sections, one dealing with Phaethon's anxiety while preparing to take the place of his father, Apollo, as driver of the chariot carrying the sun through the sky each day, and a second considering Apollo's attempt to reassure his son that he would return safely from the trip. Although Thoreau did not translate the conclusion of the story describing Phaethon's loss of control during the journey and his subsequent death, this outcome must have been in his mind as he worked with the earlier passages. Just as Phaethon had asked to drive Apollo's chariot, Thoreau had chosen to pursue a literary career. If Phaethon had died as a result of his challenge to his father, what would Thoreau's fate be if he emerged in the literary world as a competitor to Emerson?[16]

As Raymond Gozzi has pointed out, Thoreau "dreamed of a perfect friendship" with Emerson, but as he came to see him more and more as a father figure, the "unconscious feelings of love and hate he had toward his own father became controlling" in the relationship. During the winter, when Thoreau turned once again to writing lectures, the subjects he chose reflected his struggle to deal with these ambivalent feelings. Although they had been mounting within him for a decade, his present position in the Emerson home had intensified them greatly.[17]

On February 23, Thoreau informed Emerson that he had recently read a lecture before the Concord Lyceum on "The Rights & Duties of the Individual in relation to Government." In this lecture, which has since become known in essay form as "Civil Disobedience," he made it clear that he saw the individual occupying the same position in his country that a child does in the family: "'We must affect our country as our parents,'" is the opening line of a poem he quoted in the text.[18] With this statement as a guide, it becomes apparent that his objection to being "at the service of some unscrupulous man in power" has a very real meaning to him.[19] Behind the government stands the man who leads it, and that man is a parent, a father.[20] In writing of this lecture to Emerson he did not mention that he had placed at the core of his argument his brief imprisonment for nonpayment of the poll tax. Although Emerson's disapproval of Thoreau's behavior in that instance can be viewed as a legitimate manifestation of a different attitude toward activism, Emerson had also perceived it as a rebellious act directed toward himself, and the essay can be read in the same way.[21] The "tyranny" Thoreau rails against as "great and unendurable" is personified for him in the tyranny the father exercises over his son. The emotion that Thoreau poured into this lecture derived its explosive force from the anxiety aroused in him by the complex of desires surrounding his wish to supplant his friend, and in it he identified the specific apprehensions that tormented him: "Is there not a sort of bloodshed when the conscience is wounded? Through this wound a man's real manhood and immortality flow out, and he bleeds to an everlasting death. I see this blood flowing now." When the compulsion to rebel is coupled with the fear of emasculation, "hate," however well repressed, is an unavoidable by-product.[22]

Since the roots of Thoreau's feelings for Emerson reached down into the most secret recesses of his mind, no amount of conscious effort could free him for long from the conflicts provoked by their relationship. Recently, however, it appears that Thoreau had enjoyed one bright moment of respite from those conflicts owing to an expression of affection from Emerson, who had written: "I have to thank you for your letter which was a true refreshment. Let who or what pass, there stands the dear Henry,—if indeed any body had a right to call him so,—erect, serene, & undeceivable. So let it ever be!" This statement seems to have released a flow of unrestrained emotion. "Dear Waldo, For I think I have heard that that is your name,—" Thoreau began his reply. He had never previously used Emerson's first name in the salutation of a letter; in fact, it is unlikely that he had ever spoken it in his friend's presence. It was as if Emerson's words absolved him, momentarily, of the guilt that was festering within him.[23]

3

During the "beautiful winter" of 1848 the pleasant flow of experience in the Emerson home that had been so gratifying to Henry Thoreau for several months had been interrupted. For much of the time Lidian had been "confined to the bed of sickness." Although she had written despondently to an acquaintance in February that "Fatigue and care have brought me low, & will bring me lower," she had not let her husband know how ill she was. Finally, Thoreau took it upon himself to inform Emerson of the situation. Lidian had been "confined to her chamber four or five weeks, and three or four weeks, at least to her bed—with the jaundice, accompanied with *constant* nausea, which makes life intolerable to her," he wrote. "This added to her general ill health has made her *very* sick." The doctor who visited every day had given her strict orders to rest. She was not to read or even be read to except for brief intervals. When the doctor learned that she had insisted on sitting up in bed to write to Emerson, he had threatened not to come again unless she stopped.[24]

While Thoreau had been struggling covertly with the emotions aroused by his attachment to Lidian, she had been attempting to deal with the problems created for her by separation from her husband. Housekeeping with Thoreau had not compensated her for his absence, and the letters that she wrote to him from her sickbed seemed to him to be "tragic." Apparently he destroyed them, for they have not survived among the others that he carried with him on his return to Concord several months later, but from his replies to her it is clear that she had longed to receive "full and 'private' letters" from him and had been hurt by the long impersonal chronicles of his social successes that had reached her. No doubt she was interested to learn that he had been presented to the Marquis of Northhampton; viewed the art collection of Lord and Lady Palmerston; observed Prince Albert closely across a table; talked with Wordsworth, Thackery, Macaulay, and De Quincey; but what she wanted to hear was that he loved her and missed her. Emerson's reticence regarding his feelings was nothing new, of course. When Lidian persisted in her hope, he answered, "Ah you still ask me for that unwritten letter always due, it seems, always unwritten, from year to year, by me to you, dear Lidian." But he could not delude her into thinking it would ever be delivered. The "trick of solitariness," he feared, "never never can leave me."[25]

Nevertheless, he could accommodate her in one important way, and he hastened to do this. In one of his early letters, it appears, he had informed her that he intended to invite Margaret Fuller to live with them in Concord, a proposal that to Lidian had "looked calamitous." A year and a half earlier Margaret had gone to Europe with friends and after touring through England, Scotland, France, and Italy had settled in Rome. Although Emerson did not know the details of her situation there, he had learned that she was under great stress. Probably he realized that in suggesting this course to Lidian he had gone beyond the bounds of the acceptable, for when her response reached him, his letter to Margaret, which had remained in his "pocket for weeks," had still not been posted. He would not send it, he assured Lidian. Instead he had "written her only my regrets that I am not a prince, with good hope, too, that she may yet be a tenant of Mrs. Brown's house if that remains open."[26]

At this time Emerson confessed to his brother William that the strains of his marriage had been one of the considerations that had led him to come to England in the first place. He had hoped that his "absence" would prove a "relief" to Lidian's cares, but this had not proved to be the case. While he could not bring himself to regret his journey, it seemed to him, even before he received Thoreau's letter detailing Lidian's illness, "in every way to have cost too much." Now, apprised of the depth of her distress, he wrote to her of his concern that his departure had been "the cause or signal of a crop of annoyances & pains."[27]

Alone in her room in Concord Lidian brooded on her situation. Shortly after their marriage Emerson had referred to the "invisible Dominican chest with its flagellant contents" that she seemed always to carry with her. Her taste for a "knotted cord-let" never seemed more in evidence than at this time when she felt totally rejected.[28] Taking out the letters Emerson's beloved first wife, Ellen Tucker Emerson, had written to him two decades earlier, she read them. Later, in recounting a dream about herself, her husband, and Ellen, Lidian revealed what she perceived her place to be in Emerson's affections. In the dream she and Emerson found themselves in heaven where they encountered Ellen. Seeing her husband with the young wife he had loved so much, Lidian withdrew, presumably leaving them together for eternity. When told of this the next morning Emerson commented, "None but the noble dream such dreams."[29] Lidian had always been able to count on softening Emerson's feelings toward her by praising Ellen, and she took this path once again after reading her letters. In response to Lidian's glowing comments about the letters when she wrote him next, he replied, "But you should have seen Ellen. When she left this world, I valued every body who had seen her, and disliked to meet those who had not." Although it was thoughtless of him to repeat this to Lidian "who had not," he made it clear that "the kindest & best account of your reading in the precious file" had moved him. "And they deserved all you have said," he told her approvingly.[30]

With the arrival of spring, Lidian was able to transmit the reassuring news that she was "perfectly recovered." In the meantime Emerson's concern for "that poor child—Lidian" had settled him in a resolve to return home for good, not just because he felt he ought to but because he wanted to. His absence had not secured her "the perfect tranquility" he had hoped for nor had his encounters with the great been a satisfactory substitute for the leisure to write that he enjoyed in Concord.[31] Separation had not worked for either of them; instead it appears that he had come to accept Thoreau's statement that people "must accept or refuse one another" as they are. He would bring back with him, he informed his wife, "a contentedness with home, I think, for the rest of my days." To this Lidian replied: "Dear, dear friend I will try to be a good wife to you on your return, if I never was before."[32]

How much Henry Thoreau knew of the drama that had played itself out between the Emersons is unclear. But he certainly felt its effects. With the onset of Lidian's serious illness the period during which they had been "good housekeepers" together had come to a close. As she had withdrawn further into sickness and depression, he had seen less and less of her. True, he had been admitted to her room "occasionally" to speak or to read to her, but the illusion of their closeness could no longer be sustained. The "Lidian" of his early letters to Emerson suddenly became "Mrs. Emerson" again. He had left his house at Walden Pond without regret to serve her, but now with Emerson's return imminent he found himself unnecessary to her. During the winter of 1848 Henry Thoreau had learned the bitter consequences of attempting to act out the fantasy of living another's life.[33]

4

Earlier in the year Thoreau had mentioned in a letter to Emerson that a lecture "on Friendship which is new" lay before him on his desk. Thoreau's first draft of *A Week on the Concord and Merrimack Rivers* had contained a section on friendship, and he had reworked this material into a form that could be delivered before a lyceum audience. In doing so he had added considerably to it. This commentary—which appears in its revised state in the Wednesday section of *A Week*—represents an attempt by Thoreau to define the boundaries of friendship. The experience it describes is in many ways unlike the one Emerson portrayed in the essay on friendship that he had completed in 1842.[34]

Perhaps the most surprising aspect of Thoreau's treatment of friendship is that his remarks commence with a confession of guilt. The recollection of "long passed" acts of kindness by his friends, he wrote, made him "shudder to think" of the manner in which he had ignored them. He had caused his friends pain, and he was sorry for it. In defense of his actions, he could only allude to his observation that friendship is "evanescent," never assuming a "permanent form," remembered only "like heat lightning in past summers." This attempt to excuse his derelictions only served to remind him, however, that he had to take his friends' suspected distress seriously, if only because his own experience had been that friendship leads to rejection as inevitably as morning does to evening.[35]

Unlike Emerson, whose view was decidedly more optimistic, Henry Thoreau claimed that the "drama" of friendship "is always a tragedy." Thoreau even went so far as to insist that "there are none charitable, none disinterested, none wise, noble, and heroic enough, for a true and lasting Friendship." This is a dark view, and it was colored by the side of his nature that appeared to seek out injustices. Although Thoreau could write with seeming rationality that "we are paid for our suspicions by finding what we suspected," he allowed these injustices, real or fancied, to dominate his thought. Friendship, as Henry Thoreau described it in these pages, was a tense, demanding process, always overshadowed by the threat that "it will end."[36]

Despite his anxieties, Thoreau recognized that friendship is widely regarded as an essential ingredient of human life. "All men are dreaming of it," he admitted. It is "a perfectly natural and inevitable result" when "those who have an affinity for one another" meet. For him, as for most people, a special aura surrounds a friend. "I always assign to him a nobler employment in my absence than I ever find him engaged in; and I imagine that the hours which he devotes to me were snatched from a higher society," he said.[37]

The yearning that Thoreau expressed in his essay for the rewards he sought in friendship is evident on every page. It seems even more strongly rooted in him than that voiced by Emerson when he wrote about the subject. To Thoreau, friendship appeared to be nothing less than "a miracle." "What is this Love," he demanded, "that discovers a new world." "It will make a man honest; it will make him a hero; it will make him a saint. It is the state of the just dealing with the just, the magnanimous with the magnanimous, the sincere with the sincere, man with man." He pictured "endless conversations with his Friend, in which the tongue shall be loosed, and thoughts be spoken without hesitancy or end." He wrote an imaginary letter to him. "This is what I would like,—to be as intimate with you as our spirits are intimate,—respecting you as I respect my ideal."[38]

Nevertheless, in the world of everyday experience, Thoreau warned, it "is commonly far otherwise." "Men do not, after all, *love* their Friends greatly. I do not often see the farmers made seers and wise to the verge of insanity by their Friendship for one another. They are not often transfigured and translated by love in each other's presence. I do not find them purified, refined, and elevated by the love of a man." He had come up against the same barrier that had blocked Emerson's way earlier. We "are dreaming that our Friends are our *Friends,* and that we are our Friends' *Friends,*" but in doing so we are evading a greater reality. "Our actual Friends are but distant relations of those to whom we are pledged." Friendship "takes place on a level higher than the actual characters of the parties would seem to warrant."[39]

In order to account for his deep need to be "transfigured and translated" by friendship, Thoreau had been led back to the view shared by many of the transcendentalists. Friendship "is not the highest sympathy merely, but a pure and lofty society, a fragmentary and godlike intercourse of ancient date." "It requires immaculate and godlike qualities full-grown." The tension at the heart of Thoreau's comments is the same as in Emerson's essay—that between concrete experience and transcendental ideality. The trouble for Thoreau was that, as much as he would have liked to believe otherwise, the "world" of elevated friendship did "not exist" for him outside the imagination. He could not integrate the two separate domains in his thought as Emerson seemed able to. He could repeat the sacraments, but the faith was gone.[40]

The world had moved on since Emerson had written his essay on friendship. The Transcendental Club had last met in 1844. The *Dial* had ceased publication the same year. The movement had lost its force and within a year or two would recede into the past. When Thoreau attempted to return to the discourse where Emerson had left it, it was as if he was talking to his friend but not to the larger world. The language already had an old-fashioned ring to it. The voice was that of the mid-1830s to the early 1840s. There is also a difference between the two essays in tone and emphasis. Emerson was writing about unmet expectations; Thoreau was expressing anger and disappointment at the thought of real or fancied rejection, and his bitterness showed. His comments have a personal ring. "In human intercourse the tragedy begins, not when there is misunderstanding about words, but when silence is not understood." "I value and trust those who love and praise my aspiration rather than my performance." "What avails it that another loves you, if he does not understand you? Such love is a curse." In all these instances—and there are others—Thoreau was clearly referring to Emerson.[41]

If Thoreau found it difficult to refrain from blaming his friend for the sense of separation that had grown up between them, he was nevertheless aware of the role he himself had played in the estrangement. Why, he wondered, was he so apt to indulge in elevated fantasies about the nature of friendship while allowing himself to miss the real opportunities that life presented to him. "How often we find ourselves turning our backs on our actual Friends that we may go and meet their ideal cousins," he observed glumly in the early pages of his commentary. Thoreau then proceeded to cite an example of behavior on his part that seemed to have weighed on his mind for months. "Suppose you go to bid farewell to a friend who is setting out on a journey," he began. You say nothing of importance, shake his hand, wish he would set off immediately and thereby relieve you of the feeling that you are not adequate to the situation. In this apparent allusion to his reticence when he parted from Emerson the day his friend sailed for England, Thoreau indicated an awareness that his actions at times seemed to undercut his cherished desires.[42]

In the end Thoreau conceded, "We must accept or refuse one another as we are." A friend is "not of some other race or family of men," he knew. Once again he turned to his relationship with Emerson as the touchstone of the situation. "I see his nature groping yonder so like mine. We do not live far apart. Have not the fates associated us in many ways?" "It says, in the *Vishnu Purana*: 'Seven paces together is sufficient for the friendship of the virtuous, but thou and I have dwelt together.'" "As I love nature, as I love singing birds, and gleaming stubble, and flowing rivers, and morning and evening, and summer and winter, I love thee, my Friend."[43]

5

With Emerson's return planned for early summer, Thoreau could not avoid the somber realization that the time had finally come when he had to wean himself from his dependency on his "brother" and "sister." "I see that I must get a few dollars together presently to manure my roots," he wrote to James Elliot Cabot, who had recently helped establish the *Massachusetts Quarterly Review*. "Is your journal able to pay anything, provided it likes an article well enough?" Although this overture did not lead to a placement, a subsequent effort was more productive. To Horace Greeley, Thoreau sent the manuscript of his essay "Katahdin and the Maine Woods" for which Greeley—who did not plan to use it in his own newspaper, the *New-York Tribune,* but intended to place it elsewhere—advanced him twenty-five dollars. "If you will write me two or three articles in the course of the summer, I think I can dispose of them for your benefit," he advised. "But write not more than half as long as your article just sent me, for that is too long for the Magazines." Thoreau replied that he would "see to those shorter articles" as soon as he had completed a new draft of *A Week,* which, he announced, "is swelling again under my hands."[44]

Just as this correspondence was getting underway, an accident occurred

that dealt a severe financial blow to Thoreau's family. During the night of
May 20 a fire started in the steam mill where they rented space, apparently
to manufacture the wooden parts of their pencils. The flames shot so high
that their glow illuminated the nearby meadows. Before the fire subsided,
the entire structure was destroyed. Damages were estimated at "four or five
hundred dollars," and Mr. Thoreau carried no insurance. Although Henry
Thoreau needed very little money to satisfy his personal needs, his way of
life was dependent upon food and housing being provided for him. Since
he would be moving back into the family home when Emerson returned in
July, the disaster had a meaning for him apart from his natural concern for
his family's welfare. With the help of Ellery Channing, who continued to
live in Concord with his wife and child, he attempted to make up the loss
through a subscription. Lidian Emerson contributed ten dollars, which she
thought was "little enough" considering the extent of the damage. "I hope
you will not disapprove," she wrote to Emerson.[45]

With Lidian's emergence from her room, life in the Emerson house had
resumed the pattern it had followed in the autumn before her serious illness
had begun. Although Thoreau had been forced to recognize the realities of
his relationship with her, his role within the family had not changed. As he
reported to Emerson at the end of May, he continued to perform the household duties expected of him. Except for a brief note, he had not written to
his friend since February, and in his present letter, the last he would post
before Emerson's return, his tone at the start was as business-like as if he
were being paid to attend to Emerson's affairs. "Mrs. Emerson" had gone to
Boston for a few days with little Eddy leaving Ellen and Edith in his charge;
he had been "a constant foe to the caterpillars" and the "trees are doing very
well"; a neighbor, acting as agent for Emerson in purchasing "the hill field,"
had requested a right-of-way that Thoreau feared would "greatly reduce the
value" of the land; and so on. But before he put down his pen, he could not
prevent a few tart remarks from creeping in. He had read as much as he
could of the new *Massachusetts Quarterly Review*—among whose backers
Emerson had been included—and thought it was "not so good a book as
the Boston almanack." Even more provocative was his jibe that he was glad
to learn that Emerson was finding time to do some writing while on tour
since, "Lecturing is of little consequence." Emerson accepted these comments with remarkable good humor. To Lidian he wrote, "Thank Henry for

his letter. He is always *absolutely* right, and *particularly* perverse. But I always thank heaven for him."[46]

Separated from Thoreau by the Atlantic Ocean, Emerson found it easier than he had during the Walden years to accept his friend's acerbity. According to the testimony of Henry Sutton, a young Nottingham poet who met Emerson in England not long after his arrival there, he "spoke much of Thoreau, especially to the 'earnest young men' who surrounded him." When Sutton was alone with Emerson, the British poet recalled, "Again and again he talked to me of this young man, his characteristics and achievements." From Sutton's report on Emerson's remarks it is clear that in addition to the affection Emerson had always felt for Thoreau, he saw him as occupying a special place in his life in Concord: "Fond of solitary ways and unsocial silences, [Thoreau] was, though swift to hear when in company, habitually slow to speak. Sometimes he was silent when he ought to have spoken. But when he did speak, out jumped, like a Jack in a box, the plain, straight forward truth, free from all polite softenings or embellishments. The effect on the great man's mind was agreeably tonic, bracing and refreshing." During Emerson's nine-month separation from Thoreau, the positive elements in their relationship appear to have been restored to a proper perspective. At the same time, the conflicts that had begun to drive a wedge between them before Emerson's departure seem to have receded from his consciousness.[47]

Emerson sailed from Liverpool on the steamship *Europa* on July 15 and arrived in Boston at six-thirty in the morning eight days later in time to catch the early train to Concord. At home he found Lidian once again in "miserable health" and Henry Thoreau still occupying the little room at the top of the stairs.[48] A few months earlier Thoreau had been described by a woman who had met him for the first time as "not a living man" but "a phenomenal creature." What she had recognized was that he had built a defensive shell of mannerisms around him that could, when he wished, be impossible for others to penetrate. That he was "all overlaid by an imitation of Emerson" was only part of the story; his silences, his sudden verbal thrusts, his roughness of manner were all devices calculated to protect the sensitive soul ensconced behind them.[49] After having lived with Lidian and her children for almost a year "as surrogate father and husband," it would only have been natural for him to have allowed his resentment of Emerson's reappearance on the scene to cause him to withdraw still further within himself in Emerson's presence.[50] When Emerson "spoke of friendship," Thoreau therefore did not respond with the expected warmth. Rebuffed, Emerson scrawled in his journal, "As for taking T.'s arm, I should as soon take the arm of an elm tree."[51]

Thoreau remained with the Emersons for three days, then returned to his parents' home on Main Street. In need of money, he immediately sought odd jobs in the village, which he carefully recorded:

Surveyed lumber etc	half a day
Whitewashing	4 hours
Papering	8 hours
Papering & whitewashing	4 "
"	9 "
Budding	2 half days[52]

Emerson, resuming his practice of walking regularly in the countryside near Concord, turned to Ellery Channing for companionship.

The Emersons' elder daughter, Ellen, who in her teens began to assume responsibility for the running of the family home. *Photograph courtesy of the Concord Free Public Library.*

The Emersons' younger son and daughter, Edward and Edith, not long after Thoreau had completed his second stay in the Emerson home. *Photograph courtesy of the Concord Free Public Library.*

Lidian Emerson, who suffered increasingly from depression during the 1840s and 1850s as Emerson's lecture tours kept him away for long periods. *Photograph courtesy of the Concord Free Public Library.*

Emerson in 1848 when he spent nine months lecturing in England and Scotland. *Photograph courtesy of the Concord Free Public Library.*

Thoreau in Worcester while visiting a friend two years after the publication of *Walden. Photograph courtesy of the Concord Free Public Library.*

(*Above, left*) Ellery Channing, who moved to Concord with his wife to be near Emerson and became a close friend of Thoreau's as well. *Painting by John Cranch.*

(*Above, right*) Ellen Channing, Margaret Fuller's sister, whose marriage to Ellery Channing started out propitiously but ended unhappily. *Photograph courtesy of Willard P. Fuller Jr.*

Sophia Thoreau, the youngest of the four Thoreau children, shared her brother's life and helped him maintain the family business in his later years. *Photograph courtesy of the Concord Free Public Library.*

Thoreau after the death of his father had placed him at the head of the family, a responsibility he accepted but found onerous. *Photograph courtesy of the Concord Free Public Library.*

Emerson when his books were selling more briskly than ever but who felt that his creative powers were steadily waning. *Photograph courtesy of the Concord Free Public Library.*

9

Separate Paths

Three and a half years after Emerson's return from England Thoreau observed, "I never realized so distinctly as this moment that I am peacefully parting company with the best friend I ever had, by each pursuing his proper path." While Thoreau's life was mired in the struggle to achieve literary success, Emerson's was being shaped more and more by the consequences of dealing with it. Where Thoreau had turned inward to nurture the sources of his genius, Emerson had turned outward in response to public acclaim. Without either man recognizing what was taking place, a sense of separation between them had increased steadily and inexorably as their lives had moved in different directions.[1]

By stating that "success has a great charm for me," as Emerson did at this time in a letter to Thomas Carlyle, he was presenting a point of view that found expression in all aspects of his life. During his stay in England Emerson had enjoyed being "made a lion of" by the rich, the noble, and the famous, and that experience had a positive effect on his demeanor.[2] He was noticeably "happier and more joyous" than he had been previously. Less nervous in his manner and less sensitive to the intrusions of the world, he even ate more heartily. There was a consequence to this infusion of spirits, however; he found himself increasingly dissatisfied with the narrowness of daily experience in Concord. In response, he "assumed a more public life" than he had aspired to previously.[3] He plunged into the organization of a town and country club in Boston to promote "good fellowship between men of Science, Letters, and Philanthropy." He continued to extend his already voluminous correspondence. And he sought opportunities to meet a wide variety of new people. It wasn't surprising, then, that his friends found him to be "not so easy of access as formerly."[4]

Despite all this activity Emerson continued to devote a considerable part of his time to the advancement of his career. In September 1849, he published a volume that reprinted *Nature* in its entirety and included four addresses and three lectures that had appeared in the *Dial.* He was also fashioning a new book, *Representative Men,* from lectures he had delivered in the United States and in Britain. In his presentation of this material a retreat was already evident from the elevated discourse he had engaged in previously. His thoughts now focused more steadily on the practical side of experience. His writing was becoming "less abstract, less anarchically individualistic." In it, it has been observed, "Progress replaces reform; culture, self-reliance; character, greatness." His friends had begun to irk him with the frequently repeated remark that he was not telling them anything new. From now on he would hear the refrain that his latest book, whatever it was, had "less vigor and originality than the others." Nevertheless his popularity continued to rise.[5]

The pursuit of success brought with it demands and responsibilities that increased the pressures on Emerson. In the autumn of 1849, as he was preparing *Representative Men* to go to press, he once again expressed the desire "to read no more Lyceum lectures." Nevertheless, he soon found himself "driven abroad by the necessity of paying my debts." The situation was one that had plagued him for years. "Is it not a little pathetic to find genius too resting at last so much on money?" he asked. Unable to remove himself from the "Lyceum Express," as he called it, he struck out on one of the longest tours of his career, for the first time traveling as far west as St. Louis. For nearly twenty years thereafter western cities regularly found a place in his itinerary. Although he objected to the "squalor of travel" and the "mortifications" of staying in provincial American hotels, he managed by this means to maintain the lifestyle he considered appropriate for himself and his family. In time his household staff grew to seven, and he purchased a chaise to replace the hired one that Lidian had previously used to get around in the village.[6]

While Emerson's enjoyment of success and its appurtenances was giving a clear direction to his life, Thoreau was still trying to find a way to earn enough money so he could continue to write. Working now and then as a day laborer was obviously not a satisfactory course for him. He might enjoy scoffing at the manners and possessions of the well-to-do, but the conviction that his neighbors thought him "the humblest cheapest least dignified man in the village" rankled. Having spoken before the Concord Lyceum on his Walden experience while still living beside the pond, he had material for a lecture readily at hand and decided to seek opportunities to present it in other towns. With the aid of friends and acquaintants he was able to arrange several appearances, but unlike Emerson, he did not assert a charismatic presence when he stood up to speak. Of Thoreau's delivery from the platform Emerson noted sadly, "his speech falls dead & is forgotten."[7]

Luckily Thoreau had been exploring another interest during these months. Since the days when he had kept school with his brother, John, surveying had attracted him. Turning to a serious study of the subject, he made a list of fourteen books to read. Soon he was ready to issue a handbill advertising his services. It required two or three weeks of surveying to bring in as much money as a one-hour talk on the lecture circuit, but at least there was a demand for work of that kind. By combining surveying and occasional lecturing with part-time work in his father's pencil manufactory, he managed to satisfy his needs while continuing to devote part of each day to writing.

A decade earlier when Thoreau had been a recent college graduate, the marked difference between his situation in life and that of Emerson's had passed without notice. Now it inevitably assumed a greater importance. Although the difference in their social positions would not have been openly recognized by either, they were both aware of it, and it created a gulf between them. Having achieved success on his own terms, Emerson found it hard to understand the compromises that Thoreau was willing to make in a cause that, in his opinion, had not yet proven itself. His comment that Thoreau "wants a little ambition in his mixture" perfectly expressed this attitude. "Instead of being head of American Engineers," he said, "he is captain of a huckleberry party."[8]

Emerson's disappointment in Thoreau expressed itself in a subtle change in his manner toward him that Emerson himself was probably unaware of but that Thoreau felt keenly. More and more, a note of condescension crept into Emerson's tone when he was referring to him. "Will you not now say to Mr. Thoreau, that I beg he will give me a day of attention to my vines," he wrote to Lidian while lecturing in New York City. Specifically, he continued, he wished him to "further reestablish our fallen arbor," adding, "he may set new posts if he will. I shall be very glad to pay the bill." When they met, Thoreau felt that Emerson treated him with an elaborate politeness; his "diabolical formality," he called it: "Passing the time of day, as if he were just introduced! No words are so tedious. Never a natural or simple word or yawn. It produces an appearance of phlegm and stupidity in me the auditor. I am suddenly the closest and most phlegmatic of mortals, and the conversation comes to naught."[9]

Although Thoreau did not seem to recognize it, he had come up against a reality—Emerson's growing eminence—and was reacting with resentment, not toward his friend's success but toward the inevitable manifestations of it. "O would you but be simple and downright!" Thoreau apostrophized in his journal. "Would you but cease your palaver! It is the misfortune of being a gentleman and famous." His immediate response was to lash out at Emerson's lifestyle. "When I consider what my friend's relations and acquaintances are, what his tastes and habits, then the difference between us gets named. I see that all these friends and acquaintances and tastes and habits are indeed my friend's self."[10]

Simply by each following his "proper path," as Thoreau had noted, a climate for estrangement had been established, but the very ordinariness of the situation made it difficult for them to see it as a cause. Instead they ascribed their difficulties to more readily identifiable events, such as those surrounding the publication in 1849 of Thoreau's first book, *A Week on the Concord and Merrimack Rivers.*

2

Thoreau had celebrated his thirty-first birthday on July 17, 1848. At that time only a small group of people outside his intimate circle knew that he was a writer, and they thought of him merely as a minor follower of Emerson, who had recently turned forty-five. In October of that year James Russell Lowell published a satirical poem forcefully calling attention to this situation. Printed as a thin volume, "A Fable for Critics" circulated widely in

New England. Although Lowell did not mention Thoreau by name, it was clear to many of the poem's readers which of the blanks referred to him.[11]

> There comes ———, for instance; to see him's rare sport,
> Tread in Emerson's tracks with legs painfully short;
> How he jumps, how he strains, and gets red in the face,
> To keep step with the mystagogue's natural pace!
> He follows as close as a stick to a rocket,
> His fingers exploring the prophet's each pocket.
> Fie, for shame, brother bard; with good fruit of your own,
> Can't you let neighbor Emerson's orchards alone?[12]

To Thoreau the unfairness of these remarks was apparent. At that time "Katahdin," the record of his journey through the Maine woods, was being serialized in the *Union Magazine*. A reader of Thoreau's essay who was familiar with Emerson's writings would immediately have been struck by the marked differences between the two men in style, subject matter, and approach to material. Unfortunately few people took the time to make such distinctions, especially when reading occasional short pieces such as this.

Fundamental among the differences between them in their published work was the manner in which they chose to place man in relation to nature. "What is Nature unless there is an eventful human life passing within her?" Henry demanded. The "eventful human life" that he placed in his narratives was his own. He became a character in the narrative moving through the natural world as he observed it and responded to it—a process clearly demonstrated in "Katahdin." Emerson, on the other hand, approached the problem in a manner characteristic of him. While insisting that in any fully realized work of art nature "must always combine with man," he chose to "converse with" nature rather than encounter it, which resulted in his standing apart from it. The man who appears in *his* nature is engaged in an intellectual enterprise. While Thoreau was seeking union with the natural world, Emerson was seeking mastery of knowledge concerning it. In actuality this opposition, although it may have been obscured in the early days of their relationship, had always existed. Alcott alluded to this when he wrote that while "Thoreau has the profoundest passion for the aboriginal in Nature of any man I have known," Emerson "was forbidden pure companionship with Nature. He dealt rather in an intellectual grove." It was inevitable that this dichotomy in the men's approach to experience would to some extent lead them in different directions in the way in which they expressed themselves.[13]

Thoreau had never lost the hope that *A Week* would establish an independent reputation for him and for some time had been working with renewed vigor on it. Early in 1849 he decided that he could no longer ignore Emerson's advice to print it at his own expense. On these terms Ticknor and Company was willing to undertake the project but insisted on an advance of $450, a sum Thoreau could not hope to raise. Turning once again to James Munroe and Company, the booksellers who had brought out Emerson's *Poems* two years earlier, he reached an agreement under which he would pay the full cost of printing the book, but the money would come from the income from sales. By the end of May *A Week* had been printed and seventy-five copies distributed by the publisher to Thoreau's friends, Emerson's acquaintances in England, and prospective reviewers.

The volume that appeared in James Munroe's bookstore in Boston on May 26 had been revised substantially since Thoreau had read portions of it to Emerson beside the Concord River. An addition to the text that Emerson would have recognized immediately was an alteration of one of his own verses. For Emerson's "Never from the lips of cunning fell," Thoreau had substituted "From *his* 'lips of cunning fell / the thrilling Delphic oracle,'" then had proceeded to comment that: "We should not mind if in our ear there fell / Some less of cunning, more of oracle." Making it clear he was addressing Emerson directly, he wrote, "O rare Contemporary . . . let epic trade winds blow, and cease this waltz of inspirations." With their insinuation that Emerson was no longer plumbing the depths he had in *Nature* and in his first collection of essays, Thoreau's words could hardly have been expected to please him.[14]

Five days after *A Week* appeared Emerson received a letter from Theodore Parker, then editor of the *Massachusetts Quarterly*, asking him to review the book. Although Parker's letter made his opinion clear that the book must be reviewed with sympathy if it was to survive in the rough and tumble literary marketplace, Emerson declined the opportunity. While conceding in his reply to Parker that the "book had rare claims," he suggested that, since he and Thoreau were "of the same clan & parish," it would be wiser to assign the review "to a good foreigner." Although Emerson suggested several qualified reviewers, Parker turned to James Russell Lowell. The news that Emerson would not be reviewing the book in the *Massachusetts Quarterly* was a blow to Thoreau; after all, Emerson had written favorably of Ellery Channing's volume of verse. Learning in addition that his refusal had opened the door to a man who had recently ridiculed him in print only threw salt in the wound. Now Thoreau had a real injustice on which to focus the hostile feelings toward Emerson aroused in him by the sense of rejection he felt due to their growing apart.[15]

Thoreau was not the sort of person who spoke openly about his emotional life. "Others can confess and explain; I cannot," he said. Instead of confronting the situation, he withdrew still further into himself. Later in the summer when Emerson alluded to this withdrawal, Thoreau reacted with injured innocence in his journal. "I have a friend, whom I heartily love, whom I would always treat tenderly," he wrote, yet he had been "indirectly accused by this friend of coldness and disingenuousness—When I cannot speak for warmth—& sincerity." Ignoring the impact of the passage in *A Week* that had been an affront to Emerson, he declared that he desired "nothing so much as to tell my love." He had "tenderly cherished the flower" of their friendship, he said; it had been Emerson who had "treated it as a weed."[16]

In the meantime, it was becoming clear that the sales of *A Week* would not be sufficient to cover the cost of publication. The problem was not only that James Munroe and Company had no financial stake in promoting it. More important to the book's reception by the reading public was the growing perception of Thoreau's bias against established religion. The first review of *A Week,* which appeared in the *New-York Tribune* two weeks after its publication, denounced Thoreau's "misplaced Pantheistic attack on the Christian faith." This strident note continued to be sounded in succeeding reviews. Considering the obscure position of its author, *A Week* received considerable critical attention in the months following its appearance. A great deal was written about the sensitivity of Thoreau's perception and the originality of his style. Even Lowell's review, when it appeared, contained much favorable comment. But no amount of praise could outweigh the public resistance at the time to a writer who professed that "it is necessary not to be a Christian to appreciate the beauty and significance of the life of Christ."[17]

From the beginning Emerson's attitude toward the book had been ambivalent. Despite his contention that "the narrative of the little voyage, though faithful, is a very slender thread for such big beads & ingots as are strung on it," he had praised the book frequently in his correspondence. Now that its failure had become evident he changed the emphasis of his comments. Where earlier he had praised the book to Thoreau "for what was good in it," he suddenly blamed him "for all that was bad." The reasons for this unexpected reversal were complicated. Having invested so much of his own prestige in promoting Thoreau's "genius" in the last decade, Emerson undoubtedly felt let down by the book's lack of success. In addition, the friction that had been evident between Thoreau and him since his return from England may have led him to express reservations openly that he had quietly harbored all along. But it is also true that in expanding the book Thoreau had allowed his unrelated musings to overwhelm the already "slender thread" of the narrative, and Emerson may simply have been responding to this fact.[18]

Regardless of Emerson's motivation, the effect upon Thoreau was devastating. He believed he had been betrayed by the friend he had trusted most. "While my friend was my friend he flattered me, and I never got the truth from him, but when he became my enemy he shot it to me on a poisoned arrow," he said bitterly.[19]

3

As relations grew cooler between Thoreau and Emerson, Ellery Channing's presence in Concord assumed a greater importance to both of them. For Thoreau and Emerson—as for Channing and other writers such as Nathaniel Hawthorne and Bronson Alcott who had settled in the village for varying lengths of time—there was little real connection with the community itself. Alcott described their situation this way: "We are ghosts and spectres, chimeras, rumours, holding no known relations to the fields and houses where we are supposed or seen to abide; and our dealings with men have an aspect ridiculous and to be made game of at the bank and bar-room." Removed as they were from meaningful involvement with their neighbors, Thoreau and Emerson, who had depended on each other for companionship for a decade, now increasingly turned to Channing to fill this need. Ellery Channing had an elfin sense of humor that both men found appealing. Thoreau said he was "as naturally whimsical as a cow is brindled" while Emerson marveled at the fecundity of his wit, describing him as "squandering his jewels as if they were icicles, sometimes not comprehended by me, sometimes not heard." Emerson enjoyed Channing's fanciful remarks enough to preserve several examples of them in his journal. On one occasion Channing exclaimed, "What a fine day is this! Nothing about immortality here!" and on another, "Life is so short, that I should think everybody would steal." His wit was based on the simple principle, Hawthorne remarked, that he "never said anything he believed."[20]

Since Channing's reason for settling in the village in the first place had been to be near Emerson, he was delighted to be sought out by him as a walking companion. Before coming to Concord to live, Channing had had only one "personal friend," Samuel Gray Ward. Emerson, who had encouraged Channing to pursue a career as a writer and who clearly liked him, had become a major figure in his narrow world. But lacking Thoreau's innate ability and his persistence in pursuing his goals, Channing had not maintained Emerson's interest in him as a writer. Channing was intensely aware that Emerson valued him more as an amusing person than as a productive one, and this realization fed a sense of grievance against Emerson that he could not always conceal.[21]

Over the years Channing had grown equally attached to Thoreau, but in a different way. They had become friends in the manner of contemporaries and equals, an easier relationship to maintain. Since they were both failures in the eyes of their neighbors, they formed a partnership against the world, walking constantly together but in a different way than either of them walked with Emerson. With their distinguished neighbor they followed the open paths that he preferred, but alone they often attempted to pass unseen through the countryside, avoiding any encounter with other people.[22]

During these years Channing not only provided companionship to both men, he served as an important link between them. Although they were seeing less of each other than ever before, they were kept fully informed by Channing of each other's activities. There was a different tone, however, to the separate conversations. When Channing and Emerson talked about Thoreau, their remarks, while not necessarily uncritical, were contained within the framework of objective observation. They reflected an interest in him that was not overly distorted by their feelings. When Channing and Thoreau talked about Emerson, the situation was different. He was the reference point against which they measured their experience. This was fine when their mood was positive, but on those days when one or the other felt he had been mistreated by him in some way, their concern with Emerson's most minute actions could also feed their resentment of him. And then the result was to intensify their sense of him as a cold and rejecting figure.

Although for the trio their walks were an essential part of the day, they turned to them for different reasons: Emerson to recreate after writing, Thoreau to gather material for his journal, and Channing to get out of the house. The idyll of the early years of the Channings' marriage had gradually given way under the pressure of poverty and a growing family to an unhappy alliance. The Channings' meager income of about four hundred dollars a year, mostly contributed by Ellery's father, did not permit them to have regular help in the house for Ellen, who was not physically strong. In the spring of 1849, as the time neared for her to give birth to their third child, Channing's sister Barbara expressed the fear that it would be "almost too much for her." Her words were prophetic; Ellen was ill for many weeks after the delivery and under the stress of maintaining their home never completely regained her strength. Despite their removal to a larger house on Main Street the daily presence of three small children proved to be more than Channing's temperament could bear. As the months passed, he became increasingly more difficult to live with.[23]

Not long after the Channings moved, the Thoreau family did also. A shift in the market for pencils had led to prosperity for their pencil business, and in 1850 they were able to acquire a larger house in the center of town. They bought one on Main Street directly opposite the Channings whose property bordered on the Sudbury River. This permitted Thoreau to see Channing more frequently and even to moor his boat on the Channing property.

Despite their newfound nearness, the Thoreau and Channing families themselves did not grow closer. This was in part due to Channing's intense dislike for Thoreau's mother, but an additional factor was probably Thoreau's attitude toward women of his own age.[24] About this time he noted in his journal that he could not "imagine a woman no older than I." The psychological satisfactions that he derived from his association with Lidian Emerson did not flow to him from a contemporary like Ellen Channing. He continued to perform the gratefully received function of providing her husband with opportunities to spend long afternoons with him outdoors, but he did not develop an independent relationship with her. She became a negative, rather than a positive presence for him; essential to his relationship with Channing, since for him friendship seemed to flourish best in the context of a family situation, but representing the demanding rather than the nurturing aspects of a wife and mother.[25]

Shortly after the Thoreaus moved to Main Street, news reached Concord that Margaret Fuller had drowned in a shipwreck off Fire Island while returning from her five-year sojourn in Europe. While in Italy, Margaret had married and had a child, and she had been accompanied on her trip by her family. Emerson immediately commissioned Henry Thoreau and Ellery Channing, Margaret's brother-in-law, to hasten to Fire Island to recover what they could relating to them. Only a button from Margaret's husband's jacket and a small carrying case could be identified as being theirs among the salvage that still remained on the beach when Thoreau arrived. With Margaret Fuller's sudden and unexpected death, a major link with the past had been broken.

4

Although the tragedy led to a momentary sense of unity between Emerson and Thoreau, it did nothing to stem their drift apart. As time went on Thoreau began to realize more fully that their differences were intellectual as well as temperamental. After Thoreau had spent an evening at Emerson's going over his manuscripts with him, he commented in disgust, "It is dull work reading to one who does not apprehend you." Was it possible, he wondered, that in all the years of their friendship Emerson had never truly met him "thought with thought?"[26]

Although he rarely looked at Emerson's books these days, Thoreau had read a passage in Emerson's essay "Literary Ethics" recently and had been struck by the "obviousness of the moral." It seemed to Thoreau that he had "perhaps, *thought* the same thing myself twenty times during the day, and yet had not been *contented* with that account of it." "We do not believe in the same god," he decided. That Thoreau did not reach this conclusion until the 1850s, a decade and a half after his friendship with Emerson had begun, was more than anything else due to the nature of their relationship during those years. When they met, Thoreau had just read *Nature;* shortly after that

Emerson had delivered "The American Scholar," his most famous address. The influence of these works on Thoreau at age twenty was strongly reinforced by the personality and position of the famous man who had befriended him. Accepting his mentor's leadership in intellectual matters was a natural consequence of this situation. If Thoreau was to have any realistic hope of pursuing a literary career, Emerson's approval was essential. This is not to say that Thoreau was dissembling; during the 1840s there were many indications of his growing independence of thought. But a fuller understanding of the differences in their attitudes came only with the slow maturing of Thoreau's talent. By this time Thoreau's fundamental views had become much clearer in his own mind. And at the same time the shift in Emerson's writing from the idealism of his earlier years to a more practical view of life had intensified the contrast between them.[27]

How difficult it was for Thoreau, despite this basic difference in outlook, to throw off the dominance of Emerson's thought is perhaps best revealed in his vacillating attitude toward Emersonian correspondence. In *Nature* Emerson had unequivocally stated his view that "nature echoes the Ten Commandments." The clear-eyed man, he believed, would be able to read the eternal truths in nature, a conviction that is frequently mirrored in the early pages of Thoreau's journal. In spite of Thoreau's determination to adhere to this basic premise of Emerson's worldview, his natural tendency to perceive reality differently soon forced its way to the surface. "It is more proper for a spiritual fact to have suggested an analogous natural one, than for the natural fact to have preceded the spiritual in our minds," he had written in 1841. As the years passed he continued to vacillate on this subject, but at heart he believed the doctrine of correspondence to be an imposition on nature of man's opinions. By the summer of 1851 he could cry, "Farewell to those who will talk of nature unnaturally."[28]

During the years that the friends had been conversing earnestly in Emerson's study on the literary subjects that most engaged their minds, the pleasure they had taken in these exchanges had continued to overshadow the inherent dissimilarity in their views. If Thoreau had "an aversion to abstraction and a peculiar attachment to facts," Emerson was caught up in an attempt to determine the laws that would make sense of human existence. For Thoreau "the depth and intensity of the life excited" was the measure of success he sought in his work, while for Emerson the desire to pin down

eternal principles rested at the core of his intention. Where Thoreau ultimately was forced to construct a mythology of his own to express himself
adequately, Emerson had slowly evolved a philosophy to incorporate his
ideas. At bottom, as Joel Porte has pointed out, although there was only a
fourteen-year difference in their ages, their views were rooted in different
periods of history; where intellectually Emerson was "much more a man of
the eighteenth century," Thoreau stood solidly in "the nineteenth."[29]

5

The widening breech between Thoreau and Emerson did not prevent Thoreau from continuing to use the Emersons' house as a second home. John
Albee, a student at Phillips Academy in Andover, found Thoreau there one
day when he arrived for a visit. Albee's account of the occasion provides an
interesting look at the interaction between the two men. Thoreau, he observed, "was much at home with Emerson" and appeared "to belong in some
way to the household." He "was rather silent," but "when he spoke, it was
either in a critical or witty vein." The conversation turning to the general
subject of education, Emerson commented that all branches of learning
were taught at Harvard. Thoreau's response was, "Yes, indeed, all the
branches and none of the roots." It seemed to Albee that Emerson antici-
pated comments of this kind from Thoreau and for his own amusement was
intent on bringing out Thoreau's bitter wit. Nevertheless, he could see that
Emerson was "clearly fond of Thoreau," who was still seated comfortably at
the fireside when Albee left that evening.[30]

What Albee could not know was that the intimacy had gone out of the
relationship, a fact that disturbed Emerson as much as it did Thoreau. On
an earlier occasion, when Emerson had tried to "take the bull by the horns"
in a private "session" with Thoreau, the "rambling talk" that had ensued had
made it clear that the effort had failed. Emerson would try again on at least
one other occasion with a similar result. In making these attempts to recapture the sense of closeness that he and Thoreau had enjoyed in the past,
Emerson was unwittingly confronting a side of his friend's nature that Thoreau kept carefully hidden. Emerson simply did not know the extent to
which Thoreau's behavior toward him was based on feelings that Thoreau
could not bring himself to discuss openly.[31]

Thoreau had begun to suspect that he carried "into friendship the tender-ness and nicety of a lover." Certainly the introspective agonizing about his relationship with Emerson that dominated page after page of his journal lends credence to this observation. Thoreau treated each slight—real or imagined—like a wound that he refused to let heal and that he harbored in secrecy. Overburdened by anger and resentment he found it impossible to respond to Emerson's overtures. Instead it seemed to him at times as if every act of Emerson's was a betrayal. "I hear my friend say, 'I have lost my faith in men; there are none true, magnanimous, holy,' etc., etc., meaning all the while, that I do not possess those unattainable virtues; but worm as I am, this is not wise in my friend, and I feel simply discouraged so far as my relation to him is concerned." He was further discouraged when he learned that Emerson had been speaking of him to another, "not with cold words perhaps, but even with a cold and indifferent tone." At this he exclaimed, "Ah! what treachery I feel it to be!—the sum of all crimes against humanity. My friend may cherish a thousand suspicions against me, and they may but represent his faith and expectations, till he cherishes them so heartlessly that he can speak of them." When Emerson openly mentioned their loss of inti-macy, Thoreau immediately drew back. When "my friend rashly thought-lessly profanely speaks, *recognizing* the distance between us—that distance seems infinitely increased," he complained in his journal. "Here I have been on what the world would call friendly terms with one [for] fourteen years, have pleased my imagination sometimes with loving him, and yet our hate is stronger than our love," he wrote. "Why are we related, yet thus unsatis-factorily? We almost are a sore to one another."[32]

While there is no question that there were concrete reasons for the feeling of separation that had grown up between the friends, it is also clear that an extreme response to the situation was playing itself out in Thoreau's mind. Unfortunately Emerson had no inkling of the internal drama that Thoreau was experiencing. He saw only the surface manifestations of Thoreau's feel-ings, the withdrawal or the anger, without understanding what motivated them. Under the circumstances, it's difficult to see how Emerson could have acted in a way Thoreau would have found acceptable.

The situation was further exacerbated by the emotional problems that Thoreau was experiencing at this time. The failure of *A Week* had led to a disintegration of Thoreau's sense of self-worth. The symptoms are readily identifiable in his journal. Entry after entry deals with a growing doubt that he will ever achieve the level of literary performance he has been aiming for. He is filled with a growing dislike of himself that leads him to the conviction that he is powerless to improve his situation. The picture he paints of his inner life at this time is a dismal one. Despair, with no apparent hope for improvement in his circumstances, dominates his days.

Even during this period of intense emotional strain, Thoreau began to sense that he was going too far in his show of anger toward Emerson. As his behavior became more hostile, it started to worry him. "Last night I treated my dearest friend ill. Though I could find some excuse for myself, it is not such excuse as under the circumstances could be pleaded in so many words. Instantly I blamed myself, and sought an opportunity to make atonement, but the friend avoided me, and, with kinder feelings than ever I was obliged to depart." Under the pressure of this emotion Thoreau made a pledge to himself. "I am resolved to know that one centrally, through thick and thin, and though we should be cold to one another, though we should never speak to one another, I will know that inward and essential love may exist even under a superficial cold, and that the law of attraction speaks louder than words."[33]

10

Undercurrents

In the spring of 1852, Horace Greeley sent a letter to Henry Thoreau proposing that he write a long magazine article about Emerson. "Let it be calm, searching and impartial; nothing like adulation, but a just summing up of what he is and what he has done," he requested. For Thoreau to undertake such a venture would have been difficult at any time, but given the strains that had developed in his relationship with Emerson, it was not possible at this juncture. Still his refusal was unnecessarily abrupt. He could use his time "to better purpose," he informed Greeley in turning down the fifty-dollar fee.[1]

Despite the cold manner of his dismissal, Thoreau continued to be drawn to the Emerson house. But now when he entered "without knocking," as was his habit, he tended to pass quickly by the rooms in which the adults were seated to seek the children. Eddie, the youngest, was already five years old; Edith was eleven, and Ellen, thirteen. The relationship with them that had grown so close during his periods of residence with the Emersons had not been affected by the chill that had settled between him and his friend. As Thoreau strode through the Emerson's hall, he would whistle, and at this sound, the children would run out of the room where they were playing, throw their arms around his legs, and struggle with him until he reached a chair near the fireplace. There he would tell them stories and make their pencils and knives disappear only to emerge in a moment from their ears and noses. Later, as a special treat, he might retrieve the heavy copper warm-

144

ing pan "from the oblivion of the garret and unweariedly shake it over the blaze." As Edward Emerson testified, "He was to us children the best kind of an older brother."[2]

A favorite pastime of the Emerson children during the summers was to go berrying under Thoreau's guidance. Sometimes he took them alone in his boat to Conantum where the bayberries grew in abundance. On other days he led them to fields not far from Concord that were rich in huckleberries. These occasions often took on the aspect of a family outing with Emerson, his wife, and other friends joining in. For these excursions wagons were fitted up for the ladies, and baskets of food were prepared for a midday picnic. During one of these jaunts Eddie Emerson stumbled, spilling his carefully gathered huckleberries. Thoreau quickly put his arm around the weeping boy and explained to him that it was necessary that some should be scattered so that a good crop of huckleberries could be counted on in succeeding years. "We shall have a grand lot of bushes and berries on this spot, and we shall owe them to you," he told Eddie, who immediately began to smile.[3]

The antagonism that had grown up between Emerson and Thoreau did not break the social fabric that wove their lives together but remained submerged, rarely recognized openly by either of the men. That Thoreau remained one of the family was made abundantly clear when Emerson's mother died suddenly. Thoreau took charge of arrangements for the funeral to relieve his stricken friend of these difficult duties. He even traveled to Littleton, where Emerson's retarded brother Bulkeley was being cared for, to bring him to Concord for the services, a kindness that Emerson particularly appreciated since he found his brother's irritability and garrulousness hard to endure.

2

Emerson had speculated that if he, Thoreau, and Channing could find a way to deal with their "repulsions and incompatibilities," they could produce an interesting work together. The nearest he came to suggesting this as an actual project was when, in 1853, he commissioned Channing to assemble excerpts from the journals of all three men into a book to be called *Country Walking*.[4] Emerson took this step as a way of providing money to Channing, whose wife was once again pregnant. That spring only a gift of two hundred dollars from Sam Ward had "saved him from bankruptcy." Emerson's payments for his work on the book were intended to help the family through the summer and fall.[5]

Money was not the Channings' only problem, however. The birth of their fourth child created turmoil in their household. For some time Thoreau's mother and his sister Sophia had been aware that things were not going well with them. They knew of Ellen Channing's problems with her health and the difficulties she was having in raising her children with scant assistance from their father. Although the two women had kindly feelings toward her and wanted to help during periods of obvious stress, they were put off by Channing's rudeness. What particularly appalled Mrs. Thoreau was that he "showed no love for his children." Sophia, who time after time saw the youngest running out of the house crying, suspected that he was being "ill-used." This was Walter, who told the Thoreaus one day that his father was always "cross, & now he takes his meals alone in the kitchen."[6]

The pressures of family life were too great for Channing's fragile psyche. As his distress deepened, he began to be abusive. He spoke disparagingly of Ellen in front of others; accused her of teaching the children to hate him; constantly scolded and on occasion struck them, while threatening worse; threw "everything about the table" at meal time; in Ellen's words, "acted like a mad man." During the darkest days Ellen barricaded herself in her room at night fearful of what he might do. Finally she could deal with it no longer. She had already told Ellery that she intended to leave him but had allowed him to persuade her to stay on. Now, "really *afraid of him*," she decided that she had no other choice but to take the children and go away.[7]

In the 1850s it was very difficult for a woman to leave her husband regardless of the severity of the problems she was encountering in her life with him. Ellen turned to Thomas Wentworth Higginson, the husband of Ellery's sister, for support. He arranged for Channing's father, Dr. Walter Channing, to furnish her with an income of three hundred dollars a year "& *more if necessary.*" On November 17 Higginson brought her and the children to his home in Worcester and immediately began searching for a house for her there.[8]

Returning to Concord the next day, Higginson found Channing "perfectly cool & quiet." He was "very willing to talk upon indifferent subjects, but entirely refused to say anything about himself or Ellen."[9] Channing's friends were coalescing around him. Thoreau had walked across the street to sit with him during his first evening alone in the house. The Emersons asked him if he would like to take his meals with them, and for a time he dined there regularly. After spending an afternoon with Channing on the river, Thoreau reported that he seemed "affable as usual." His newfound freedom seemed to release him from depression, but as winter passed into spring, he became increasingly more lonely and embittered.[10]

In the spring, he packed a trunk and left Concord for Niagara Falls with the intention of spending six months traveling. He did not stay away that long but his desperate need for a reconciliation with Ellen dominated his life for the next year, and when he finally succeeded in persuading her to agree to it, he settled with her and the children near Worcester. Channing's departure from Concord was more of a blow to Thoreau than to Emerson. Since Thoreau had only two intimate friends, the loss of one greatly increased his sense of isolation. Thoreau's need for Emerson's companionship grew proportionately, which made his friend's remoteness even more difficult for him to bear.

3

During the winter of 1852 Thoreau had become concerned that the "groves" beside Walden Pond were being "invaded" by loggers. The "thick and lofty pine and oak woods" that had once completely surrounded the pond were being cut off so quickly, he complained, that the eastern shore would soon be "laid waste."[11] Thoreau had had a preference for "this recess among the pines" since riding past the pond with his grandmother as a five-year-old.[12] For more than twenty years he had visited it "almost daily." He had lived beside it for two years. Now the site that had played such an important role in his life was being ravaged. To him this was a visible symbol of the loss of his youth.[13]

Six years earlier, while Thoreau was still living on the shores of the pond, he had begun the process of taking his journal entries about his life in his cabin and turning them into the book-length *Walden*. The commercial failure of *A Week on the Concord and Merrimack Rivers* had prevented the publication of his second book, however, and in the intervening years he had worked on it only fitfully. Now he returned to it, recognizing that time was passing quickly and that his hopes for recognition centered on his improving it and getting it published.

Thoreau approached *Walden* with an awareness that the effect he wanted to achieve was different from that sought by Emerson in his work. "All that interests the reader," he observed, "is the depth and intensity of the life excited."[14] This was not a new goal, but he understood better than he had in the past how to create the effects he desired on the page. Like Emerson, he wanted to instruct his readers, but he chose to do so through the dramatization of examples rather than by admonition. As material he selected "those parts of [his] life" that he "would gladly live again."[15] To realize the "depth and intensity" he strove for placed great pressure on him. "The strains from my muse are as rare nowadays, or of late years, as the notes of the birds in winter," he said. But despite this he kept at it, day after day, for two years.[16]

Toward the end of that time Thoreau began to seek a publisher for the manuscript. Ticknor and Company, which had offered to bring out the earlier draft at Thoreau's expense, was in the process of being reorganized under the name Ticknor and Fields. James T. Fields who was to become a partner in the company had worked for Ticknor for many years and had recently been associated with the firm's drive to establish itself as a leading literary publisher by printing such authors as Nathaniel Hawthorne, Henry Wadsworth Longfellow, James Russell Lowell, Oliver Wendell Holmes, and James Greenleaf Whittier.[17] In Fields's opinion *Walden* belonged in the same category as these, in fact, "to the same class of works with Mr. Emerson's writing," and would "be likely to attract attention."[18] The contract that Ticknor and Fields offered Thoreau for *Walden* placed him among their "first class authors," a small group to whom they paid 15 percent royalties.[19]

Thoreau had read the manuscript of *A Week* to Emerson before seeking a publisher, but that does not appear to have been the case with *Walden*. Although Emerson had heard Thoreau lecture on the subject and was certainly familiar with the excerpts from the book that had appeared in the *Union Magazine* in 1852, he was essentially in the dark about the book as a whole until early in 1854 when Thoreau was readying it for publication. Emerson had apparently read it by then, for in March he expressed his enthusiasm for the book in a letter to his English publisher in an attempt to persuade him to release it in that country. Describing Thoreau as "a man of rare ability," he went on to say that he had "great confidence in the merit & in the success of the work."[20]

When *Walden* appeared in August 1854, Emerson displayed "as much pleasure as if his brother had written it."[21] The book was "cheerful, sparkling, readable, with all kinds of merits," he said. His praise was not unstinted, however. While noting that Thoreau "writes always with force," he was restrained in his appraisal of the book as a whole. He saw the prose as "rising sometimes to very great heights"; he saw that Thoreau wrote "sometimes with wonderful depth & beauty," but he withheld any comment about the work in its entirety that would place it high in the ranks of literary achievement. Thoreau, he said, is "a good scholar, & a good naturalist"; he carefully refrained from calling him a great writer.[22]

A review of *Walden* in the *National Era,* that appeared shortly after its publication summed up the general attitude toward the book in one sentence that praised it and then quickly limited that praise: "In its narrative, this book is unique, in its philosophy quite Emersonian." The view of Thoreau expressed by James Russell Lowell in 1848 as stealing literary apples from Emerson's orchard was firmly entrenched in the public mind. Readers were not yet able to see Thoreau's accomplishment clearly for what it was. He was universally viewed as a disciple, rather than as a writer with an original view.[23]

Thoreau was not kind to Emerson in *Walden.* After enthusiastically describing the visits Alcott, Channing, and Horace Hosmer, a neighboring farmer, had paid him at the pond, he merely commented that Emerson had "looked in upon me from time to time." This was an obvious slight, but even harsher was an omission he made in the text. Although he stated in the book that nothing had been given to him during his stay "of which I have not rendered some account," he nowhere indicated that the land on which he had lived for two years was owned by Emerson and that Emerson had made it available to him. Instead he described himself as a "squatter"—according to Webster, "one that settles on land without a right or title." This seems particularly lacking in generosity since Emerson had even gone to the extent of changing his will to leave the land to Thoreau when it looked as if his friend would remain there permanently.[24]

4

Over the years Emerson had created an image of himself that he presented to the world as the real man. In intercourse with others he became the public figure whose fame had spread from the United States to Europe. Tall to begin with, he held himself with an assurance that emphasized his importance. Although he was never in any way pretentious, there was something in the correctness of his manner that established a distance between him and those with whom he spoke. The voice that had enthralled crowds from the lecture platform for decades did not have to be raised to command attention. There was no need for him to dominate a conversation to be the dominant figure in a group.

Encountering the public "Emerson" deeply angered Thoreau. He complained that his friend had become "ridiculously stately." "You are so grand that I cannot get within ten feet of you," he sputtered in his journal. No matter how hard he tried, he did not seem able to get past this facade to the sensitive friend whose companionship had meant so much to him in the past. He was convinced that Emerson adopted this manner purposely to frustrate his desire for a closer relationship with him. In those rare moments when Thoreau could put his feelings aside and see the situation more objectively, he was aware that Emerson was not unique in his assumption of a public manner. He had met many others, he admitted, who could not "afford to be simple and true men, but personate, so to speak, their own ideal of themselves." However, in thinking about this, it did not occur to him that he himself had been hard at work building a public image, at least since the time when he had moved to Walden, and that it must have seemed just as false to Emerson as Emerson's did to him.[25]

It has been remarked that in *Walden* Thoreau created a character named "Henry Thoreau" that readers often confuse with the writer himself.[26] Although the book is based on Thoreau's experience, the way that experience is presented paints a picture of a man who is bigger than life. This "Henry Thoreau" lives apart from the social and economic system that dominates the lives of others. He has a mystical relation with nature and at the same time is a naturalist who observes with scientific precision. He is completely in control of his environment. He never despairs of life; instead he finds abundant reasons in his day-to-day activities to be optimistic about experience.

Thoreau's creation of a mythical "Henry Thoreau" put him in the position of having to defend the reality of that image to the world at large through his behavior. The need to do this began with his removal to the pond, which was in itself an announcement to his neighbors that he was different from them. It increased as more and more people learned of his experiment and he began to lecture about it. After a decade the process was capped by the publication of *Walden*. People who had read it saw the character from the book when they met Thoreau, and this naturally influenced not only his manner at the moment but also his general view of how he ought to comport himself.

Emerson did not enjoy his encounters with the public "Henry Thoreau" any more than Thoreau liked to encounter Emerson's alter ego. It seemed to Emerson that Thoreau's pose of independence could be ridiculous at times. He "says he values only the man who goes directly to his needs, who, wanting wood, goes to the woods & brings it home; or to the river, & collects the drift, & brings it in his boat to his door, & burns it: not him who keeps shop, that he may buy wood."[27] From a man in his thirties who lived in his parents' home and ate from their table, this sort of talk seemed a bit foolish to Emerson. But what bothered him even more was the exaggerated pride "Henry Thoreau" took in his knowledge about plants and animals. When Emerson lent him a book about an arctic journey, Thoreau returned it with the comment that "most of the phenomena noted could have been observed in Concord."[28] When he presented him with a type of "berry he had not seen," Thoreau could "hardly suppress his indignation." The "Henry Thoreau" who was an authority on nature was a prideful person indeed.[29]

Although Thoreau and Emerson responded negatively to each other's public image, there was a major difference in the way they responded to their own. Emerson apparently believed that he was "Emerson." His adopted persona was the product of the life he had built for himself and reflected the world's view of his accomplishments. He had needed the applause of others to establish his importance. He had received it in abundance and still continued to receive it. He had no reason to question the reality of this view of himself. If he knew about the struggle that had been required for him to attain this position, he also knew that the accomplishments were real.

But it is doubtful that Thoreau ever truly believed that he was the "Henry Thoreau" described in *Walden*. In fact, since the myth was so far from the reality, the idea probably contained in it a kernel of self-reproach. Unlike Emerson, he presented himself as a person whose experience did not accurately represent his own. Instead his new layer of definition represented what he had condemned in others: the personation of an "ideal of themselves." Whenever he was presenting himself as the man from Walden, whether in a room or on the lecture stage, he became this person. But inside he knew himself for what he was: a man who, unlike "Henry Thoreau," did not rationally control his world.

Nevertheless, Thoreau's public image was very useful to him and he continued to employ it just as Emerson employed his, as a mask. Under these circumstances, it became even more difficult than it had been previously for Thoreau and Emerson to "meet" each other. This new layer of definition acted to separate Thoreau from Emerson just as much as Emerson's sense of self-importance distanced Thoreau. At any given moment neither knew whether he would encounter his friend or his friend's double.

5

"I need hardly say to any one acquainted with my thoughts that I have no system," Emerson had observed in 1839 three years after the publication of *Nature*. Nothing he had written since then had challenged the truth of this statement. Neither he nor Henry Thoreau had attempted to "rebuild the Universe in a model." In actuality, Emerson insisted, "I am & always was a painter," while Thoreau declared that his aim was "to give the within outwardness." Not having set out to erect a philosophical system, neither Emerson nor Thoreau felt the need to be absolutely consistent line by line. The appearance of an observation on one page in the writings of either man does not preclude the possibility that an opposite position will be articulated on another of his pages. Nevertheless, a reader of their journals, letters, poems, essays, and books quickly becomes caught up in a flow of thought that moves forcefully in a discernible direction. There is a decided coherence to their views, in the whole if not necessarily in all the details.[30]

The fact that Emerson and Thoreau did not attain the summit of their mature thought and creative effort at the same historical moment is not always made clear in studies of their intellectual lives. Critics generally agree that *Nature* and the first collection of essays were Emerson's major achievements, just as Thoreau's work is commonly recognized as having reached a culminating point with the publication of *Walden*. In other words, the periods of greatest accomplishment for the two men occurred a decade apart; Emerson's between 1836 and 1842, Thoreau's between 1845 and 1854. If their paths of achievement were to be graphed for the years since their first meeting, the lines would chart different curves for most of that time.

By the mid-1850s, however, those lines had begun to move together. By then it had become increasingly accepted, at least in intellectual circles in New England, that the change in subject matter in Emerson's lectures and essays was evidence of a lessening of his creative powers. As for Thoreau, although it was not yet apparent to anyone except himself, a major shift in emphasis in his work was also occurring. A convergence was taking place in their intellectual lives that, as it happened, did not create a happy situation for either of the friends.

Emerson admitted somewhat ruefully that he was no longer attempting to confront experience at the same level as formerly. "There were questions, I believe, which I was to solve. But I never do; I know better than to try," he said.[31] He had set out to explore "the forgotten Good, the unknown Cause in which we sprawl & sin." He had wanted to communicate "the Ideal and Holy Life, the life within life." How thoroughly his intellectual orientation had changed in recent years is made clear by the titles of some of the lectures he had completed in the early 1850s: "Property," "Power," "The Laws of Success," "Wealth," and "Economy." He had also been working for some time on *English Traits,* a book rooted in the observations he had made during his stay in England. The material that engaged his mind now was qualitatively different from that which had interested him as a younger man.[32]

The focus of Thoreau's work was changing also. He had embarked on his career with an aim similar to Emerson's. His intention had been to "find God in nature," to "commune with the spirit of the universe."[33] During the early years of the 1850s he had continued to defend his preference for being a poet, if only a poet in prose. His "desire," he had said, was "to bear my head through atmospheres and over heights unknown to my feet." But Thoreau no longer had ready access to the mystical states that had enabled him to transcend the humdrum experience of daily life. With these increasingly beyond his reach, the engine that fired his creativity lacked fuel.[34]

In addition, the dissolution of the transcendental movement had deprived both Emerson and Thoreau of the sense of solidarity that comes from being part of a larger group with similar, if not identical, interests and objectives. With the attention of their peers having shifted to other areas of interest, the difficulty of continuing along the established path had increased. While Emerson had begun to disassociate himself from transcendentalism early on, Thoreau had not. He saw himself not only as a mystic and natural philosopher but as a transcendentalist to boot.

In the early 1850s the phrase "natural philosopher" seemed to hold the key to Thoreau's future. Although he had probably thought of himself in this way since the outset of his career, he was now struggling within himself to define more carefully what those words meant to him. In the beginning he had not thought of a "natural philosopher" as pursuing "natural science."[35] At that time his position had been simple and straightforward. "It is impossible for the same person to see things from the poet's point of view and that of the man of science. The poet's second love may be science, not his first." But as his moments of epiphany became rarer and more widely spaced he found himself revisiting this argument. He discovered that he could accept the pursuit of natural science as "a condition of mind" that might interest "others" as they grew older and confronted "the decay of their poetic faculties." But he was disturbed by the possibility that he had reached that point himself. "Once I was part and parcel of Nature; now I am observant of her." "I fear that the character of my knowledge is from year to year becoming more distinct & scientific—that, in exchange for views as wide as heaven's cope I am being narrowed down to the field of the microscope."[36]

While the change that was taking place in Emerson's work was open for all to see, for Henry Thoreau the shift in orientation was occurring quietly in his journal, not simply in the comments that clarified his struggle but also, and more importantly, in the material he chose to record. After Thoreau's death, Emerson referred to the "volumes of 'Field notes,' as he called them" that Thoreau kept during "the last ten years of his life."[37] In these volumes entries concerning birds and plants had become more precise in their descriptions and more detailed in their content. The journal had grown "more 'scientific'—rigorous and methodical—with a consequent deemphasis on lyrical mysticism."[38] For Thoreau, who originally conceived of a journal as a book containing "a record of all your joy, your ecstasy," this was a radical shift.[39]

The pursuit of knowledge had reached a fork in the road for both men, and each had chosen a new path for himself. Emerson had concluded that "knowledge is the knowing that we cannot know." In his writings he had shifted his attention to a consideration of the practical aspects of human behavior that can be observed and discussed. Thoreau, who had claimed earlier that "knowledge amounts to" little more than "an indefinite sense of the grandeur & glory of the Universe," now had to alter that view since it offered him little support in his new situation. "I see details not wholes nor the shadow of the whole," he said. "I count some parts, & say, 'I know.'"[40]

6

Emerson's most recent book, *Representative Men,* had found a wide public, and *English Traits,* the new volume he was working on, promised to do the same. Celebrity continued to be a source of solid satisfaction for Emerson. It compensated in some measure for the tedium and difficulty of everyday life. But for Thoreau, the story was different. The modest success of *Walden* had created strains on him that he did not know how to cope with.

The publication of *Walden* was an achievement that Thoreau had been working toward since he had begun keeping his journal in 1837. The book received broader and more favorable notice by reviewers than *A Week on the Concord and Merrimack Rivers.* Although Ticknor and Fields was disappointed when *Walden* sold only 738 copies in its first year, Thoreau was encouraged by the continued interest shown in it month after month. A Harvard student reported to him that a question repeatedly asked in Cambridge was, "Who is Mr. Thoreau?" By the time of his death eight years later, about 2,000 copies had been sold. Since the largest part of these copies had been purchased in New England, and most particularly in Massachusetts, he found that he was becoming well known in the part of the world that mattered most to him.[41]

A certain sign of Thoreau's importance as a writer was the gradual coalescing around him of a group of men who were interested in his ideas. The first to approach him had been Harrison G. O. Blake, an austere bachelor librarian who lived in Worcester and who had begun to exchange letters and visits with him in 1848. The publication of *Walden* also spurred the interest of three others of diverse backgrounds. Thomas Cholmondeley, an Englishman who was staying in Concord with Emerson at the time of *Walden's* appearance, became deeply interested in what Thoreau had to say. Daniel Ricketson, an independently wealthy resident of New Bedford, wrote days after the book's publication expressing his admiration, and a few months later Franklin Sanborn, a Harvard student from New Hampshire, sent an enthusiastic letter. The interest that these men showed in his ideas was tangible proof that Thoreau's message had struck a nerve among people sensitive to the social and economic conditions of the era. Within a short period of time Thoreau had established long-term relationships with each of these men.

Even more indicative of the increased interest in Thoreau was the sudden demand for his services as a lecturer. In the previous two years he had been invited to lecture only once, and that was by the Concord Lyceum. Now he found that he was suddenly sought after. In the six months between October 1854 and March 1855 he lectured more frequently than in any other six-month period of his life. He appeared in New Bedford and Concord, Plymouth and Worcester, even Providence and Philadelphia. Although the absence of invitations in the past had been a blow to his ego, the reality of appearing before audiences intensified an old conflict for him. He knew from experience that when he presented his material in his own way his listeners quickly lost interest in what he was saying. Now he felt increased pressure to find ways to hold their attention. When, in response to this demand, he added more humor to his talks, he felt that he was "in danger of cheapening" himself "to become a successful lecturer." He began to brood about the compromises he had begun to make.[42]

After so many years of dedicated but mostly unrewarded labor, even the modest success he was experiencing placed more pressure on Thoreau than he could bear, and he began to show signs of deepening depression and a breakdown in his health. That process was already becoming evident in the fall of 1854 when, as William Howarth points out, his journal entries had begun to show that he was "regressing to earlier ideas and modes of writing." In February he began entering the listless notes on the daily weather that occupy so much space in his journal from then on.[43]

By spring, after the lecture season had ended, he succumbed to a nameless sickness. "I should feel a little less ashamed if I could give any name to my disorder but I cannot, and our doctor cannot help me to it," he said. He no longer even had the strength to enjoy his long daily walks. He could only "lie on my back and wait for something to turn up." By June, Emerson had become alarmed. "Henry Thoreau is feeble, & languishes this season, to our alarm," he wrote to his brother in Staten Island. "We have tried to persuade him to come & spend a week with us for a c[h]ange." Proud and stubborn, Thoreau declined the invitation.[44]

11

Between Narrow Walls

Until Emerson read Thoreau's journal after his death, it's unlikely that he understood how deeply their drift apart affected his friend. Thoreau's remark that "there is one who almost wholly misunderstands me and whom I too probably misunderstand" correctly described the situation in the late 1850s. Each man misread the actions of the other. But it was Emerson's failure of perception at this crucial period in Thoreau's life that would lead Thoreau to conclude despondently that their friendship had "ended."[1]

Emerson was aware that Thoreau was having a difficult time emotionally and he was concerned about it. But when he thought about the situation, which he did frequently, he lay the blame on Thoreau for not taking the necessary steps to build a better life for himself. He was exasperated by Thoreau's seeming inability to examine the plain facts of his existence and reach rational conclusions about how to deal with them successfully. He thought he lacked realism when it came to everyday matters.

In considering Thoreau's quandary in this way, Emerson was thinking of it in terms of his own experience and capabilities. In his opinion, certain conditions in life had to be confronted, no matter how difficult it might be to do so. His year abroad, for instance, which had been an experiment in separation from Lidian, had taught him the fundamental importance of being in his own home with his family. He had returned to Concord determined to deal with circumstances as they existed there. Lidian's depression, withdrawal, and constant illness had made life in the Emerson home difficult for him and his children since the early 1840s, but he continued to seek solutions that would enable them to get by. Recently he had taken his fourteen-year-old daughter Ellen out of school so she could remain at home and run the household for Lidian until her mother's mood lightened and she was able to manage the servants on her own once more. This had not been a pleasant decision to make, but the maintenance of the family structure had been his goal, and he had achieved it.[2]

Emerson was also keenly aware of the importance of worldly success to an individual's sense of self-worth in a competitive society like that of New England. In his own case, he knew that he had to keep constant pressure on himself if he hoped to maintain the reputation and income that were so important to his view of himself. Despite his fear that his most productive days as a writer were behind him, he continued to produce collections of essays derived from his lectures. Recently he had published *English Traits* based on his observations in England. The book hadn't been easy for him to complete, but it had been a success. It sold seventeen hundred copies in the first four days after publication and went into a second printing a few weeks later.[3] Emerson had accomplished this while continuing to lecture throughout the country, even though these trips were not as easy to arrange as people thought. Due to the difficulty audiences had in understanding Emerson's rhetoric, lyceum managers often felt they could invite him back only after an interval of three or four years. He traveled widely, not because he wanted to but because that was the only way he could put together a profitable tour.[4]

One of the most intractable problems Emerson had to face in his life was an internal one. He considered himself shy and "cold at the surface." Casual encounters were difficult for him. He didn't find it easy to make small talk nor did he enjoy being with groups. But he couldn't spend all his time in his study writing or reading. He needed the stimulation of being with other people, particularly his peers. Since their companionship was not so easily arranged for, for the second time since his return from England he joined with a group of other intellectuals to form a club where they could meet on a regular basis, this time with greater success than on the first occasion. The Saturday Club, which had its first meeting in 1856, soon enlisted Lowell, Longfellow, Holmes, Hawthorne, Prescott, and Whittier as members. Once a month, regardless of the other pressures on him, Emerson boarded the train to Boston to attend its regular meeting.[5]

Since Emerson was able to work out solutions to the problems he faced, he could not understand why Thoreau did not do the same thing. He had no doubt, for instance, that Thoreau was a man "of great ability and industry"; what concerned him was that his energies appeared to be misdirected. Despite the recognition *Walden* had gained for Thoreau, he had not yet built a major reputation for himself as a writer, and Emerson was not convinced that Thoreau would ever do so. For a long time Emerson had felt that Thoreau would be wise to pursue a different career, one that would employ his practical talents and provide him with a respectable income. While it might be too late for him to become "the head of American engineers," there was still time for him to capitalize on "the universal impulse toward natural science" so evident in the nineteenth century. By approaching the subject in a scholarly fashion as Louis Agassiz had at Harvard, Thoreau might use his interest in nature to earn himself a prominent place in the world.[6]

An equally important problem for Thoreau, in Emerson's view, was his isolation. Emerson thought he was "more solitary even than he wished." Although Thoreau claimed it was necessary "to get away from men" for him to be free to pursue his interests, it seemed to Emerson that the price Thoreau paid for his freedom was too high, that it led to loneliness and reinforced his tendency toward depression. With Ellery Channing spending most of his time away from Concord, Thoreau's isolation had increased. To Emerson it seemed essential that Thoreau make the effort to involve himself more in the world. While Thoreau would have been welcome as a member of the Saturday Club, Emerson knew his friend would never travel to Boston to attend its meetings. But he thought that to achieve some sensible balance in his life, Thoreau needed to form relationships with more men and women who were his intellectual equals.[7]

Above all, however, Emerson was persuaded that Thoreau needed "to fall in love, to sweeten him and straighten him." Twice married himself and a father four times, Emerson believed that only in family life could his friend find the support he needed for him to achieve emotional balance. A decade and a half had passed since the episode with Ellen Sewall without any further romantic attachment on Thoreau's part. This "disappointment in early love" had by now achieved the status of myth among those who knew and cared for Thoreau. His celibacy was always referred to in terms of the crushing blow Ellen's rejection had dealt him. While on the surface it may have seemed that Thoreau had "no appetites, no passions," Emerson found it hard to accept the thought that he did not secretly harbor yearnings of the kind that are so much a part of the lives of most men. It appeared to him that for Thoreau it was a simple matter of choice. His life would be better if he married, and therefore he should find a partner.[8]

None of these demands seemed unreasonable to Emerson. Having been able to deal with his own problems through the strength of his will, he thought his friend should act in the same fashion. If Thoreau would only focus his energies on a different career, enter more into social activities, and marry, his days would no longer be dominated by bitterness and despair. Thoreau's failure to heed Emerson's words ultimately had an effect on Emerson's attitude toward him. Emerson found it increasingly difficult to hide his impatience.

2

Thoreau didn't disagree with Emerson's basic premise. He tried to convince himself that he possessed "force enough to overcome" the depression that plagued him, that he should not "despair of life." But his own view of his capability for real change was very different from Emerson's. "I am under an awful necessity to be what I am," he said, leaving no doubt that the essential outlines of his experience could not be altered. The challenge he faced each morning when he got out of bed was to shape a day for himself that provided him with some degree of satisfaction. To do this, however, had become increasingly more difficult for him.[9]

The collapse of Thoreau's health in the spring of 1855 had been the culmination of a process of breakdown that had commenced at the start of the decade. It was then, in his early thirties, that Thoreau began to experience less and less frequently the ecstatic states that had characterized his youth. Of these mystical experiences he had written: "There comes into my mind or soul such an indescribable infinite all-absorbing divine heavenly pleasure, a sense of elevation & expansion—and [I] have nought to do with it. I perceive that I am dealt with by superior powers." The diminishing frequency of these moments of epiphany came as a severe blow to him. Where he had previously felt himself to be "part and parcel of Nature," he now seemed to be merely "observant of her."[10]

It was at this time that his journal began to record aspects of his behavior on his walks that could be seen as additional evidence of distress. Removing his clothes and carrying them in his arms as he forded a river was a practical way to get to the other side without soaking them. But walking upstream with only his hat and shirt on was another matter. While the heat of the day may have been his excuse, such conduct in the vicinity of Concord was reckless to say the least. He had also developed a predilection for striking out alone after dark, often at midnight, that puzzled those who knew him. What satisfaction was he seeking as he made his way alone "through the wilds"? Was he hoping to induce one of those mystical experiences that now visited him so rarely?[11]

To Henry Thoreau who could say simply, "My work is writing," the loss of what had seemed to be a special relation to the universe was a severe blow. Although he had been able to summon up the energy to finish *Walden,* his inability any longer to "communicate with the gods" almost at will shut a door in his mind.[12] Seemingly barred from functioning at the level of his best work, he turned to less demanding projects. He filled notebooks with facts to be used in a study of the American Indian, and he slowly gathered information for a treatise on the propagation of seeds. Ironically, the latter was the kind of effort that Emerson felt he should have been concentrating on all along, one that might lead to the establishment of his reputation as a natural scientist. However, while these projects filled his hours, they did not satisfy his inner needs. Deprived of a sense of mission, he found himself dreading the "barren and worthless" days that stretched in front of him.[13]

Dissatisfied with the present, Thoreau looked back in time for happiness. For many years he had been convinced that "no experience which I have today comes up to, or is comparable with, the experiences of my boyhood." Then he had been "all alive," inhabiting his "body with inexpressible satisfaction."[14] In an attempt to recapture that sense of well-being he had begun reading Mayne Reid's "Books of Adventures for Boys," immersing himself in each volume of the series as it appeared throughout the 1850s.[15] Instead of seeking to expand his social horizon in the way that Emerson did, he sought boy companions for his walks. With them the "lost Child," as he described himself, could recover a sense of serenity. While a boy who had been one of his favorites recalled later that he had been "jolly and social" during these excursions, the outings provided him with no more than an occasional respite, a momentary lift; they could not solve the problem of his pervading loneliness.[16]

Thoreau had a pessimistic view of adulthood. "After the era of youth is passed, the knowledge of ourselves is an alloy that spoils our satisfactions," he said. For him, self-knowledge led in only one direction: to self-reproach. "I should be shunned by my fellow-men if they knew me better" is a typical remark. In a letter to H. G. O. Blake on the occasion of Blake's marriage Thoreau hinted at his reasons for being so harsh with himself. Referring to some "thoughts" he had included "on chastity and sexuality," he noted that he sent them "with diffidence and shame, not knowing how far I speak to the condition of men generally, or how far I betray my peculiar defects."[17] Regardless of how one interprets his reference to his "peculiar defects," these words make one thing clear: Thoreau was conscious of a difference between himself and others that deeply concerned him, and this situation had a harmful effect on his life. "If I could wholly cease to be ashamed of myself, I think that all of my days would be fair," he claimed.[18]

His "impurity" was Thoreau's central concern. "I am impure and vicious," he insisted. Any reference to sexuality seemed to offend him. His ire was raised in particular when Channing spoke casually about his relations with his wife. Thoreau's anger at his friend's disrespect masked deeper feelings, as did his indignation when he encountered obscene drawings on privy walls that he assumed had been scribbled there by boys. Boys who performed outrageous acts, he fumed, should be whipped by their mothers just as they would have been for "impurity."[19] There are indications that when he was fourteen he had been similarly punished for his own "sins," probably in that instance masturbation. If impurity and masturbation were connected in his mind, it would not have been the act, but the fantasies accompanying it, that caused such intense feelings of guilt on his part.[20]

The nature of the "peculiar defects" that underlay these fantasies is not important, but the inhibitions they imposed on him are, since they had a lasting effect on his life. Marriage, for instance, was ruled out for Thoreau. Not that he didn't want to marry; on the contrary he saw just how important it could be "to perform the pilgrimage of life in the society of a mate."[21] "If you fail in this respect, in what respect will you succeed?" he asked. But he could not master the forces at work within him; he could not free himself of their effect, which was to cause him to recoil at sexuality. "The marriage which the mass of men comprehend is but little better than the marriage of the beasts," he complained. Believing as he did that true love "mortifies and triumphs over the flesh, and the bond of its union is holiness," he was confined to dreaming of a relationship with a woman "transcending marriage," a hope that had little chance of being realized.[22]

The one refuge from these conflicts that the world offered Thoreau was friendship. It was, he wrote, "a glowing furnace in which all impurities are consumed." Since he considered sexuality to be excluded from friendship, he saw it as providing a safe harbor for him. But there was a danger even here. Having limited himself to friendship as the arena in which he was free to express his feelings, it had become the focus of his emotional life.[23]

3

The reality of Thoreau's situation was that his problems were too deeply rooted to be dealt with in the simple, direct way that Emerson advised. In fact, they had begun to overwhelm him. In looking back over his life it appeared to Thoreau that his "waking experience" had "*always*" oscillated between "Insanity and Sanity," but while the shifts from one state to the other had been sharp, he had experienced frequent periods of fulfillment. Now he found himself powerless to escape the all-pervading sense of emptiness that accompanies severe depression. "What are all these years made for?" he wondered. Try as he might, he could find no purpose in his existence.[24]

Emerson, who had a deep understanding of the human condition, was aware of his own "dark spots." He knew that within himself he was "not united," that he was prone to "bite & tear" himself. But he was alert to the effect of the unconscious on behavior and believed that health lay in accepting the reality of its power and deferring to it. In trying to deal with the problems in his life, he never attempted to turn himself into a different person. Unfortunately, that was exactly what he was demanding of Thoreau. If he had admitted this to himself, he might have seen Thoreau's situation with a more sympathetic eye. Under the circumstances, however, when Thoreau needed emotional support most from the man he still considered his best friend, it was not forthcoming.[25]

If anything, Emerson seemed irritated by Thoreau's silent demand for attention. "Yes, I know he needs cherishing and care. Yet who can care and cherish, when we are so driven with our own affairs?" he demanded.[26] They went for walks through the woods as usual; they visited each other's homes; set out trees together on Emerson's newly purchased cemetery plot; even attended an auction together. But none of this changed the situation that had existed for several years. Each privately continued to record his sense of estrangement from the other. Emerson noted tersely that Thoreau was "quite inattentive to any comment or thought," "merely interrupted by it," while Thoreau complained that Emerson "would not meet me on equal terms, but only be to some extent my patron."[27]

Winters were always a busy time for Emerson, and the winter of 1857–58 was particularly active. In December he began a lecture tour that took him to sixteen Massachusetts cities and towns. Then early in January he left for New York City, Philadelphia, and an extended tour in the west. In the next month he appeared before audiences in Buffalo, Cortland, Rochester, and Syracuse, New York; Chicago and Waukegan, Illinois; Lafayette, Indiana; Cincinnati, Columbus, Sandusky, and Cleveland, Ohio; and Covington, Kentucky. As usual, he complained bitterly in his letters to Lidian that he could find "no compensations for the waste & discomfort of this journeying" or for "the stultification of brain which it causes," but he continued to meet his engagements, slowly accumulating the sum he needed to see his family through the remainder of the year.[28]

As Emerson hurried from city to city, the loneliness and isolation of winter in Concord increased Thoreau's depression. His friend's absence tinged his days with an irrational but pervasive feeling of abandonment. The "sense of degradation" he had come to feel in Emerson's presence had become consuming.[29] He found himself dwelling on the grievances against Emerson that he had been accumulating for so many years. It seemed clear to him that he must face an inevitable fact: their friendship had "ended." All that was left of it was an unsatisfactory series of encounters springing not from interest but from habit. This conclusion filled his whole being with anguish. "Morning, noon, and night, I suffer a physical pain, an aching of the breast which unfits me for my tasks," he confided to his journal. He felt as if there was no longer a center to his life. "I could better have the earth taken away from under my feet, than the thought of you from my mind," he wrote.[30]

Emerson, of course, knew nothing about this. When he returned from his lecture tour the second week in February, he picked up the strands of his life as usual. There were letters to write, bills to be paid, Lidian's concerns to be attended to. And, of course, there were the children who were growing up and, like all adolescents, asserting their individuality. If Emerson noticed that Thoreau seemed to have closed a door between them, there was little time for the thought to linger. Too many other pressing matters demanded his attention.

Emerson's burst of activity was cut short, however, not long after his return to Concord by "a sudden & pretty serious attack" of illness that the doctor identified as measles. At that time any sickness accompanied by fever was a matter for serious concern, considering the limited means for treatment available to doctors. For Thoreau the situation had a frightening familiarity. It echoed the events leading up to his brother's sudden death while they were still at odds regarding Ellen Sewall. Struggling with these thoughts as Emerson lay sick, Thoreau wrote, "At the very instant that I seem to be saying farewell forever to one who has been my friend, I find myself unexpectedly near to him, and it is our very nearness and dearness to each other that gives depth and significance to that forever."[31]

The fear that he might lose Emerson as he had lost John caused something to shift in Thoreau's mind. It wasn't that the anger had disappeared or that the sting had gone out of Emerson's behavior. It was rather an adjustment of priorities. He realized that he could not live without the sustenance of the friendship. "I am a helpless prisoner, and these chains I have no skill to break. While I have broken one link, I have been forging another."[32]

Emerson recovered quickly, but the effect of his illness on their relationship was permanent. Thoreau had been shocked into realizing that he had to accept reality as it was instead of constantly bemoaning a past that could not be resurrected. He had no other choice. Years earlier in *A Week* Thoreau had written, "We must accept or refuse one another as we are." It had taken him a long time to apply that concept to his changing relationship with Emerson, but in doing so at last he was laying the foundation for a new phase in their friendship, one that would provide him with essential support during the few, increasingly more difficult years that remained of his life.[33]

12

The Final Years

In the spring of 1857, finding himself in better health than he had enjoyed for two years, Thoreau resumed his long walks with Emerson. Typical of these excursions was one that led them to Ebba Hubbard's swamp. Emerson's report of the hours they spent together in the countryside that afternoon recalls his enthusiastic descriptions of similar occasions in the early years of their friendship. They watched pigeons and marsh hawks swooping across the sky, Emerson noted, as he and Thoreau slowly made their way "through the savage & fertile houseless land." Later, when a mist began to rise, it seemed to him that they had entered "the haunt of the elder gods." As had happened so often in the past, Emerson recorded a remark of Thoreau's that particularly pleased him. "Henry said of the railroad whistle, that nature had made up her mind not to hear it, she knew better than to wake up." On the surface, as Emerson's journal entry indicates, their relationship had quietly resumed its old rhythms. Nonetheless, a new and unexpected element had entered it.[1]

Behind the undeniable fact of their commitment to each other lay a mystery that puzzled Thoreau and Emerson. Here they were, middle-aged men, neither of whom much resembled his younger self. It had become more and more difficult for either of them to understand how the stiff and insular person he glimpsed across a room or encountered in the street could have been so important a factor in his life for so long. Neither of them could easily bring the memory he cherished of the other into focus with the actuality. This sense of dislocation was perplexing enough for both Thoreau and Emerson to feel the need to deal with it in their journals, although Emerson approached the subject indirectly through a series of oblique remarks, while Thoreau confronted it head on.

The attempt to answer the question—"Why has Henry Thoreau been so important to me for so many years?"—underlay many of the comments about Thoreau that Emerson recorded in the late 1850s. During this period Thoreau's behavior often seemed to heighten Emerson's confusion. One day in 1858, for instance, as Emerson walked in his woodlot beside Walden Pond, he encountered Thoreau who had arrived earlier and was experiencing one of his moments of union with nature. When Thoreau was in a mood of this kind, he could be overpoweringly dogmatic in his manner. On this occasion he informed his friend that if the "bit of mould" on which Emerson stood was "not sweeter to you to eat, than any other in this world, or in any world," then there was no hope for him. It was this kind of posturing that led Emerson to write a note to Thoreau in the privacy of his journal, a note that clearly expressed his impatience with Thoreau's manner on occasions like this: "My dear Henry, A frog was made to live in a swamp, but a man was not made to live in a swamp. Yours ever, R."[2]

However, Emerson had only to compare Thoreau with the rich and successful Bostonians whose acquaintance he had cultivated in recent years for Thoreau's merits to stand out with sudden and persuasive clarity. When Emerson talked with the successful businessmen from "State Street," they all seemed alike to him. But when he conversed with Henry Thoreau, Emerson realized he could be talking with no one else: "he brings his own deep force," he remarked. Emerson also admired the democratic tenor of Thoreau's approach to people. He "talks birchbark to all comers, & reduces them all to the same insignificance," he said approvingly. This was the Thoreau with whom he had been linked for two decades, not the truculent man who confronted him across the dinner table on Sunday afternoons. The difficulty for Emerson lay in remembering the former Thoreau when encountering the latter. Only when he was able to set aside the sense of alienation that often nagged him when he was with Thoreau was Emerson able to accept his companion as his friend.[3]

Emerson was not alone in feeling this way. Henry Thoreau had always brought large expectations to his encounters with Emerson, but so often these days when they met face to face, Thoreau had the sense that he "imagined something that was not there." He felt balked by these meetings. Emerson was "not thinking, not believing, not doing as I do," Thoreau said. He gave Thoreau the impression that his presence "interrupted" some more important activity. Emerson simply did not seem to be the friend who figured so prominently in Thoreau's imagination. It was as if two strangers were dealing with one another. Nevertheless, as soon as they were no longer in each other's company, Thoreau found his thoughts returning to Emerson as if by an implacable magnetism. He was puzzled by the persistence of his intense attachment to Emerson despite the difficulty he encountered in making contact with his ideal friend, the one he carried with him in his heart. At times Thoreau felt as if he were in the grips of an illusion. Ultimately, Thoreau decided, "It may be enough that we have met *some time,* and now can never forget it." In other words, he was willing to accept the memory of the exhilarating intimacy of the earlier years of their relationship as the validation of his present feelings.[4]

Despite this sense of dislocation, neither of the men could deny that over time their friendship had become deeply embedded in the structure of their lives. As this mutual dependency had grown, they had developed distinctive patterns of support for each other that had become important underpinnings for their lives, patterns that reflected their personalities and priorities. Emerson, for instance, had habitually shown his concern through a thoughtfulness that could take many forms, a custom that was still characteristic of his behavior. In the spring of 1858 sensing that Thoreau would find the *Documentary History of New York* useful in his study of the American Indian, Emerson wrote to the editor of the four-volume work asking him to send a copy to his friend. On another occasion, impressed by Thoreau's latest lecture, "Autumnal Tints," he invited a group of neighbors including the Alcotts and Ellery Channing to his home to hear Thoreau read it. When James Russell Lowell mentioned in a letter to Emerson that he would like to publish a piece by Thoreau in a new magazine he was editing, the *Atlantic Monthly,* Emerson carried the proposal to his friend. The result was the appearance in the magazine of three installments describing Thoreau's excursion to the Maine woods in 1853. Actions like these were a more important expression of the depth of Emerson's feeling for Thoreau than any spoken sentiments could have been.

Thoreau reciprocated these kindnesses in a manner typical of him, by performing practical duties for Emerson. He built an arbor to ornament the Emersons' garden. He planted four hundred pines and one hundred larches on Emerson's land at Walden where his cabin had stood. Although Emerson paid him to perform these tasks, the money was not the important thing at this point in Thoreau's life; it was the desire to help his friend that mattered. This was made clear when Emerson's retarded brother Bulkeley died suddenly in Littleton, Massachusetts. Thoreau immediately relieved Emerson of responsibility for arranging the funeral, handling all the details himself.

Clearly, Thoreau and Emerson had experienced the loneliness inherent in life sufficiently to realize the importance of connectedness despite the difficulty they had at times in locating their "friend" in the person with whom they were talking. Thoreau put his finger on the situation when he said, "We are attracted toward a particular person, but no one has discovered the laws of this attraction." While the mature friendship they were now experiencing could never be as satisfying as the intimacy of their earlier years, the foundation of trust established between them when they were younger had become a primary source of security for both men as they confronted the problems that middle age began to press upon them.[5]

2

Thoreau's father, John Thoreau Sr., who had been declining in health for two years, had reached the point in the winter of 1858–59 where he could no longer leave his bedroom. Unwilling to give in to invalidism until the last few days of his life, he insisted upon getting up each day and spending some time in his chair. He died so quietly that the family members who were in the room with him did not immediately realize what had happened.

His father's death placed Thoreau in a position similar to the one Emerson had occupied for many years. Suddenly he was head of the family, with all the cares inherent in that role. He not only had to be concerned with the welfare of his mother and his sister Sophia but also with the running of the family business.[6] The Thoreaus' business had changed greatly in character since the mid-1840s when twenty-six-year-old Henry Thoreau had perfected a method for manufacturing a better pencil. In that time the development of electrotype printing had led to a dramatic growth in the need for high quality lead. Since the Thoreaus were known for the fine quality of the lead they produced, a demand had arisen for their product, and after 1852, they had made few pencils, preferring to supply the electrotyping market instead.[7]

For some time Sophia Thoreau had handled the accounts, taken care of the correspondence, and seen to the shipping of the lead while Thoreau had done the heavy work, which included overseeing activity at the mill in East Acton, transporting the processed lead to the work area at the back of their house, and then packaging it for shipment.[8] Manual labor had never been a problem for Henry Thoreau. When he was finished with his chores, he would turn, refreshed, to his work as a writer. But the problems associated with running the business were a different matter. These were "irksome affairs" in his opinion, but being "a martinet in the family service," as Ellery Channing said, he attended to them dutifully.[9]

In the preceding decade Thoreau's dependence on Sophia for companionship had increased steadily. They had always been important to each other, but as they grew older, they found themselves growing closer in a variety of ways. Running the family business on their own was just one facet of this intensifying involvement. The balance of responsibility for daily matters in the household had changed. Although their mother was still alive and healthy, Henry and Sophia Thoreau were effectively in charge of affairs. Together they saw to it that family life maintained the level of comfort the Thoreaus had come to expect. They also spent much of their leisure time together, visiting neighbors or making excursions into the countryside. In his relationship with his sister Sophia, Thoreau had at last attained the companionate marriage he had dreamed about as a youth.

If the passage of time had altered Henry Thoreau's circumstances at home profoundly, its effect on Emerson's affairs, although more subtle perhaps, had been no less consequential. Lidian Emerson's unending battle with her servants and with herself in her role as a homemaker had, if anything, sharpened. Lidian's conscience demanded that she maintain a well-kept house despite the fact that housework itself and the supervision of servants oppressed her. More and more frequently her solution was to avoid the situation entirely by secluding herself in her room. In time, the fact that she had come downstairs became an event worth reporting in the letters exchanged among family members. In a note the Emersons' eldest daughter, Ellen, wrote to her sister, Edith, it was reported as a startling development that "mother was downstairs" the day the letter was written and, in addition, that Lidian "had been down in the evening Thursday to see Mr. Sanborn, and Friday to see Mrs. Forbes."[10]

Lidian's inclination to sequester herself led to a continuing dilemma for Emerson. The family had tried on several occasions to arrange for someone to manage the household, but without success. Ellen Emerson, who was then in her late teens, had demonstrated that she was happy to take over for her mother whenever it was necessary but had not yet completed her schooling. For several years Emerson found himself concurring in an endless back and forth: Lidian forcing herself to accept her responsibilities, then withdrawing from housekeeping activities; servants leaving or being fired; Ellen temporarily giving up school to take charge; Lidian slowly regaining control of the situation; Ellen returning to school; and then full circle again.

The Emersons' growing dependence on Ellen had an unfortunate effect on the lives of all three of them. For Ellen, who never married, the consequences were particularly severe. She remained at home for the rest of her life to devote herself to her parents. This may have seemed like an ideal situation for the Emersons, but in actuality it skewed their own relationship. Emerson began more and more to depend on his daughter as if she were his mate, and Lidian no longer had any external brakes to slow her retreat into herself. The mysterious processes of life had placed Thoreau and Emerson in unexpected situations in their middle years. Neither would have sought these outcomes; neither found his circumstances completely satisfying. But this was where the continuing struggles of their lives had led them, and having learned a healthy realism in regard to their expectations, they accepted their situations with resignation, not only as they related to their personal lives but also as they regarded their careers.

"I have now for more than a year, I believe, ceased almost wholly to write in my Journal, in which I formerly wrote almost daily," Emerson admitted in 1859, adding, "I . . . sometimes believe that I have no new thoughts, and that my life is quite at an end." His *Conduct of Life*, which was published in 1860, was based on earlier lectures and centered its interest on power and the means by which individuals attain it. The book, which was written in a straightforward style and was easier to read than his earlier books, quickly became a popular success. Still it did not please Henry Thoreau. He told

Bronson Alcott that he thought it only "moderate" in its accomplishment and that it lacked "the fire and force of the earlier books."[11]

That summer Thoreau had described a series of lectures he was scheduled to deliver as *"transcendental,"* which could not have been said of *The Conduct of Life*. It has been suggested that the reason Thoreau still considered himself a transcendentalist was so that he could continue to associate himself and his work "with the quest for a morally significant universe."[12] The lion's share of his present activity, however, was related to his interest in natural science, most importantly to a study of the dispersion of seeds. He had been gathering this information in a systematic way for several years and ultimately produced 354 pages of manuscript on the subject. Part of this material had been printed recently in his essay "The Succession of Forest Trees." Aware of the scope of Thoreau's effort, Emerson noted after his death that the "scale on which his studies" had been conducted was "so large as to require longevity." But Thoreau was not given that boon; his work on the dispersion of seeds would never be completed.[13]

3

The forces that were leading the United States inexorably toward civil war were being felt in Concord, Massachusetts, just as surely as they were in every other corner of the nation. On September 15 the governor of Massachusetts called for a statewide muster of militia to be held in Concord. Several thousand troops converged on the village for a three-day encampment. Infantry and cavalry maneuvered on the parade ground in a display that left a deep mark on the consciousness of the town's citizens. Although there was a holiday atmosphere about the occasion, no one present could escape the sense that there was a momentum building in the country toward a violent confrontation.[14]

A month later the news reached Concord that John Brown, accompanied by a small group of armed men, had raided Harpers Ferry and had subsequently been overcome by forces under the command of Col. Robert E. Lee. Emerson, Thoreau, and Alcott were gathered together at the Emerson home when they learned of the events. From the dispatch reaching them it was unclear whether Brown had been killed. To say that they were shocked would be to understate the case. They knew John Brown. He had visited

Concord twice, once in February 1857 and more recently in May 1859. Thoreau and Emerson had sat in the town hall with their neighbors and listened as he spoke of his efforts to prevent the institution of slavery from becoming rooted in Kansas. Each of the men had entertained him in his home. They admired him, and they supported his cause.[15]

As more information began to trickle into Concord, the initial confusion about what had actually happened at Harpers Ferry began to clear. Word soon reached Thoreau and Emerson that Brown had not been killed by Lee's forces but was under arrest and would shortly be tried for treason. They also learned that letters had been found at Brown's staging ground in West Virginia that threatened to implicate their neighbor Franklin Sanborn in Brown's plot.[16] Sanborn, a young Harvard graduate who had reopened the Concord Academy three years earlier, had long been a supporter of Brown's and was a member of the Secret Six, a group of Massachusetts men who had aided Brown's antislavery activities up to and including the raid.[17]

Both Thoreau and Emerson responded immediately to the crisis, each in his own characteristic way. Thoreau sat down at his desk and began to write what has since become known as "A Plea for Capt. John Brown," an address that formalized sentiments he had expressed at Emerson's house the day news of Brown's raid reached the friends there. Thoreau delivered his talk on October 30 in the town hall over the objections of Concord's selectmen who refused to order the bell rung at the hall to announce the meeting. Emerson, concerning himself at first primarily with Franklin Sanborn's dilemma, acted quickly to intervene in the situation. The young teacher had fled to Quebec, convinced that if he remained in Concord he would be arrested and tried in a federal court for complicity with Brown. Emerson inquired into the legal situation facing Sanborn and, satisfied that he could return safely to Concord, wrote urging him to do so. Emerson also helped with the arrangements to keep Sanborn's school open until the young man reached home and could go back to work.

John Brown was tried on November 1, convicted of treason, and sentenced to be hanged. Neither Thoreau nor Emerson had known in advance of Brown's plan.[18] In fact it seems unlikely that either man had been aware of the dark side of his earlier activities in Kansas, such as his involvement in the massacre at Potawatomie. By now, however, newspapers were printing the details of his previous activities in their reports of the Harpers Ferry raid, and there is every likelihood that Thoreau and Emerson learned about it from them.[19] In spite of this, they continued to support Brown because they believed in the purity of his character.[20] On the day of Brown's trial Thoreau repeated his "Plea" in Boston, and two days later he delivered it again in Worcester. Not long afterward Emerson also defended Brown publicly while addressing an audience in Boston and then spoke fervently in his behalf at a rally for the relief of Brown's family held in the same city.

After the announcement of Brown's sentence the two men agreed that speaking out was not enough; some positive action had to be taken to save Brown's life. They decided that an attempt should be made to persuade Governor Wise of West Virginia to show leniency to his prisoner. Emerson explored the question with various like-minded people of his acquaintance in Boston hoping to find someone there "who might have private influence" with the governor, but he was unsuccessful in this undertaking.[21] At the same time Thoreau discussed their concerns with Bronson Alcott who thought that either Emerson or Thoreau should take the initiative and write personally to Governor Wise. Sanborn was of the opinion that helping Brown to escape offered the best chance for saving his life but admitted to Emerson that Brown had no desire to pursue such a path. In the end Emerson drafted a letter to Governor Wise, but it appears that, convinced of the futility of the effort, he did not send it.[22]

By this time the friends had come to the conclusion that there was nothing more they could do except to arrange for services to be held on the day of Brown's execution. Thoreau spearheaded the effort. On the evening of November 28 he and Emerson addressed a meeting held at the Concord Town Hall to discuss the subject, and the next evening they met with the other members of the four-man committee that had been formed to make plans for the service. At that meeting it was decided that Thoreau would read selections from the poets while Emerson would read from Brown's words and that Alcott, Sanborn, and others would also participate. December 2, the day of Brown's execution, was "a beautiful mild winter day, suitable for boating" on the Concord River. The large group that attended the service that afternoon included many people from adjoining towns.[23]

The initial report of Brown's raid on Harpers Ferry had brought Thoreau and Emerson together in a common effort. The arrival of the news two weeks later that Brown had been sentenced to death had had the effect of intensifying this involvement. In their desire to provide whatever support they could to Brown and his family, Thoreau and Emerson had become engaged with each other in a manner they had not experienced in over a decade. They had thrust their ego concerns aside and had met with each other day after day without being weighed down by the baggage of the past. It had taken a tragic event to achieve this result, but the effect was to clear the air between them once and for all.

4

In June 1860 Nathaniel Hawthorne and his wife, Sophia, who had lived abroad for seven years moved back to Concord. To celebrate Hawthorne's return, Emerson arranged for a small gathering at his home to which he invited Thoreau. As the guests ate strawberries with cream, there was no special consciousness in the room that the leading American writers of their era were present. Emerson, Thoreau, and Hawthorne talked quietly among themselves and with the others as they would have on any ordinary occasion. Nevertheless, it was a special moment in time. With the recent publication of Hawthorne's *Marble Faun,* all three men had completed the work on which their reputations would rest. These reputations had not been earned without a tremendous investment of energy. Although they were not aware of it as they enjoyed their strawberries and cream, Emerson, Thoreau, and Hawthorne were among that small group of Americans destined to achieve lasting international reputations. Ultimately their works would contribute largely to defining their country's view of human experience in the pre–Civil War era.

A month after the strawberry party, William Dean Howells, a young Ohio journalist with literary aspirations, came to Concord with the intention of calling on all three of the men. He visited Hawthorne first and was impressed by his encounter with him, but his meetings with Thoreau and Emerson left him with less positive feelings. Thoreau, at whose house he appeared next, kept him so much at a distance that the young man was offended, and Emerson showed little interest in his conversation. Howells's reactions to Thoreau and Emerson are unclouded by sentiment. In his reminiscences, Howell presented Thoreau and Emerson as self-absorbed and barely able to repress their impatience to be rid of him. He painted them as tired, withdrawn men who had been left behind by the vital force.[24]

The personal pressures Thoreau and Emerson were experiencing in their lives had indeed begun to wear on them, and their behavior showed it. It was Thoreau, however, who was having the more difficult time of the two. He was the one who said at this period, "I do not know how to distinguish between our waking life and a dream. Are we not always living the life that we imagine we are." Thoreau was not temperamentally suited to the burden of being head of a family. Being forced to give up his freedom placed a great strain on him.[25] Retreating into his imagination had always been his way of escaping from the stresses of everyday life. Now the responsibilities he had to confront daily made it far more difficult for him to do this. As the months passed, his system began to show evidence of the strain imposed on it. A severe cold he caught late in the autumn of 1860 kept him indoors until spring except for "a very few experimental trips as far as the P. O. in some particularly mild noons."[26]

Concern about Thoreau's health began to mount among his friends. In writing to an acquaintance of Thoreau's about the situation, Ellery Channing said: "His trouble appears to him bronchial, the cold air brings on coughing . . . [and] he is reduced much in stature." Emerson refused to countenance the forebodings of the others that Thoreau might not recover, insisting, there was "too much resistance" in him for that to be the case. When the situation had not improved perceptibly by spring, Thoreau's doctor recommended that he take a trip in the hope that a change of climate would be helpful. After thinking this advice over, Thoreau decided "to try the air of Minnesota." It was arranged that he would be accompanied on the journey by seventeen-year-old Horace Mann Jr., son of the well-known educator, who had recently moved to Concord with his family. The date of their departure was set for May 11.[27]

Emerson called on Thoreau that morning to say good-bye. Before they parted he gave him a formal note of introduction to carry with him on the road and a list of people to visit who might be helpful to him. In the note, he allowed his emotions to break through only once, at the point where he referred to Thoreau as an invalid. He spoke of him then as "so dear and valued by me and all good Americans." The phrase was revealing in two ways. It indicated the fullness of his understanding of Thoreau's importance to him and also his growing awareness of the importance of Thoreau's achievement as a literary man.[28]

Toward the end of June, Thoreau reported from Redwing, Minnesota: "I am considerably better than when I left home, but still far from well." Within two months of his departure, Thoreau was back in Concord. While the trip was probably beneficial in that it removed him from the daily cares of his life at home, it could not arrest the progress of what was beginning to be recognized as, in the words of a Concord neighbor, "the first stage of consumption."[29]

On the evening of July 10, Thoreau's second day home from his trip, he joined Ellery Channing at the Emersons for dinner. Emerson had recently suffered severe financial losses due to his purchase of railroad securities on the advice of Abel Adams, a Boston banker who had been his unofficial investment adviser for many years. To compensate for this, Adams had offered to pay for young Edward Emerson's college education, and Edward was slated to take his entry examination shortly. In remembering that evening years later, Edward wrote: "When we left the table and were passing into the parlour, Thoreau asked me to come with him to our East door— our more homelike door, facing the orchard. It was an act of affectionate courtesy, for he had divined my suppressed state of mind and remembered that first crisis in his own life, and the wrench that it seemed in advance, as a gate leading out into an untried world. With serious face, but with a very quiet, friendly tone of voice, he reassured me, told me that I should be really close to home; very likely should pass my life in Concord. It was a great relief."[30]

Thoreau also dined at the Emersons' in September, the day before Edward commenced his course of study in Cambridge. Thoreau had recently said, "I have been sick so long that I have almost forgotten what it is to be well." By this time even Emerson, who did not want to admit the truth, could not deny the seriousness of the situation. Thoreau's appearance spoke volumes about his condition. An acquaintance described a visit with him this way: "By evening a flush had come to his cheeks and an ominous beauty and brightness to his eyes, painful to behold. His conversation was unusually brilliant, and we listened with a charmed attention which perhaps stimulated him to continue talking until the weak voice could no longer articulate."[31]

5

One fine day followed another in the autumn of 1861, making it possible for Thoreau to enjoy being out of doors. Several times a week his sister Sophia arranged to take him riding in a shay to "his familiar haunts, far away in the thick woods, or by the ponds." He took pleasure in introducing her to places she had never visited and appeared to benefit from the outings. His appetite improved, his energy level increased, and he was able to devote more time to his work. His friends' letters were suddenly filled with the news that Thoreau seemed to be getting better. By the middle of October, Franklin Sanborn was able to report that there was "hope of his recovery."[32]

Still, Thoreau's appearance was shocking to someone who had not encountered him recently. George William Curtis was visiting with Emerson in his study one afternoon in November when Thoreau walked in unannounced to borrow a volume of Pliny's letters. Curtis was appalled by the progress of Thoreau's disease, noting particularly that he "was much wasted." With the advent of cold weather, the promising signs of recovery began to reverse themselves. New England's harsh winters were notoriously hard on people suffering from tuberculosis, and medicine at that time could do little to ameliorate the situation. Thoreau's cough increased, and he found himself confined to the house. Soon Bronson Alcott was reporting to a friend that Thoreau was growing "feebler day by day," slowly "failing and fading from our sight."[33]

Despite the seriousness of his situation, Thoreau faced the future serenely, continuing to work as long each day as his steadily increasing weakness permitted. In February 1862, he received a heartening letter from James Fields, who had recently replaced James Russell Lowell as editor of the *Atlantic Monthly*. Fields wrote to tell Thoreau of his interest in printing some of his shorter works in the magazine. The details were quickly arranged and Thoreau began editing three of his unpublished pieces.

Thoreau's declining strength made it necessary for him to seek Sophia's assistance in preparing the manuscripts for Fields. Thoreau would first correct the text, then Sophia would read it aloud to him for his review and copy it neatly so it could be sent to the *Atlantic*. In this way Thoreau was able to pull together "Autumnal Tints," "Walking," and "Life without Principle" and send them off by the end of the month. Fields, who remained active as a partner in the publishing firm of Ticknor and Fields, also suggested that it was time to reprint *Walden,* a proposal that was eminently agreeable to Thoreau, although he was also concerned about the fate of *A Week on the Concord and Merrimack Rivers.* He still had 146 bound and 450 unbound copies of the latter book stored in the Thoreau house. Although Fields resisted reissuing it, Thoreau persevered, finally persuading him to do so.

As spring approached, Thoreau was finding it difficult to converse with others, although he still enjoyed receiving visitors. A neighbor commented that he "never saw a man dying with so much pleasure and peace." Emerson, who had recently returned from a short lecture tour, came to see him regularly. He read to him; brought him a duck to be prepared for his dinner; carried news of the appearance of the first purple finch of spring and of how near the ice was to breaking up on Walden pond. Forced to face the imminence of Thoreau's death, Emerson chose an unexpected word to describe his attitude toward its inevitability; he felt "threatened" by it, he said.[34] For a quarter of a century his relationship with Henry Thoreau had been a central feature of his life. Although Emerson had often found Thoreau's attachment to him burdensome, he was aware that their friendship had been a source of great strength in his own struggle to achieve his personal goals. His "Henry brave and good" had always been there when he needed him. Not surprisingly, a world in which he would be denied this support was a frightening prospect for him to anticipate. Returning from a talk with Thoreau during these last weeks of his life, Emerson marveled, as he had since the beginning of their friendship, at the force of his intellect. He is "full of compensations, resources and reserved funds," he wrote.[35]

Aware that he would shortly be going "up country," Thoreau concentrated the little energy left to him on the disposition of his remaining material. He decided that his notes on the American Indians, which he had spent many years developing, would not yield a publishable volume but concluded that his three essays on Maine could be successfully combined into a book. By providing transitional material to link the Maine essays, he was able to create the volume that would appear posthumously as *The Maine Woods.*[36]

Although Thoreau's last days were wearisome, he did not experience great pain and preserved his good humor to the last. On the morning of May 6 Thoreau asked Sophia, who was attending him, to read aloud from the last chapter of *A Week*. After she had read the sentence, "We glided past the mouth of the Nashua, and not long after of Salmon Brook, without more pause than the wind," Thoreau murmured, "Now comes good sailing." A short time later he died.[37]

6

Although Sophia Thoreau did not think that her brother's funeral service should be held in church, Emerson insisted that this be done and that he himself deliver the eulogy. On the afternoon of Friday, May 9, the bell at the First Parish Church tolled forty-four times in commemoration of Thoreau's age at his death. The schools had closed early that day to allow the children of the town to attend the funeral, which was scheduled to begin at two o'clock, and many of them joined the adults who filed past the open coffin in the vestibule in which Thoreau's body lay strewn with wild flowers.

The large crowd that slowly assembled in the pews included the Thoreau family, the Emersons and their children, the Alcotts, the Hawthornes, and James Fields with his wife. Reverend Grindall Reynolds opened the service by reading selections from the Bible; the choir sang a hymn written for the occasion by Ellery Channing; and then Emerson entered the pulpit.

Standing erect before the crowd, Emerson spoke at length about the man with whom he had been intimately associated for a quarter of a century. As might have been expected from Emerson, the appraisal was balanced. He did not try to present a Thoreau who had no faults; instead he memorialized the man he and those gathered before him had known so well. If his tone seemed detached at times, it was because he had stepped back to achieve a clearer view of Henry Thoreau, not because of a lack of feeling for his friend.

Emerson reminded his listeners that Thoreau had focused his energies on "the art of living well." Thoreau's determination to "reconcile his practice with his own belief" set him apart from others. He had chosen "to be rich by making his wants few, and supplying them himself." He did not bow to "opposition or ridicule"; it carried no "weight with him." He was "sincerity itself," "a person incapable of any profanation, by act or by thought." His originality lay as much in his manner of confronting experience as in the words he set down to record his observations.[38]

But the "severity of his ideal" erected a wall between him and his friends that could be hard to breech, Emerson said. He was "a born protestant" whose "first instinct on hearing a proposition" was inevitably "to controvert it." In fact, it often appeared "as if he did not feel himself except in opposition." This practice was "a little chilling to the social affections"; it dampened the conversational impulse. But it had more to do with the quickness of his mind than anything else. He "understood the matter at hand at a glance" and immediately grasped "the limitations and poverty of those he talked with." Nothing, it seemed, could be "concealed from such terrible eyes."[39]

Why was it, then, that so many of those who knew Henry Thoreau "almost worshipped" him? There was no mystery, Emerson said. These were the people who recognized both "the deep value of his mind" and his "great heart." Thoreau was the possessor of "an excellent wisdom" reserved for "a rare class of men." He was "a speaker and actor of the truth." He had "no appetites, no passions, no taste for elegant trifles." While this might mean that his "virtues . . . sometimes ran into extremes," his "holy living" set an example for all.[40]

Although Emerson paid abundant tribute to Thoreau the man, he was less forthcoming about his friend's accomplishments as a writer. He mentioned two poems of Thoreau's that he particularly liked, "Sympathy" and "Smoke," but declared that as a poet he lacked "a lyric facility and technical skill." Although he referred to Thoreau's sojourn at Walden Pond, he mentioned *Walden* only once, and then in passing. He read short passages from Thoreau's journal but did not comment on the achievement that the journal represented. His judgment on his friend's literary career was stated elliptically, in terms of the loss caused by his early death. "It seems an injury," Emerson said, that Thoreau's life should have ended while he was still engaged in "his broken task which none else can finish." It was an "indignity to so noble a soul that he should depart out of Nature before yet he has been really shown to his peers for what he is."[41]

Toward the end of the eulogy, Emerson shifted his attention from the man whose body lay in the coffin in the foyer of the church. With carefully chosen words he began the work of creating the mythical Henry Thoreau, the naturalist whose remarkable powers had permitted him to move as easily among animals as among humans. "Snakes coiled round his legs; the fishes swam into his hand, and he took them out of the water; he pulled the woodchuck out of its hole by the tail, and took the foxes under his protection from the hunters." The words have a biblical ring, and they set the tone for much that would be written about Henry Thoreau in subsequent years. This was the Thoreau people wanted to believe in, and Emerson was clearly first among them.[42]

Not until Emerson reached the final paragraph of his text did he permit himself to show the emotion that lay beneath the surface of the controlled demeanor he presented to his auditors. "The country knows not yet, or the least part, how great a son it has lost," he said. Then he added from the depth of his being, "His soul was made for the noblest society; he had in a short life exhausted the capabilities of this world; wherever there is knowledge, wherever there is virtue, wherever there is beauty, he will find a home."[43]

Notes

Introduction

1. Tilton, "Emerson's Lecture Schedule," 387–88.
2. R. Emerson, *Journals and Miscellaneous Notebooks,* 5:293.
3. Cooke, *Historical and Biographical Introduction to the Dial,* 13.

1. An Extraordinary Young Man

1. L. Emerson, *Selected Letters,* 51.
2. On March 15, 1837, Emerson delivered his only recorded lecture of the year in Concord. See Charvat, "A Chronological List," 501.
3. J. Hawthorne, *Memoirs,* 94.
4. *Thoreau, Man of Concord,* 29; J. Hawthorne, *Memoirs,* 95.
5. R. Emerson, *Journals and Miscellaneous Notebooks,* 5:163. This account of the events leading to the meeting is based on Emerson's recollection as recorded by Franklin Sanborn, whose version of the story was published in 1882 shortly before Emerson's death, and the family tradition as made public by Emerson's son, Edward Waldo Emerson, six years later. See Sanborn, *Henry D. Thoreau,* 59–60, and Edward Emerson, *Emerson in Concord,* 110. The meeting is placed before Thoreau's graduation from Harvard on August 30, 1837, by Emerson's statement that Thoreau "was not quite out of college, I believe, when I first saw him." See R. Emerson, *Letters,* 5:424. Mrs. Lucy Brown's having returned to Plymouth by the end of the summer corroborates this statement. See Rusk, *The Life of Ralph Waldo Emerson,* 531, notes to p. 266.
6. Strauch, "Emerson As Literary Middleman," 4.
7. Cameron, "Emerson in the Diaries of S. K. Lothrop and E. E. Hale," 63; Whicher, *Freedom and Fate,* 56; Strauch, "Emerson As Literary Middleman," 4; Thoreau, *Walden,* 107.
8. In 1837 Harvard's spring vacation began on Thursday, April 6; see Cameron, "Chronology of Thoreau's Harvard Years," 108. On the following Sunday, April 9, Emerson entered a description of an "extraordinary young man" in his journal who appears to have been Henry Thoreau; see R. Emerson, *Journals and Miscellaneous Notebooks,* 5:293–94.
9. Weiss, "Thoreau," 6–7; R. Emerson, *Journals and Miscellaneous Notebooks,* 5:293.

10. R. Emerson, *Journals and Miscellaneous Notebooks,* 5:293.

11. Cabot, *A Memoir,* 1:362; R. Emerson, *Journals and Miscellaneous Notebooks,* 5:294.

12. For Thoreau's early encounters with *Nature,* see Cameron, "Thoreau Discovers Emerson," 331–32; on Emerson's influence on Thoreau's thinking, see Adams, "Thoreau's Literary Apprenticeship," 617–29; Kwiat, "Thoreau's Philosophical Apprenticeship," 61–69; Paul, *The Shores of America,* 45–46.

13. R. Emerson, "New Poetry," 221.

14. Students with high grades who were asked to take part in exhibitions of oratorical skill were given grants of money to help with the cost of their education; Quincy is quoted in Sanborn, *Henry D. Thoreau,* 54; for details of Thoreau's awards, see Harding, *The Days of Henry Thoreau,* 36.

15. For an eyewitness account of the gathering, see Keyes, "Autobiography," 37.

16. Thoreau, *Journal,* 1:9.

17. On Thoreau's commencement address, see Kwiat, "Thoreau's Philosophical Apprenticeship," 64; Paul, *The Shores of America,* 14.

18. Thoreau's experience as instructor at the Concord school is described in Miss Prudence Ward to Caroline Ward Sewall, September 25, [1837], Transcript, Thoreau Society Collection, Concord Free Public Library, Concord, Massachusetts.

19. Cabot, *A Memoir,* 1:69; R. Emerson, *Letters,* 1:106; R. Emerson, *Journals and Miscellaneous Notebooks,* 5:403. Emerson's journal entry of October 19, 1837, concerning a "young man" who "finds the present hostile & cold" was written three days before his second known meeting with Thoreau and clearly expresses his attitude toward his young neighbor's recent experience.

20. The quotations are from Ossoli, *Memoirs,* 242, and R. Emerson, *Collected Works,* 1:68; on Thoreau's exposure to Goethe, see Cameron, *The Transcendentalists and Minerva,* 1:86.

21. Thoreau, *Journal,* 1:5.

22. R. Emerson, *Early Lectures,* 2:261.

23. Tilton, "Emerson's Lecture Schedule," 387–88.

24. The circumstances leading up to Thoreau's inclusion in the party invited to hear Emerson lecture at home and other information regarding those evenings appears in Tilton, "Emerson's Lecture Schedule," 387–88. The quotation about the Hoar family is in Hosmer, *Remembrances,* 3. Emerson's characterization of Elizabeth Hoar appears in R. Emerson, *Correspondence of Emerson and Carlyle,* 233.

25. Porte, *Emerson and Thoreau,* 84.

26. Myerson, "Frederick Henry Hedge," 400.

27. R. Emerson, *Early Lectures,* 2:240, 296–97.

28. R. Emerson, *Journals and Miscellaneous Notebooks,* 5:453, 7:131, 5:452; Thoreau, *Journal,* 1:16. For identification of Emerson as Thoreau's "friend," see Emerson, *Journals and Miscellaneous Notebooks,* 5:265–66.

29. Thoreau, Henry D. Thoreau to Henry Vose, 6; R. Emerson, *Journals and Miscellaneous Notebooks,* 5:453.

30. Channing, *Thoreau,* 21.

31. Thoreau, *Correspondence,* 654; Channing, *Thoreau,* 18.

32. Thoreau, *Correspondence,* 24.

33. Harding, "Thoreau in Emerson's Account Books," 1; Thoreau, *Correspondence,* 26.

34. Thoreau, *Correspondence,* 25–26.

35. R. Emerson, *Journals and Miscellaneous Notebooks*, 5:453; Haskins, *Ralph Waldo Emerson*, 118–19.

36. Porte, "'God Himself Culminates in the Present Moment,'" 1; Thoreau, *Journal*, 1:49.

37. For a thoughtful discussion of Emerson's resignation, see Richardson, *Emerson*, 125–26; R. Emerson, *Correspondence of Emerson and Carlyle*, 171.

38. Whicher, *Freedom and Fate*, 42.

39. For a discussion of the reasons for the vehement response to Emerson's address, see Edrich, "The Rhetoric of Apostasy," 547–60.

40. R. Emerson, *Letters*, 2:160; the newspaper quotation (Andrews Norton, *Boston Daily Advertiser* [August 27, 1838]) is cited in Miller, *The Transcendentalists*, 195–96.

41. Rusk, *The Life of Ralph Waldo Emerson*, 271; R. Emerson, *Journals and Miscellaneous Notebooks*, 7:60.

42. R. Emerson, *Journals and Miscellaneous Notebooks*, 7:143–44.

43. Ibid., 155.

44. Alcott, *Journals*, 107.

45. Rusk, *The Life of Ralph Waldo Emerson*, 255; R. Emerson, *Journals and Miscellaneous Notebooks*, 12:350.

46. Hoeltje, "Thoreau and the Concord Academy," 108; Thoreau, *Journal*, 1:67; R. Emerson, *Letters*, 2:182.

47. Margaret Fuller Ossoli, "Works," 3, p. 81, MS, Houghton Library, Harvard University.

48. T. Higginson, *Margaret Fuller Ossoli*, 64–65.

49. Margaret Fuller Ossoli, "Works" 1, pp. 419–21, MS, Houghton Library, Harvard University.

50. Blanchard, *Margaret Fuller*, 142; R. Emerson, *Letters*, 2:182.

2. A Troubled Dream

1. Cameron, "Young Henry Thoreau," 115–16.

2. Details of Ellen Sewall's visit are given by her in Ellen Sewall to Edmund Q. Sewall, July 31, 1839, Huntington Library, San Marino, California. Transcript courtesy of the Thoreau Society, Lincoln, Massachusetts; the quotation from Thoreau's journal is cited in Harding, *The Days of Henry Thoreau*, 95.

3. Harding, *The Days of Henry Thoreau*, 96.

4. Ibid.

5. Thoreau, *A Week on the Concord and Merrimack Rivers*, 15.

6. Harding, *The Days of Henry Thoreau*, 97; Ellen Sewall to Prudence Ward, September 29, 1839, Huntington Library, San Marino, California. Transcript courtesy of the Thoreau Society, Lincoln, Massachusetts.

7. Edward Emerson, *Henry Thoreau*, 23, 129.

8. Ibid., 128, 22.

9. R. Emerson, *Journals and Miscellaneous Notebooks*, 7:230–31.

10. Myerson, *New England Transcendentalists*, 32. For a detailed history of the establishment of the *Dial*, see Myerson, *New England Transcendentalists*, 19–99.

11. Myerson, "Frederick Henry Hedge," 400; Cooke, "Emerson and Transcendentalism," 264–80.

12. R. Emerson, *Letters,* 2:225; Myerson, "A Calendar of Transcendental Club Meetings," 204.

13. Harding, *The Days of Henry Thoreau,* 98.

14. Ibid, 98–99.

15. Myerson, "Frederick Henry Hedge," 403–4; Clarke, *Autobiography, Diary, and Correspondence,* 133; R. Emerson, *Letters,* 2:271.

16. R. Emerson, *Letters,* 2:280–81, 287; see Fink, *Prophet in the Marketplace,* 30, for the suggestion that the letter to Fuller was incorrectly dated by Rusk and therefore does not refer to "Persius."

17. R. Emerson, *Letters,* 2:290, 293.

18. Myerson, "A Calendar of Transcendental Club Meetings," 205.

19. Thoreau, *Correspondence,* 39; Paul, *The Shores of America,* 1.

20. R. Emerson, *Letters,* 2:311.

21. Higginson, *Margaret Fuller Ossoli,* 159.

22. Frothingham, *Transcendentalism in New England,* 138–39.

23. Gohdes, *Periodicals of American Transcendentalism,* 71.

24. Cabot, *A Memoir,* 1:266.

25. Harding, *The Days of Henry Thoreau,* 100.

26. Thoreau, *Journal,* 1:95, 52; Sanborn, *The First and Last Journeys of Thoreau,* 1:106.

27. R. Emerson, *A Correspondence between John Sterling and . . . Emerson,* 28; Thoreau, *Journal,* 1:99, 103.

28. Thoreau, *Journal,* 1:99, 100.

29. Ibid, 110.

30. Harding, *The Days of Henry Thoreau,* 101–2.

31. See Miller, *Consciousness in Concord,* 68; Thoreau, *Journal,* 1:233.

32. Thoreau, *Journal,* 277.

33. Ibid., 230.

3. The Beautiful and the Brave

1. R. Emerson, *Letters,* 3:216.

2. R. Emerson, *Collected Works,* 2:121.

3. R. Emerson, *Letters,* 2:143, 205.

4. Ossoli, *Letters,* 1:273; R. Emerson, *Journals and Miscellaneous Notebooks,* 8:318; Blanchard, *Margaret Fuller,* 133.

5. R. Emerson, *Journals and Miscellaneous Notebooks,* 7:48.

6. Baldwin, "The Emerson-Ward Friendship," 316. Tilton, in "The True Romance of Anna Hazard Barker and Samuel Gray Ward," 61, argues, however, that "Emerson did not meet Ward until the summer of 1839 and then twice by accident."

7. R. Emerson, *Journals and Miscellaneous Notebooks,* 7:46; R. Emerson, *Letters . . . to a Friend,* 9.

8. R. Emerson, *Correspondence of Emerson and Carlyle,* 310; Baldwin, "Puritan Aristocrat," 143.

9. R. Emerson, *Letters . . . to a Friend,* 27, 15.

10. R. Emerson, *Journals and Miscellaneous Notebooks,* 7:259, 260.

11. R. Emerson, *Letters,* 2:143.

12. R. Emerson, *Journals and Miscellaneous Notebooks,* 7:273.

13. Capper, *Margaret Fuller,* 1:246.

14. Baldwin, "Puritan Aristocrat," 106. See 106 n. 3 for a discussion of evidence that Margaret Fuller loved Ward. Baldwin's dissertation is a comprehensive source for biographical information about Ward. Ossoli, *Letters,* 2:81.

15. Tilton, "The True Romance of Anna Hazard Barker and Samuel Gray Ward," 63.

16. Ossoli, *Letters,* 2:81, 93.

17. R. Emerson, *Letters,* 2:245; Ralph Waldo Emerson to Caroline Sturgis, January 10, 1840, MS, Houghton Library, Harvard University.

18. R. Emerson, *Letters . . . to a Friend,* 19–20.

19. McNulty, "Emerson's Friends and the Essay on Friendship," 393.

20. Perry Miller suggested that the transcendentalists "found in their idealization of friendship an escape analogous to that which the younger romantics of France found in sexual promiscuity and in plucking the flowers of evil." See Miller, *Consciousness in Concord,* 92. In support of this view see Thoreau's suggestive remarks: "[Friends] are like two boughs crossed in the wood, which play backwards and forwards upon one another in the wind, and only wear into each other, but never the sap of the one flows into the pores of the other, for then the wind would no more draw from them those strains which enchanted the wood. They are not two united, but rather one divided," *Journal,* 1:236–37.

21. R. Emerson, *Collected Works,* 2:121, 115.

22. Ibid., 121.

23. Ibid., 121, 114, 115.

24. Ibid., 114, 117.

25. Ibid., 118, 121, 117.

26. Ibid., 118, 116.

27. Ibid., 118, 126, 116, 119, 123.

28. Ibid., 116, 120.

29. Ibid., 123, 126.

30. Ibid., 125.

31. Strauch, "Hatred's Swift Repulsions," 70.

32. R. Emerson, *Letters,* 7:402.

33. Ibid., 400, 2:328.

34. Ibid., 7:402; R. Emerson, *Correspondence of Emerson and Carlyle,* 277.

35. R. Emerson, *Journals and Miscellaneous Notebooks,* 7:509.

36. Ibid; R. Emerson, *Letters,* 2:325.

37. R. Emerson, *Letters,* 2:325.

38. Ibid., 7:404.

39. Ibid., 2:336; R. Emerson, *Journals and Miscellaneous Notebooks,* 7:400.

40. Strauch, "Hatred's Swift Repulsions," 69–70.

41. Caroline Sturgis to Ralph Waldo Emerson, October 17, 184[?], MS, Houghton Library, Harvard University; R. Emerson, *Letters,* 2:352–53.

4. The Womb of Zeus

1. Cabot, *A Memoir,* 1:231; "The Emerson House in Concord," 186–87; L. Emerson, *Selected Letters,* 92.

2. Thoreau, *Correspondence,* 53; R. Emerson, *Letters,* 2:403–4.

3. Edward Emerson, *Emerson in Concord,* 124; Thoreau, *Correspondence,* 44.

4. R. Emerson, *Journals and Miscellaneous Notebooks,* 8:375.

5. R. Emerson, *Letters,* 2:403, 402.

6. R. Emerson, *Correspondence of Emerson and Carlyle,* 300; R. Emerson, *Letters,* 2:402.

7. R. Emerson, *Journals and Miscellaneous Notebooks,* 7:454–55.

8. Rusk, *Life of Ralph Waldo Emerson,* 215; L. Emerson, *Selected Letters,* 96.

9. R. Emerson, *Journals and Miscellaneous Notebooks,* 8:165; L. Emerson, *Selected Letters,* 93.

10. R. Emerson, *Journals and Miscellaneous Notebooks,* 8:165.

11. Ellen Emerson, *The Life of Lidian Jackson Emerson,* 78.

12. Thoreau, *Correspondence,* 46.

13. Cameron, "Ralph Cudworth and Thoreau's Translations of an Orphic Hymn," 31–36; Canby, *Thoreau,* 185; Albee, *Remembrances of Emerson,* 14.

14. R. Emerson, *A Correspondence between John Sterling and . . . Emerson,* 36.

15. R. Emerson, *Letters,* 2:432.

16. Chevigny, *The Woman and the Myth,* 121.

17. R. Emerson, *Journals and Miscellaneous Notebooks,* 8:97, 7:442.

18. Ibid., 8:96, 118.

19. Ossoli, *Letters,* 3:162.

20. Hoeltje, *Sheltering Tree,* 27; Thoreau, *Journal,* 1:243, 51.

21. See Moss, "'So Many Promising Youths,'" 46–64.

22. R. Emerson, *Journals and Miscellaneous Notebooks,* 8:149.

23. Shelburne, "A Reminiscence of Emerson and Thoreau," 5.

24. R. Emerson, *Journals and Miscellaneous Notebooks,* 8:140.

25. Sattelmeyer, "Thoreau's Projected Work on the English Poets," 242.

26. Thoreau, *Journal,* 1:337.

27. Cameron, "Thoreau and Stearns Wheeler," 73; Sattelmeyer, "Thoreau's Projected Work on the English Poets," 243.

28. Thoreau, *Journal,* 1:337.

29. Ibid., 347.

30. Harding, *The Days of Henry Thoreau,* 134.

31. L. Emerson, *Selected Letters,* 99–100.

32. Harding, *The Days of Henry Thoreau,* 134.

33. Edward Emerson, *Henry Thoreau,* 29.

34. R. Emerson, *Letters,* 3:4.

35. Ellen Emerson, *The Life of Lidian Jackson Emerson,* 88.

36. R. Emerson, *Letters,* 3:8; Rusk, *The Life of Ralph Waldo Emerson,* 287.

37. R. Emerson, *Letters,* 3:13–14.

38. Ibid., 22; Thoreau, *Journal,* 1:365.

39. Thoreau, *Journal,* 1:368, 383.

40. Henry David Thoreau, Journal, vol. 6, entry for March 20, 1842, MS, Pierpont Morgan Library, New York. Sentence added in pencil above inked line.

5. One of the Family

1. R. Emerson, *Complete Works,* 3:30, 40, 27.

2. R. Emerson, *Correspondence of Emerson and Carlyle,* 184; Ellen Emerson, *The Life of Lidian Jackson Emerson,* 83, 79.

3. Rusk, *The Life of Ralph Waldo Emerson*, 294.

4. R. Emerson, *Journals and Miscellaneous Notebooks*, 8:165; Thoreau, *Collected Poems*, 81.

5. R. Emerson, *Letters*, 3:39, 47.

6. R. Emerson, *Correspondence of Emerson and Carlyle*, 321; R. Emerson, *Letters*, 3:33; Allen, *Waldo Emerson*, 358–59.

7. R. Emerson, *Letters*, 3:47, 54.

8. Thoreau, "Natural History of Massachusetts," 5:107; Harding, *Days of Henry Thoreau*, 116.

9. Myerson, "Thoreau and *The Dial*, 5; R. Emerson, *Letters*, 3:75; Richardson, *Henry Thoreau*, 116.

10. Porte, *Emerson and Thoreau*, 137; Thoreau, *Writings*, 5:106.

11. For information about William Ellery Channing, see McGill, *Channing of Concord*.

12. R. Emerson, *Journals and Miscellaneous Notebooks*, 7:469.

13. This account of the events surrounding Margaret Fuller's stay with the Emersons is drawn mainly from Myerson, "Margaret Fuller's 1842 Journal," 320–40.

14. R. Emerson, *Letters*, 1:434; Ellen Emerson, *The Life of Lidian Jackson Emerson*, 51; R. Emerson, *Journals and Miscellaneous Notebooks*, 7:168.

15. Ellen Emerson, *The Life of Lidian Jackson Emerson*, 79–80; R. Emerson, *Letters*, 2:112; R. Emerson, *Journals and Miscellaneous Notebooks*, 7:463.

16. R. Emerson, *Letters*, 3:75; Myerson, "Margaret Fuller's 1842 Journal," 326–27; R. Emerson, *Journals and Miscellaneous Notebooks*, 7:463.

17. Myerson, "Margaret Fuller's 1842 Journal," 331.

18. Ibid., 332.

19. R. Emerson, *Journals and Miscellaneous Notebooks*, 7:468, 469.

20. J. Hawthorne, *Nathaniel Hawthorne and His Wife*, 271.

21. N. Hawthorne, *American Notebooks*, 8:353–54.

22. N. Hawthorne, *Letters, 1813–1843*, 15:656–57.

23. Thoreau, *Correspondence*, 77.

24. R. Emerson, *Letters*, 3:18; R. Emerson, *Correspondence of Emerson and Carlyle*, 332.

25. Whicher, *Freedom and Fate*, 103, 111.

26. R. Emerson, *Journals and Miscellaneous Notebooks*, 8:313.

27. R. Emerson, *Correspondence of Emerson and Carlyle*, 332.

28. Porte, *Emerson and Thoreau*, 129; R. Emerson, *Journals and Miscellaneous Notebooks*, 8:100; Thoreau, *Writings*, 9:38.

29. Porte, *Emerson and Thoreau*, 109.

30. Ibid.

31. R. Emerson, *Collected Works*, 1:26; Thoreau, *Journal*, 1:315, 382.

32. Porte, *Emerson and Thoreau*, 121.

33. R. Emerson, *Letters*, 3:134.

34. Thoreau, *Correspondence*, 78.

35. R. Emerson, *Letters*, 3:139; Thoreau, *Correspondence*, 84.

36. L. Emerson, *Selected Letters*, 118, 123. The word "law," which appears in the manuscript, is printed as "last" in the *Selected Letters*.

37. Thoreau, *Correspondence*, 92.

38. L. Emerson, *Selected Letters*, 115, 128.

39. Ibid., 129; Thoreau, *Correspondence*, 86.

40. Thoreau, *Correspondence,* 85, 87–88, 91.

41. Ibid., 89; R. Emerson, *Letters,* 3:158.

42. R. Emerson, *Letters,* 3:159, 158; N. Hawthorne, *American Notebooks,* 369.

43. Perry, *The Thought and Character of William James,* 1:49.

44. R. Emerson, *Letters,* 3:127, 130, 147, 143.

45. Giles Waldo to Ralph Waldo Emerson, April 27, 1842, MS, Houghton Library, Harvard University. Internal evidence makes it clear this letter was written in 1843, not 1842. Giles Waldo to Ralph Waldo Emerson, April 18, 1843, MS, Houghton Library, Harvard University; N. Hawthorne, *American Notebooks,* 371.

6. Into the World

1. Walter Harding, *The Days of Henry Thoreau,* 147–48; Thoreau, *Correspondence,* 99.

2. Thoreau, *Correspondence,* 100, 114.

3. For the location of Tappan's office, see *New-York Business Directory for 1843–1844* (New York: John Doggert Jr.). Tappan, *The Life of Arthur Tappan,* 345.

4. Giles Waldo to Ralph Waldo Emerson, April 7, May 14, 15, 1843, MS, Houghton Library, Harvard University.

5. Giles Waldo to Ralph Waldo Emerson, May 14, 15, 1843, MS, Houghton Library, Harvard University; William A. Tappan to Ralph Waldo Emerson, December 12, 1844, MS, Houghton Library, Harvard University.

6. Thoreau, *Correspondence,* 111.

7. Perry, *The Thought and Character of William James,* 1:45.

8. R. Emerson, *Letters,* 3:166.

9. Perry, *The Thought and Character of William James,* 1:45.

10. Poe, "Our Magazine Literature," 302. The article is signed "L"; for identification of the author as Edgar Allan Poe, see Tassin, *The Magazine in America,* 148.

11. Thoreau, *Correspondence,* 102, 107, 111.

12. Perry, *The Thought and Character of William James,* 1:45.

13. Thoreau, *Correspondence,* 114.

14. Ibid., 122.

15. Ibid., 118.

16. R. Emerson, *Journals and Miscellaneous Notebooks,* 8:435–36.

17. McGill, *Channing of Concord,* 72.

18. R. Emerson, *A Correspondence between John Sterling and . . . Emerson,* 77; Thoreau, *Correspondence,* 108.

19. R. Emerson, *Journals and Miscellaneous Notebooks,* 8:351.

20. Poe, "Our Amateur Poets," 113–17; R. Emerson, *A Correspondence between John Sterling and . . . Emerson,* 83.

21. R. Emerson, *Journals and Miscellaneous Notebooks,* 8:165.

22. Thoreau, *Correspondence,* 103.

23. Ellen Emerson, *The Life of Lidian Jackson Emerson,* 64. Although the exact date of this incident has not been established, it probably occurred after Lidian Emerson's receipt of Henry Thoreau's affectionate letter of May 21, 1843, but before Mrs. Emerson received his letter of June 20, 1843 in which he revealed his feelings for her with less restraint.

24. Thoreau, *Correspondence,* 119–20.

25. Ibid., 126.

26. Giles Waldo to Ralph Waldo Emerson, April 18, 23, 1843, MS, Houghton Library, Harvard University.

27. R. Emerson, *Letters,* 3:130.

28. Giles Waldo to Ralph Waldo Emerson, January 16, 23, 25, 1843, MS, Houghton Library, Harvard University.

29. Emerson, who had expressed himself in a similar manner on many occasions had written, "I am not a sickly sentimentalist though the name of a friend warms my heart & makes me feel as a girl." R. Emerson, *Journals and Miscellaneous Notebooks,* 5:449. As Perry Miller points out, even in American gift books of the period the friend is often referred to as a lover. See Miller, *Consciousness in Concord,* 92.

30. Giles Waldo to Ralph Waldo Emerson, August 19, 1843, MS, Houghton Library, Harvard University; R. Emerson, *Letters,* 3:185.

31. Giles Waldo to Ralph Waldo Emerson, August 19, 1843, MS, Houghton Library, Harvard University.

32. Thoreau, *Correspondence,* 126.

33. Ibid., 128, 133.

34. Ibid., 133–34, 130.

35. Ibid., 118.

36. Blanding, "Beans, Baked and Half-Baked," 21.

37. Thoreau, *Correspondence,* 134–35, 139.

38. *New-York Daily Tribune,* August 23, 1843, p. 2.

39. Giles Waldo to Ralph Waldo Emerson, August 19, 1843, MS, Houghton Library, Harvard University; R. Emerson, *Journals and Miscellaneous Notebooks,* 9:9.

40. R. Emerson, *Journals and Miscellaneous Notebooks,* 9:65; Thoreau, *Correspondence,* 131.

41. Thoreau, *Correspondence,* 137, 139, 147; Poe, "Our Magazine Literature," 303.

42. Giles Waldo to Ralph Waldo Emerson, March 14, August 19, 1843, MS, Houghton Library, Harvard University.

43. William A. Tappan to Ralph Waldo Emerson, December 12, 1844, MS, Houghton Library, Harvard University.

44. Giles Waldo to Ralph Waldo Emerson, February 25, 12, 1844, September 26, 1843, MS, Houghton Library, Harvard University.

45. R. Emerson, *Journals and Miscellaneous Notebooks,* 9:7.

46. Thoreau, *Correspondence,* 112.

7. A Beautiful Asylum

1. R. Emerson, *Letters,* 2:447; R. Emerson, *Journals and Miscellaneous Notebooks,* 8:257.

2. Sanborn, *Henry D. Thoreau,* 286–87.

3. R. Emerson, *A Correspondence between John Sterling and . . . Emerson,* 68.

4. See Harding, *Days of Henry Thoreau,* 157–59, for a detailed account of Thoreau's pencil-making activities.

5. Johnson, "Historical Introduction," 446.

6. Channing, "Selected Letters," 205.

7. N. Hawthorne, *Letters, 1813–1843,* 16:47.

8. R. Emerson, *Letters,* 3:268.

9. McGill, *Channing of Concord*, 83.

10. R. Emerson, *Letters*, 3:262.

11. Myerson, "Margaret Fuller's 1842 Journal," 332; Thoreau, *Correspondence*, 161.

12. Thoreau, *Walden*, 45.

13. Skinner, *With Feet to the Earth*, 58–59.

14. Thoreau, *Journal*, 1:455.

15. Thoreau, *Walden*, 11; R. Emerson, *Letters*, 8:26.

16. Thoreau, *Walden*, 58–59.

17. R. Emerson, *Journals and Miscellaneous Notebooks*, 9:378–79; R. Emerson, *Letters*, 3:290.

18. Hopkins, *Spires of Form*, 37.

19. William Dean Howells, "May-Day and Other Pieces," *Atlantic Monthly* 20 (September 1867), 376, quoted in Henney, "The Craft of Genius," 8.

20. R. Emerson, *Journals and Miscellaneous Notebooks*, 9:295.

21. R. Emerson, *Letters*, 3:301.

22. Ellen Emerson, *The Life of Lidian Jackson Emerson*, 105.

23. Alcott, *Journals*, 179.

24. Thoreau, *Journal*, 3:154.

25. Alcott, *Journals*, 179.

26. R. Emerson, *Journals and Miscellaneous Notebooks*, 9:47.

27. R. Emerson, *Letters*, 3:338.

28. Johnson, "'A Natural Harvest,'" 306; R. Emerson, *Letters*, 8:121–22.

29. Edward Waldo Emerson, "Notes of Interviews re HDT," MS, Concord Free Public Library, Concord, Massachusetts, transcript courtesy of Thomas Blanding; Edward Emerson, *Henry Thoreau*, 64; R. Emerson, *Complete Works*, 10:612. In the MS "Notes of Interviews re HDT" under the heading "1891—Staples," Edward Waldo Emerson recorded a different version of this exchange: "'I ain't a-going to pay it, Sam,' says he. 'I'll go to jail first.' 'Well, come along,' says I, '& so I locked him up.'"

30. Jones, "Thoreau's Incarceration," 100, 102.

31. Harding, *The Days of Henry Thoreau*, 205.

32. R. Emerson, *Journals and Miscellaneous Notebooks*, 9:447; Alcott, *Journals*, 183–84.

33. R. Emerson, *Journals and Miscellaneous Notebooks*, 9:269, 101–2.

34. For a different view of the motivations of Thoreau and Emerson concerning this incident, see Gougeon, *Virtue's Hero*, 123–25.

35. R. Emerson, *Journals and Miscellaneous Notebooks*, 9:445.

36. Ibid., 367; R. Emerson, *Letters*, 3:366.

37. Alcott, *Journals*, 192.

38. Thoreau, *Correspondence*, 146.

39. R. Emerson, *Correspondence of Emerson and Carlyle*, 413 n. 5; R. Emerson, *Letters . . . to a Friend*, 65.

40. R. Emerson, *Letters*, 3:384.

41. R. Emerson, *Journals and Miscellaneous Notebooks*, 10:106–7, 10:116.

42. Thoreau, *Correspondence*, 188.

43. Thoreau, *Journal*, 2:223, 226.

44. Ibid., 159.

45. R. Emerson, *Journals and Miscellaneous Notebooks*, 9:383.

46. Ibid., 466.

47. R. Emerson, *Letters,* 8:121–22.

48. Shanley, *The Making of Walden,* 18.

8. At Home with Lidian

1. Thoreau, *Walden,* 323.

2. Canby, *Thoreau,* 243.

3. Thoreau, *Correspondence,* 191, 222.

4. R. Emerson, *Letters,* 3:416–17.

5. Thoreau, *Correspondence,* 187.

6. Ibid., 188, 195.

7. L. Emerson, *Selected Letters,* 136.

8. Thoreau, *Correspondence,* 245.

9. Ibid., 189.

10. Sattelmeyer, "'When He Became My Enemy,'" 198; Thoreau, *Correspondence,* 189.

11. Seybold, *Thoreau,* 67 n. 4.

12. Thoreau, *Journal,* 3:17–18.

13. Cummings, "Thoreau's Poems," 11–15.

14. Thoreau, *Correspondence,* 194, 200.

15. Ibid., 191, 195.

16. Thoreau, *Journal,* 2:367–69.

17. Gozzi, "Tropes and Figures," 320.

18. Thoreau, *Correspondence,* 208; Thoreau, "Civil Disobedience," 383. For a discussion of the history of the inclusion of this poem in the essay, see Thoreau, *Reform Papers,* 325.

19. Thoreau, *Writings,* 4:359.

20. See Lebeaux, *Thoreau's Seasons,* 78.

21. See Gougeon, *Virtue's Hero,* 123–25.

22. Thoreau, *Writings,* 4:360, 371–72.

23. Thoreau, *Correspondence,* 205, 207.

24. Channing, "Selected Letters,"173; L. Emerson, *Selected Letters,* 139; Thoreau, *Correspondence,* 207.

25. R. Emerson, *Letters,* 4:28, 3:454, 4:33.

26. Ibid., 4:32.

27. Ibid., 37, 32, 41.

28. Ibid., 2:111, 114.

29. Ellen Emerson, *The Life of Lidian Jackson Emerson,* 77.

30. R. Emerson, *Letters,* 4:54.

31. L. Emerson, *Selected Letters,* 146; R. Emerson, *Letters,* 4:37, 32.

32. Thoreau, *A Week on the Concord and Merrimack Rivers,* 283; R. Emerson, *Letters,* 4:74; L. Emerson, *Selected Letters,* 158.

33. Thoreau, *Correspondence,* 207.

34. Ibid., 208.

35. Thoreau, *A Week on the Concord and Merrimack Rivers,* 259, 261.

36. Ibid., 264, 277.

37. Ibid., 264, 269, 271.

38. Ibid., 272, 268, 267, 273, 270.

39. Ibid., 273, 265–66, 271.

40. Ibid., 276, 268.

41. Ibid., 278, 280.

42. Ibid., 265, 273.

43. Ibid., 283–85.

44. Thoreau, *Correspondence*, 210, 218, 225.

45. Ibid., 228, 226; L. Emerson, *Selected Letters*, 157.

46. Thoreau, *Correspondence*, 226, 227; R. Emerson, *Letters*, 4:81–82.

47. Cameron, "Emerson, Thoreau, and the Poet Henry Sutton," 10, 13, 14.

48. Allen, *Waldo Emerson*, 519.

49. Sanborn, *Recollections of Seventy Years*, 2:469.

50. See Sattelmeyer, "'When He Became My Enemy,'" 198.

51. R. Emerson, *Journals and Miscellaneous Notebooks*, 10:343.

52. Thoreau, *Journal*, 3:3.

9. Separate Paths

1. Thoreau, *Journal*, 3:214.

2. R. Emerson, *Letters*, 4:115; Thoreau, *Correspondence*, 230.

3. William Ellery Channing, Notebook, pp. 57–64, MS, Houghton Library, Harvard University.

4. Cameron, "Emerson, Thoreau, and the Town and Country Club," 2; J. Hawthorne, *Nathaniel Hawthorne and His Wife,* 323.

5. Staebler, *Ralph Waldo Emerson*, 187; Whicher, *Freedom and Fate,* 164; Rusk, *The Life of Ralph Waldo Emerson*, 377.

6. R. Emerson, *Letters*, 4:172, 185; R. Emerson, *Journals and Miscellaneous Notebooks,* 10: 174; R. Emerson, *Letters,* 4:131; Cabot, *A Memoir,* 2:565–66; R. Emerson, *Journals and Miscellaneous Notebooks,* 11:248.

7. Thoreau, *Journal*, 3:287; R. Emerson, *Journals and Miscellaneous Notebooks,* 11:404.

8. R. Emerson, *Journals and Miscellaneous Notebooks,* 11:400.

9. R. Emerson, *Letters*, 4:187; Thoreau, *Writings*, 3:141–42.

10. Thoreau, *Writings*, 3:141–42, 62.

11. Nichols, "Identification of Characters in Lowell's 'A Fable for Critics,'" 191–94.

12. Ibid.

13. Thoreau, *Writings,* 5:472; R. Emerson, *Journals and Miscellaneous Notebooks,* 11:266; Alcott, *Journals,* 253–54.

14. Johnson, "'A Natural Harvest,'" 234.

15. Theodore Parker to Ralph Waldo Emerson, June 1, 1849, MS, Houghton Library, Harvard University; R. Emerson, *Letters*, 4:151.

16. Thoreau, *Writings,* 3:146; Thoreau, *Journal,* 3:18–20.

17. Johnson, "Historical Introduction," 472; Porte, "'God Himself Culminates in the Present Moment,'" 1.

18. R. Emerson, *Letters,* 3:384; Thoreau, *Journal,* 3:26.

19. Thoreau, *Journal,* 3:26.

20. Alcott, *Journals,* 205; Thoreau's comment on Channing is found in Harding, *Days of*

Henry Thoreau, 305; R. Emerson, *Journals and Miscellaneous Notebooks*, 11:193, 13:20, 11:283; Hawthorne's comment on Channing is found in Ellen Emerson, *Letters*, 1:259.

21. Channing, "Selected Letters," 156; see McKee, "'A Fearful Price I Have Had to Pay for Loving Him,'" 251–69.

22. Canby, *Thoreau*, 310–11.

23. McGill, *Channing of Concord*, 97; [Barbara Channing] to Mrs. William W. Russel, June 28, 1848, MS, Channing Family Papers, Massachusetts Historical Society, Boston; B[arbara] H[?] C[hanning] to Aunt, March 5, 1849, MS, Channing Family Papers, Massachusetts Historical Society.

24. Harding, *The Days of Henry Thoreau*, 306.

25. Thoreau, *Journal*, 3:44.

26. Thoreau, *Writings*, 3:216.

27. Ibid., 135, 61.

28. Porte, *Emerson and Thoreau*, 122, 123, 114.

29. Ibid., 138, 177, 11.

30. Albee, *Remembrances of Emerson*, 18–19, 22.

31. R. Emerson, *Journals and Miscellaneous Notebooks*, 11:283.

32. Thoreau, *Journal*, 3:46, 193; Thoreau, *Writings*, 3:61–62.

33. Thoreau, *Writings*, 3:167–68.

10. Undercurrents

1. Thoreau, *Correspondence*, 279, 281.

2. Edward Emerson, *Henry Thoreau*, 1, 3.

3. Conway, *Autobiography, Memories, and Experiences*, 133–34.

4. R. Emerson, *Journals and Miscellaneous Notebooks*, 11:216; Harding, "Two F. B. Sanborn Letters," 230–34.

5. Baldwin, "Puritan Aristocrat," 134.

6. Thomas Wentworth Higginson, Notes on Interview with Mrs. John Thoreau, MS, Channing Family Papers, Massachusetts Historical Society.

7. Ellen C[hanning] to [Thomas] Wentworth [Higginson], [November?] [1853?], MS, Channing Family Papers, Massachusetts Historical Society.

8. T[homas] W[entworth] H[igginson] to [Mary Higginson], [November 15, 1853], MS, Channing Family Papers, Massachusetts Historical Society.

9. T[homas] W[entworth] Higginson to [Dr. Walter Channing?], November 18, [1853?], MS, Channing Family Papers, Massachusetts Historical Society.

10. Barzillai Frost to T[homas] W[entworth] Higginson, November 30, 1853, MS, Channing Family Papers, Massachusetts Historical Society.

11. Thoreau, *Writings*, 3:345–46, 228, 336.

12. Thoreau, *Journal*, 2:174.

13. Thoreau, *Walden*, 193.

14. Thoreau, *Writings*, 9:121.

15. Thoreau, *Journal*, 1:393.

16. Thoreau, *Writings*, 3:312. See Shanley, *The Making of Walden*.

17. Tryon, *Parnassus Corner*, 208.

18. Thoreau, *Correspondence*, 328.

19. Tryon, *Parnassus Corner,* 170.

20. R. Emerson, *Letters,* 8:399.

21. Edward Emerson, *Henry Thoreau,* 109.

22. R. Emerson, *Letters,* 4:459–60, 8:399.

23. Review of *Walden.*

24. Thoreau, *Walden,* 270, 60, 54.

25. Thoreau, *Writings,* 6:199–200.

26. Gozzi, "Tropes and Figures," xiii.

27. R. Emerson, *Journals and Miscellaneous Notebooks,* 13:251–52.

28. Conway, "Thoreau," 463.

29. R. Emerson, *Letters,* 4:388.

30. R. Emerson, *Journals and Miscellaneous Notebooks,* 7:302, 9:49; Thoreau, *Journal,* 1:243.

31. R. Emerson, *Letters,* 4:449.

32. R. Emerson, *Journals and Miscellaneous Notebooks,* 7:27.

33. Thoreau, *Writings,* 2:472; Thoreau, *Journal,* 3:185.

34. Thoreau, *Writings,* 2:150–51.

35. R. Emerson, *Journals and Miscellaneous Notebooks,* 11:277.

36. Thoreau, *Writings,* 3:311–12, 378, 380.

37. R. Emerson, *Letters,* 9:186.

38. Howarth, *The Book of Concord,* 80.

39. Thoreau, *Writings,* 4:223.

40. Thoreau, *Journal,* 3:198.

41. Harding, "The First Year's Sales of Thoreau's *Walden,*" 1.

42. Harding, "A Check List of Thoreau's Lectures," 78–87; Harding, "The Influence of Thoreau's Lecturing upon His Writing," 78; Thoreau, *Writings,* 7:79.

43. Howarth, *The Book of Concord,* 103.

44. Thoreau, *Correspondence,* 376; R. Emerson, *Letters,* 4:512.

11. Between Narrow Walls

1. Thoreau, *Writings,* 4:313, 9:249.

2. R. Emerson, *Letters,* 4:454; Ellen Emerson, *Letters,* 1:78.

3. R. Emerson, *Letters,* 5:30, 34.

4. Wagner, "No Tumult of Response," 130, 133.

5. Henney, "The Craft of Genius," 74; Rusk, *The Life of Ralph Waldo Emerson,* 392.

6. Sanborn, *Life of Henry David Thoreau,* 239; R. Emerson, *Journals and Miscellaneous Notebooks,* 11:400, 277.

7. R. Emerson, "Thoreau," 10:478.

8. Sanborn, *Life of Henry David Thoreau,* 239; Edward Emerson, *Henry Thoreau,* 111; R. Emerson, *Complete Works,* 10:454.

9. Thoreau, *Writings,* 10:228, 3:146.

10. Ibid., 3:306, 378.

11. Harding, *The Days of Henry Thoreau,* 296, 110.

12. Thoreau, *Writings,* 15:121; Thoreau, *A Week on the Concord and Merrimack Rivers,* 145–46.

13. Thoreau, *Writings,* 10:227.

14. Thoreau, *Journal,* 3:305–6.

15. Christie, *Thoreau As World Traveller,* 126.

16. Thoreau, *Journal,* 3:319; Edward Waldo Emerson, "Notes of Interviews re HDT," MS, Concord Free Public Library, Concord, Massachusetts, transcript courtesy of Thomas Blanding.

17. Thoreau, *Journal,* 3:124, 212; Thoreau, *Correspondence,* 288.

18. Thoreau, *Writings,* 2:77.

19. Thoreau, *Journal,* 3:311, 332.

20. *Thoreau, Man of Concord,* 90.

21. Thoreau, *Journal,* 3:209.

22. Thoreau, *Writings,* 5:369, 6:75, 3:211.

23. Ibid., 1:142.

24. Ibid., 9:211; Thoreau, *Correspondence,* 444.

25. R. Emerson, *Journals and Miscellaneous Notebooks,* 7:140, 8:236–37.

26. Sanborn, *The Personality of Emerson,* 1:95.

27. R. Emerson, *Journals and Miscellaneous Notebooks,* 14:76; Thoreau, *Writings,* 8:199.

28. R. Emerson, *Letters,* 5:56.

29. Thoreau, *Journal,* 8:199.

30. Thoreau, *Writings,* 9:276, 250.

31. R. Emerson, *Letters,* 5:63; Thoreau, *Writings,* 9:276.

32. Thoreau, *Writings,* 9:276.

33. Thoreau, *A Week on the Concord and Merrimack Rivers,* 283.

12. The Final Years

1. R. Emerson, *Journals and Miscellaneous Notebooks,* 14:162.

2. Ibid., 195, 204.

3. Ibid., 45, 166.

4. Thoreau, *Writings,* 11:281–82.

5. Ibid., 282.

6. Edward Waldo Emerson, "Notes of Interviews re HDT," MS, Concord Free Public Library, Concord, Massachusetts, transcript courtesy of Thomas Blanding.

7. Edward Emerson, *Henry Thoreau,* 35–36.

8. Ibid., 36–37.

9. Thoreau, *Correspondence,* 557; Sanborn, "A Concord Notebook," 271–72.

10. Ellen Emerson, *Letters,* 1:179.

11. R. Emerson, *Journals and Miscellaneous Notebooks,* 14:248; Alcott, *Journals,* 331.

12. Thoreau, *Correspondence,* 584; Walls, *Seeing New Worlds,* 54.

13. Thoreau, *Faith in a Seed,* 4–5.

14. Ellen Emerson, *Letters,* 1:195.

15. Sanborn, *The Personality of Emerson,* 1:87–88.

16. Sanborn, *Recollections of Seventy Years,* 1:187.

17. Gougeon, *Virtue's Hero,* 229.

18. Thoreau, *Journal,* 12:437.

19. Meyer, "Thoreau's Rescue of John Brown from History," 302–4.

20. Ostrander, "Emerson, Thoreau, and John Brown," 724.

21. Sanborn, *Recollections of Seventy Years,* 1:200.

22. Gougeon, *Virtue's Hero,* 242.

23. Sanborn, *Recollections of Seventy Years,* 1:202.

24. Howells, *Literary Friends and Acquaintances,* 55–64.

25. Thoreau, *Writings,* 12:443; Gozzi, "Tropes and Figures," 445; Edel, *Henry D. Thoreau,* 12, 14.

26. Thoreau, *Correspondence,* 609.

27. Channing, "Selected Letters," 289; Thoreau, *Correspondence,* 615.

28. Thoreau, *Correspondence,* 616.

29. Ibid., 622; Brown, "Simon Brown's Journal," 3.

30. Edward Emerson, *Henry Thoreau,* 147.

31. Thoreau, *Correspondence,* 625; "Reminiscences of Thoreau," 820.

32. Thoreau, *Writings,* 6:396; Clarkson, "Mentions of Emerson and Thoreau in the Letters of Franklin Benjamin Sanborn," 404.

33. Curtis, "Editor's Easy Chair," 271; Alcott, *Letters,* 326.

34. Edward Emerson, *Henry Thoreau,* 117; R. Emerson, *Journals and Miscellaneous Notebooks,* 15:165.

35. Edward Emerson, *Henry Thoreau,* 148.

36. Ricketson, *Daniel Ricketson and His Friends,* 214.

37. Blanding, "A Last Wind from Thoreau," 16.

38. R. Emerson, *Complete Works,* 10:452–54, 458, 477–78.

39. Ibid., 479, 452, 455–56, 465.

40. Ibid., 478, 464, 457, 454, 478.

41. Ibid., 474, 484–85.

42. Ibid., 472.

43. Ibid., 485.

Selected Bibliography

The most important primary sources are manuscripts and other materials in the possession of the Houghton Library at Harvard University, the Massachusetts Historical Society, and the Concord Free Public Library. I also consulted manuscripts at the Pierpont Morgan Library, the Berg Collection of the New York Public Library, and the Abernathy Library at Middlebury College.

Adams, Raymond. "Thoreau at Harvard." *New England Quarterly* 13 (1940): 24–33.

——. "Thoreau's Burial." *American Literature* 12 (1940): 105–7.

——. "Thoreau's Literary Apprenticeship." *Studies in Philology* 29 (1932): 617–29.

Albee, John. *Remembrances of Emerson.* New York: Robert G. Cooke, 1901.

Alcott, A. Bronson. *Concord Days.* Boston: Roberts Brothers, 1872.

——. *The Journals of Bronson Alcott.* Ed. Odell Shepard. Boston: Little, Brown, 1938.

——. *The Letters of A. Bronson Alcott.* Ed. Richard L. Herrnstadt. Ames: Iowa State University Press, 1969.

Allen, Gay Wilson. *Waldo Emerson: A Biography.* New York: Viking Press, 1981.

Austin, James C. *Fields of the Atlantic Monthly: Letters to an Editor, 1861–1870.* San Marino, California: Huntington Library, 1953.

Baldwin, David. "The Emerson-Ward Friendship: Ideals and Realities." In *Studies in the American Renaissance,* ed. Joel Myerson, 199–324. Charlottesville: University Press of Virginia.

——. "Puritan Aristocrat in the Age of Emerson: A Study of Samuel Gray Ward." Ph.D. diss., University of Pennsylvania, 1961. Ann Arbor, Mich.: University Microfilms.

Bellew, Frank. "Recollections of Ralph Waldo Emerson." *Lippincott's Magazine* 34, no. 1 (July 1884): 45–50.

Bishop, Jonathan. *Emerson on the Soul.* Cambridge: Harvard University Press, 1964.

Blanchard, Paula. *Margaret Fuller: From Transcendentalism to Revolution.* New York: Dell, 1979.

Blanding, Thomas. "Beans, Baked and Half-Baked (13)." *Concord Saunterer* 15, no. 1 (spring 1980).

——. "A Last Wind from Thoreau." *Concord Saunterer* 2, no. 4 (winter 1976): 16.

———. "Passages from John Thoreau, Jr.'s Journal." *Thoreau Society Bulletin,* no. 136 (summer 1976): 4–6.

Bode, Carl. "The Hidden Thoreau." In *The Half-World of American Culture,* 3–15. Carbondale: Southern Illinois University Press, 1965.

Bridgeman, Richard. *Dark Thoreau.* Lincoln: University of Nebraska Press, 1982.

Bridges, William E. "Transcendentalism and Psychotherapy: Another Look at Emerson." *American Literature* 41 (May 1969): 157–77.

Broderick, John. "Thoreau, Alcott, and the Poll Tax." *Studies in Philology* 53 (1956): 612–26.

Brooks, Van Wyck. *Life of Emerson.* New York: Literary Guild, 1932.

Brown, Mary Hosmer. *Memories of Concord.* Boston: Four Seas, 1926.

Brown, Simon. "Simon Brown's Journal." *Thoreau Society Bulletin,* no. 76 (summer 1961): 3.

Cabot, James Elliot. *A Memoir of Ralph Waldo Emerson.* 2 vols. Boston: Houghton, Mifflin, 1887.

Cameron, Kenneth. W. "Chronology of Thoreau's Harvard Years." *Emerson Society Quarterly,* no. 15 (1959): 13–108.

———. "Emerson in the Diaries of S. K. Lothrop and E. E. Hale," *Emerson Society Quarterly,* no. 11 (1958): 63.

———. *Emerson the Essayist.* Raleigh, N.C.: Thistle Press, 1945.

———. "Emerson, Thoreau, and the Poet Henry Sutton." *Emerson Society Quarterly,* no. 1 (1955): 10–16.

———. "Emerson, Thoreau, and the Town and Country Club." *Emerson Society Quarterly,* no. 8 (1957): 2–17.

———. "Ralph Cudworth and Thoreau's Translations of an Orphic Hymn." *Emerson Society Quarterly,* no. 8 (1957): 31–36.

———. "The Solitary Thoreau of the Alumni Notes." *Emerson Society Quarterly,* no.7 (1957): 2–17.

———. "Thoreau and Emerson in Channing's Letters to the Watsons." *Emerson Society Quarterly,* no. 14 (1959): 77–85.

———. "Thoreau and Stearns Wheeler: Four Letters and a Reading Record." *Emerson Society Quarterly,* no. 8 (1957): 31–36.

———. "Thoreau Discovers Emerson: A College Reading Record." *Bulletin of the New York Public Library* 57 (1953): 319–34.

———. "Thoreau in the Memoirs of the Concord Social Circle." *Emerson Society Quarterly,* no. 19 (1960): 45–46.

———. "Thoreau's Three Months Out of Harvard and His First Publication." *Emerson Society Quarterly,* no. 5 (1956): 2–12.

———. *The Transcendentalists and Minerva.* 3 vols. Hartford: Transcendental Books, 1958.

———. "Young Henry Thoreau in the Annals of the Concord Academy (1829–1833)." *Emerson Society Quarterly,* no. 9 (1957): 1–19.

Canby, Henry Seidel. *Thoreau.* Boston: Houghton Mifflin, 1939.

Capper, Charles. *Margaret Fuller: An American Romantic Life.* Vol. 1. New York: Oxford University Press, 1992.

Cestre, Charles. "Thoreau et Emerson." *Revue Anglo-Americaine* 7 (1930): 215–30.

Channing, William Ellery. "The Selected Letters of William Ellery Channing the Younger (Parts One to Four)," ed. Francis B. Dedmond. In *Studies in the American Renaissance,* ed. Joel Myerson. Charlottesville: University Press of Virginia, 1989–92.

————. *Thoreau: The Poet-Naturalist.* Boston: Roberts Brothers, 1873.

Charvat, William. "A Chronological List of Emerson's American Lecture Engagements." *Bulletin of the New York Public Library,* no. 64 (1960); no. 65 (1961).

Chevigny, Bell Gale. *The Woman and the Myth: Margaret Fuller's Life and Writings.* New York: Feminist Press, 1976.

Christie, John Aldrich. *Thoreau As World Traveller.* New York: Columbia University Press, 1965.

Clarke, James Freeman. *Autobiography, Diary, and Correspondence.* Ed. Edward Everett Hale. Boston: Houghton, Mifflin, 1890.

Clarkson, John W., Jr. "Mentions of Emerson and Thoreau in the Letters of Franklin Benjamin Sanborn." In *Studies in the American Renaissance,* ed. Joel Myerson, 387–420. Boston: Twayne, 1978.

Conway, Moncure Daniel. *Autobiography, Memories, and Experiences.* London: Cassell, 1904.

————. *Emerson at Home and Abroad.* Boston, 1882; London: Treubner, 1883.

————. "Thoreau." *Fraser's Magazine* 73 (April 1866): 447–65.

Cook, Reginald L. *Passage to Walden.* Boston: Houghton Mifflin, 1949.

Cooke, George Willis. "'The Dial': An Historical and Bibliographical Introduction with a List of Contributors." *Journal of Speculative Philosophy* 19, no. 3 (July 1885).

————. "Emerson and Transcendentalism." *New England Magazine* 28 (May 1903): 264–80.

————. *An Historical and Biographical Introduction to the Dial.* Cleveland: Rowfant Club, 1902.

————. "The Two Thoreaus." *Independent* 48 (December 10, 1896): 1671–72.

Cosman, Max. "Apropos of John Thoreau." *American Literature* 12 (1940): 241–43.

————. "Thoreau and Staten Island." *Staten Island Historian* 6, no. 1 (January–March 1943).

Croeby, R. C. "Thoreau at Work: The Writing of 'Ktaadn'." *Bulletin of the New York Public Library* 65 (1961): 21–30.

Cummings, Lawrence A. "Thoreau's Poems in Bixby Washington University Manuscripts." *Emerson Society Quarterly,* no. 26 (1962): 9–28.

Curtis, George William. *Early Letters of George William Curtis to John S. Dwight: Brook Farm and Concord.* Ed. George Willis Cooke. New York: Harper and Brothers, 1898.

————. "Editor's Easy Chair." *Harper's New Monthly Magazine* 25 (July 1862): 270–71; 38 (February 1869): 415.

Davis, Rebecca Harding. *Bits of Gossip.* Boston: Houghton Mifflin, 1904.

————. "A Little Gossip." *Scribner's Magazine* 28 (November 1900): 565–66.

Downs, Annie Sawyer. "Mr. Hawthorne, Mr. Thoreau, Miss Alcott, Mr. Emerson, and Me." Ed. Walter Harding. *American Heritage* 30, no. 1 (December 1978): 94–105.

Edel, Leon J. *Henry D. Thoreau.* Minneapolis: University of Minnesota Press, 1970.

Edrich, Mary W. "The Rhetoric of Apostasy: The Divinity School Address." *Texas Studies in Literature and Language* 8 (winter 1967): 547–60.

Eidson, John Olin. *Charles Stearns Wheeler: Friend of Emerson.* Athens: University of Georgia, 1991.

Emerson, Edward Waldo. *Early Years of the Saturday Club, 1855–1870.* Boston: Houghton Mifflin, 1918.

————. *Emerson in Concord.* Boston: Houghton, Mifflin, 1889.

————. *Henry Thoreau As Remembered by a Young Friend.* Concord, Mass.: Thoreau Foundation, Thoreau Lyceum, 1968.

Emerson, Ellen Tucker. *The Letters of Ellen Tucker Emerson*. Ed. Edith E. W. Gregg. 2 vols. Kent, Ohio: Kent State University Press, 1982.

————. *The Life of Lidian Jackson Emerson*. Ed. Delores Bird Carpenter. Boston: Twayne, 1980.

"The Emerson House in Concord." *American Transcendental Quarterly* 14 (spring 1972): 186–87.

Emerson, Lidian Jackson. *The Selected Letters of Lidian Jackson Emerson*. Ed. Delores Bird Carpenter. Columbia: University of Missouri Press, 1987.

Emerson, Ralph Waldo. *The Collected Works of Ralph Waldo Emerson*. Ed. Joseph Slater. 5 vols. to date. Cambridge: Harvard University Press, 1971–.

————. *The Complete Works of Ralph Waldo Emerson*. Ed. Edward Waldo Emerson. Centenary Edition. 12 vols. Boston: Houghton, Mifflin, 1903–1904.

————. *A Correspondence between John Sterling and Ralph Waldo Emerson*. Cambridge: Houghton, Mifflin, 1897.

————. *The Correspondence of Emerson and Carlyle*. Ed. Joseph Slater. New York: Columbia University Press, 1964.

————. *The Early Lectures of Ralph Waldo Emerson*. Ed. Stephen E. Whicher, Robert E. Spiller, Wallace E. Williams. 3 vols. Cambridge: Harvard University Press, Belknap Press, 1959–72.

————. *Emerson-Clough Letters*. Ed. Howard F. Lowry and Ralph L. Rusk. Hamden, Conn.: Archon Books, 1968.

————. *The Journals and Miscellaneous Notebooks of Ralph Waldo Emerson*. Ed. William H. Gilman et al. 16 vols. Cambridge: Harvard University Press, 1960–82.

————. *The Letters of Ralph Waldo Emerson*. Ed. Ralph L. Rusk (vols. 1–6); ed. Eleanor M. Tilton (vols. 7–10). New York: Columbia University Press, 1939–95.

————. *Letters of Ralph Waldo Emerson to a Friend (1838–1853)*. Ed. Charles Eliot Norton. Boston: Houghton, Mifflin, 1899.

————. "New Poetry." *Dial* 1, no. 2 (October 1840): 220–32.

————. *Records of a Lifelong Friendship*. Ed. Horace Howard Furness. Boston: Houghton Mifflin, 1910.

Fields, James T. "Our Poet-Naturalist." *Baldwin's Monthly* 14, no. 4 (April 1877): 1.

Fink, Steven. *Prophet in the Marketplace: Thoreau's Development As a Professional Writer*. Princeton: Princeton University Press, 1992.

Foster, Charles Howell. *Emerson's Theory of Poetry*. Iowa City, Iowa: Midland House, 1939.

Frothingham, Octavius Brooks. *Transcendentalism in New England*. New York: G. P. Putnam's Sons, 1880.

Fuller, Richard F. "The Younger Generation in 1840: From the Diary of a New England Boy." *Atlantic Monthly* 136 (August 1925): 216–24.

Gabriel, R. H. "Emerson and Thoreau." In *The Transcendentalist Revolt against Materialism*, ed. George F. Whicher, 18–28. Boston: Heath, 1949. Reprint, 1968.

Gittleman, Edwin. *Jones Very: The Effective Years, 1833–1840*. New York: Columbia University Press, 1967.

Glick, Wendell. "Thoreau Rejects an Emerson Text." *Studies in Bibliography* 25 (1972): 213–16.

Gohdes, Clarence. "Some Remarks on Emerson's Divinity School Address." *American Literature* 1 (March 1929): 27–31.

Gohdes, L. F. *The Periodicals of American Transcendentalism*. Durham, N.C.: Duke University Press, 1931.

Gougeon, Len. *Virtue's Hero: Emerson, Antislavery, and Reform.* Athens: University of Georgia Press, 1990.

Gozzi, Raymond D. "Tropes and Figures: A Psychological Study of David Thoreau." PhD. diss., New York University, 1957. Ann Arbor, Mich.: University Microfilms.

Graham, Phillip. "Some Lowell Letters." *Texas Studies in Literature and Language* 3 (1962): 557–82.

Greenberger, Evelyn Barish. "The Phoenix on the Wall: Consciousness in Emerson's Early and Late Journals." *American Transcendental Quarterly* 21 (winter 1974): 45–56.

Harding, Walter. "A Check List of Thoreau's Lectures." *Bulletin of the New York Public Library* 52, no. 2 (February 1948): 78–87.

———. *The Days of Henry Thoreau.* New York: Alfred A. Knopf, 1970.

———. "The First Year's Sales of Thoreau's *Walden.*" *Thoreau Society Bulletin,* no. 117 (fall 1971): 1.

———. "The Influence of Thoreau's Lecturing upon his Writing." *Bulletin of the New York Public Library* 60 (February 1956): 74–80.

———. *A Thoreau Handbook.* New York: New York University Press, 1959.

———. "Thoreau in Emerson's Account Books." *Thoreau Society Bulletin,* no. 159 (spring 1982): 1–3.

———. "Thoreau in Jail." *American Heritage* 26, no. 5 (August 1975): 36–37.

———. "Two F. B. Sanborn Letters." *American Literature* 25, no. 2 (May 1953): 230–34.

Harding, Walter, and Michael Meyer. *The New Thoreau Handbook.* New York: New York University Press, 1980.

Harris, William T. "The Dialectic Unity of Emerson's Prose." *Journal of Speculative Philosophy* 18 (April 1884): 195–202.

Haskins, David Greene. *Ralph Waldo Emerson: His Maternal Ancestors with Some Reminiscences of Him.* Boston: Cupples, Upham, 1887.

Hawthorne, Julian. *The Memoirs of Julian Hawthorne.* Ed. Edith Garrigues Hawthorne. New York: Macmillan, 1938.

———. *Nathaniel Hawthorne and His Wife.* 1884. Hamden, Conn.: Archon Books, 1968.

Hawthorne, Nathaniel. *The American Notebooks.* Ed. Claude M. Simpson. Centenary Edition. Vol. 8. Columbus: Ohio State University Press, 1972.

———. *The Letters, 1813–1843.* Ed. Thomas Woodson, L. Neal Smith, and Norman Holmes Pearson. Centenary Edition. Vol 16. Columbus: Ohio State University Press, 1984.

Henney, Thomas G. "The Craft of Genius: A Study of Emerson's Poetic Development, 1823–1846." Ph.D. diss., Princeton University, June 1946. Ann Arbor, Mich.: University Microfilms.

Higginson, Mary Thacher. *Thomas Wentworth Higginson: The Story of His Life.* Cambridge: Houghton Mifflin, 1914.

Higginson, Storrow. "Henry D. Thoreau." *Harvard Magazine* 8 (May 1862): 313–18.

Higginson, Thomas Wentworth. *Cheerful Yesterdays.* Cambridge: Houghton, Mifflin, 1898.

———. *Letters and Journals of Thomas Wentworth Higginson.* Cambridge: Houghton Mifflin, 1921.

———. *Margaret Fuller Ossoli.* Boston: Houghton, Mifflin, 1884.

Hoar, George F. *Autobiography of Seventy Years.* New York: Charles Scribner's Sons, 1903.

———. *A Boy Sixty Years Ago.* Boston: Perry Mason, [1898?].

Hoeltje, Hubert H. *Sheltering Tree: A Story of the Friendship of Ralph Waldo Emerson and Amos*

Bronson Alcott. Durham, N.C.: Duke University Press, 1943. Reprint, Port Washington, N.Y.: Kennikat Press, 1965.

———. "Thoreau and the Concord Academy." *New England Quarterly* 21 (March 1948): 103–9.

———. "Thoreau as Lecturer." *New England Quarterly* 19 (1946): 485–94.

Hopkins, Vivian C. *Spires of Form: A Study of Emerson's Aesthetic Theory.* New York: Russell and Russell, 1965.

Hosmer, Horace. *Remembrances of Concord and the Thoreaus: Letters of Horace Hosmer to Dr. S. A. Jones.* Ed. George Hendrick. Urbana: University of Illinois Press, 1977.

Hosmer, James Kendell. *The Last Leaf.* New York: G. P. Putnam's Sons, 1912.

Hosmer, Joseph. "Some Recollections of Henry D. Thoreau." *Thoreau Society of America Booklet,* no. 10 (1955).

———. "Thoreau and the Concord Academy." *New England Quarterly* 21 (March 1949): 103–9.

Hovde, Carl. "Nature into Art: Thoreau's Use of His Journals in *A Week.*" *American Literature* 30 (1958): 165–84.

Howarth, William. *The Book of Concord: Thoreau's Life As a Writer.* New York: Viking Press, 1982.

———. *The Literary Manuscripts of Henry David Thoreau.* Columbus: Ohio State University Press, 1974.

Howells, William Dean. *Literary Friends and Acquaintances.* New York: Harper and Brothers, 1902.

———. "My First Visit to New England, Fourth Part." *Harper's Monthly* 89 (August 1894): 441–51.

Hudspeth, Robert N. "A Perennial Springtime: Channing's Friendship with Emerson and Thoreau." *Emerson Society Quarterly,* no. 54 (1969): 30–36.

Jacques, John F. "'Ktaadn'—A Record of Thoreau's Youthful Crisis." *Thoreau Journal Quarterly* 1, no. 4 (October 15, 1969): 1–6.

Johnson, Linck C. "Historical Introduction." In Thoreau's *Week on the Concord and Merrimack Rivers,* ed. Carl F. Hovde, 433–500. Princeton: Princeton University Press, 1980.

———. "'A Natural Harvest': The Writing of 'A Week on the Concord and Merrimack Rivers,' with the Text of the First Draft." Ph.D. diss., Princeton University, 1975. Ann Arbor, Mich.: University Microfilms.

———. *Thoreau's Complex Weave.* Charlottesville: University Press of Virginia, 1986.

Jones, Samuel Arthur. "Thoreau and His Biographers." *Lippincott's Monthly Magazine* 48 (August 1891): 224–28.

———. "Thoreau's Incarceration." *Inlander* 9, no. 3 (December 1898): 96–103.

Keyes, John Shepard. "Autobiography." *Emerson Society Quarterly,* no. 11 (1958): 36–38.

Koopman, Louise Osgood. "The Thoreau Romance." *Massachusetts Review* 4 (autumn 1962): 61–67.

Koster, Donald N. *Transcendentalism in America.* Boston: Twayne, 1975.

Krutch, Joseph Wood. *Henry David Thoreau.* New York: William Morrow, 1948.

Kwiat, Joseph J. "Thoreau's Philosophical Apprenticeship." *New England Quarterly* 18 (March 1945): 51–69.

Lane, Lauriat. "Thoreau at Work: Four Versions of 'A Walk to Wachusett.'" *Bulletin of the New York Public Library* 69, no. 1 (January 1965): 3–16.

Lathorp, Rose Hawthorne. *Memories of Hawthorne*. Cambridge: Houghton, Mifflin, 1897.

Lebeaux, Richard. "'Sugar Maple Man': Middle-Aged Thoreau's Generativity Crisis." In *Studies in the American Renaissance*, ed. Joel Myerson, 359–77. Boston: Twayne, 1981.

———. *Thoreau's Seasons*. Amherst: University of Massachusetts Press, 1984.

———. *Young Man Thoreau*. Amherst: University of Massachusetts Press, 1977.

Lowell, James Russell. *Letters of James Russell Lowell*. Ed. C. E. Norton. New York: Harper and Brothers, 1894.

———. "Review of *A Week*." *Massachusetts Quarterly Review* 3 (1850): 40–51.

Marble, Annie Russell. *Thoreau: His Home, Friends, and Books*. 1902. New York: AMS Press, 1969.

Mathews, James W. "George Partridge Bradford: Friend of Transcendentalists." In *Studies in the American Renaissance*, ed. Joel Myerson, 133–56. Boston: Twayne, 1981.

Matthiessen, F. O. *American Renaissance: Art and Experience in the Age of Emerson and Whitman*. New York: Oxford University Press, 1941.

Maxfield-Miller, Elizabeth. "Emerson and Elizabeth of Concord." *Harvard Library Bulletin* 19 (July 1971): 290–306.

McAleer, John. *Ralph Waldo Emerson: Days of Encounter*. Boston: Little, Brown, 1984.

McGill, Frederick T. *Channing of Concord: A Life of William Ellery Channing II*. New Brunswick, N.J.: Rutgers University Press, 1967.

McKee, Kathryn B. "'A Fearful Price I Have Had to Pay for Loving Him': Ellery Channing's Troubled Relationship with Ralph Waldo Emerson." In *Studies in the American Renaissance*, ed. Joel Myerson, 251–69. Charlottesville: University Press of Virginia, 1993.

McNulty, John B. "Emerson's Friends and the Essay on Friendship." *New England Quarterly* 19 (September 1946): 390–94.

Mellow, James R. *Nathaniel Hawthorne in His Times*. Boston: Houghton Mifflin, 1980.

Meltzer, Milton, and Walter Harding. *A Thoreau Profile*. New York: Thomas Y. Crowell, 1962.

Meyer, Michael. "Thoreau's Rescue of John Brown from History." In *Studies in the American Renaissance*, ed. Joel Myerson, 301–16. Boston: Twayne, 1980.

Miller, Perry. *Consciousness in Concord*. Boston: Houghton Mifflin, 1958.

———. *The Transcendentalists*. Cambridge: Harvard University Press, 1950.

Milne, Gordon. *George William Curtis and the Genteel Tradition*. Bloomington: Indiana University Press, 1956.

Moore, John Brooks. "Thoreau Rejects Emerson." *American Literature* 4 (1932): 241–56.

Moss, William M. "'So Many Promising Youths': Emerson's Disappointing Discoveries of New England Poet-Seers." *New England Quarterly* 49 (March 1976): 46–64.

Myerson, Joel A. "A Calendar of Transcendental Club Meetings." *American Literature* 44 (May 1972): 197–207.

———. "Caroline Dall's Reminiscences of Margaret Fuller." *Harvard Library Bulletin* 22 (October 1974): 414–28.

———. "Eight Lowell Letters from Concord in 1838." *Illinois Quarterly* 38 (winter 1975): 20–42.

———. "Frederick Henry Hedge and the Failure of Transcendentalism." *Harvard Library Bulletin* 23, no. 4 (October 1975): 396–410.

———. "Lowell on Emerson: A New Letter from Concord in 1838." *New England Quarterly* 44 (December 1971): 649–52.

———. "Margaret Fuller's 1842 Journal: At Concord with the Emersons." *Harvard Library Bulletin* 21, no. 3 (July 1973): 320–40.

———. "More Apropos John Thoreau." *American Literature* 45 (March 1973): 104–6.

———. *The New England Transcendentalists and The Dial: A History of the Magazine and Its Contributors*. Rutherford: Farleigh Dickinson University Press, 1980.

———. "Thoreau and *The Dial:* A Survey of the Contemporary Press." *Thoreau Journal Quarterly* 5, no. 1 (January 1973): 4–7.

———. "A Union List of *The Dial* and Some Information about Its Sales." *Papers of the Bibliographical Society of America* 67 (1973): 322–28.

Newfeldt, Leonard. "The Severity of the Ideal: Emerson's 'Thoreau.'" *Emerson Society Quarterly*, no. 59 (1970): 77–84.

Newfield, Christopher J. "Loving Bondage: Emerson's Ideal Relationships." *ATQ*, n. s., 5, no. 3 (September 1991): 183–93.

Nichols, E. J. "Identification of Characters in Lowell's 'A Fable for Critics.'" *American Literature* 4 (1932): 191–94.

Ossoli, Margaret Fuller. *The Letters of Margaret Fuller*. Ed. Robert N. Hudspeth. 6 vols. Ithaca: Cornell University Press, 1983–94.

———. *Memoirs of Margaret Fuller Ossoli*. Boston: Phillips, Sampson, 1852.

Ostrander, Gilman. "Emerson, Thoreau, and John Brown." *Mississippi Valley Historical Review* 39, no. 4 (March 1953): 713–26.

Paul, Sherman. *The Shores of America: Thoreau's Inward Exploration*. Urbana: University of Illinois Press, 1958.

Perry, Ralph Barton. *The Thought and Character of William James*. 2 vols. Boston: Little, Brown, 1935.

Poe, Edgar Allan. "Our Amateur Poets. No. 3—William Ellery Channing." *Graham's Magazine* (August 1843): 113–17.

———. "Our Magazine Literature." *New World*, Saturday, March 11, 1843, 302–3.

Pommer, Henry F. *Emerson's First Marriage*. Carbondale: Southern Illinois Press, 1967.

Porte, Joel. *Emerson and Thoreau: Transcendentalists in Conflict*. Middletown, Conn.: Wesleyan University Press, 1965.

———. "Emerson, Thoreau, and the Double Consciousness." *New England Quarterly* 41 (March 1968): 40–50.

———. "'God Himself Culminates in the Present Moment': Thoughts on Thoreau's Faith." *Thoreau Society Bulletin*, no. 144 (summer 1978): 1–4.

———. *Representative Man: Ralph Waldo Emerson*. New York: Oxford University Press, 1979.

Raysor, T. M. "The Love Story of Thoreau." *Studies in Philology* 23 (1926): 457–63.

"Reminiscences of Thoreau." *Outlook* 63 (December 2, 1899): 815–21.

Review of *Walden. The National Era*, September 28, 1854. Reprinted in *Thoreau Society of America Booklet*, no. 14.

Richardson, Robert D., Jr. *Emerson: The Mind on Fire*. Berkeley: University of California Press, 1995.

———. *Henry Thoreau: A Life of the Mind*. Berkeley: University of California Press, 1986.

Ricketson, Daniel. *Daniel Ricketson and His Friends*. Ed. Anna Ricketson and Walton Ricketson. Cambridge: Houghton, Mifflin, 1902.

Robinson, William S. *"Warrington" Pen-Portraits*. Ed. Mrs. W. S. Robinson. Boston: Mrs. W. S. Robinson, 1877.

Rusk, Ralph L. *The Life of Ralph Waldo Emerson.* New York: Scribner's Sons, 1949; New York: Columbia University Press, 1957.

Sampson, Edward C. "Three Unpublished Letters by Hawthorne to Epes Sargent." *American Literature* 34, no. 1 (March 1962): 102–5.

Sanborn, Franklin. B. "A Concord Notebook: Papers 1–10." *Critic* 47 (July–December 1905); 48 (January–June 1906); 49 (July 1906).

———. "Emerson and His Friends in Concord." *New England Magazine* 3, no. 40 (December 1890): 411–31.

———. *Henry D. Thoreau.* Cambridge: Houghton Mifflin, 1882.

———. *Life of Henry David Thoreau.* 1917. Detroit: Gale Research, 1968.

———. *The Personality of Emerson.* Boston: Charles E. Goodspeed, 1903.

———. *The Personality of Thoreau.* Boston: C. E. Goodspeed, 1901.

———. *Recollections of Seventy Years.* 2 vols. Boston: Gorham Press, 1909.

———. "Thoreau and Emerson." *Forum* 23 (April 1897): 218–27.

———. "An Unpublished Concord Journal," ed. George S. Hellman. *Century Magazine* no. 103 (April 1922): 825–35.

———, ed. *The First and Last Journeys of Thoreau.* 2 vols. Boston: Bibliophile Society, 1905.

Sattelmeyer, Robert. "The Remaking of *Walden.*" In *Writing the American Classics,* ed. James Barbour and Tom Quirk, 53–78. Chapel Hill: University of North Carolina Press, 1990.

———. "Thoreau's Projected Work on the English Poets." In *Studies in the American Renaissance,* ed. Joel Myerson, 239–57. Boston: Twayne, 1980.

———. "'When He Became My Enemy': Emerson and Thoreau, 1848–49." *New England Quarterly* 62, no. 2 (June 1989): 187–204.

Sayre, Robert F. *Thoreau and the American Indians.* Princeton: Princeton University Press, 1977.

Schwaber, Paul. "Thoreau's Development in Walden." *Criticism* 5 (winter 1963): 64–77.

Scudder, Townsend. *Concord: American Town.* Boston: Little, Brown, 1847.

———. *The Lonely Wayfaring Man: Emerson and Some Englishmen.* New York: Oxford University Press, 1936.

Sebouhian, George. "A Dialogue with Death: An Examination of Emerson's 'Friendship.'" In *Studies in the American Renaissance,* ed. Joel Myerson, 219–39. Charlottesville: University Press of Virginia, 1989.

Seybold, Ethel. *Thoreau: The Quest and the Classics.* New Haven: Yale University Press, 1951.

Shanley, J. Lyndon. *The Making of Walden.* Chicago: University of Chicago Press, 1957; reprint, Chicago: Midway, 1973.

Shelburne, Steven R. "A Reminiscence of Emerson and Thoreau." *Thoreau Society Bulletin,* no. 197 (autumn 1991): 5.

Shepard, Odell. *Pedlar's Progress: The Life of Bronson Alcott.* Boston: Little, Brown, 1937.

Silver, Rollo G. "Ellery Channing's Collaboration with Emerson." *American Literature* 7 (March 1935): 84–86.

Simmons, Edward. *From Seven to Seventy.* New York: Harper and Brothers, 1922.

Simpson, Lewis P. "The Crisis of Alienation in Emerson's Early Thought." *American Transcendental Quarterly* 9 (winter 1971): 35–42.

Skinner, Charles M. *With Feet to the Earth.* Philadelphia: J. B. Lippincott, 1898.

Smith, Henry Nash. "Emerson's Problem of Vocation: A Note on 'The American Scholar.'" *New England Quarterly* 12 (March 1939): 52–67.

Staebler, Warren. *Ralph Waldo Emerson.* New York: Twayne, 1973.

Strauch, Carl F. "Emerson As Literary Middleman." *Emerson Society Quarterly,* no. 19 (1960): 2–9.

———. "Hatred's Swift Repulsions: Emerson, Margaret Fuller, and Others." *Studies in Romanticism* 7 (winter 1968): 65–103.

———. "The Importance of Emerson's Skeptical Mood." *Harvard Library Bulletin* 11 (winter 1957): 117–39.

———. "The Mind's Voice: Emerson's Poetic Styles." *Emerson Society Quarterly,* no. 60 (summer 1970): 43–58.

Tappan, Lewis. *The Life of Arthur Tappan.* New York, 1870.

Tassin, Algernon. *The Magazine in America.* New York: Dodd, Mead, 1916.

Thayer, James B. *Reverend Samuel Ripley of Waltham.* Cambridge, 1897.

Thoreau, Henry D. "Civil Disobedience." In *The Writings of Henry David Thoreau.* Vol. 4. Boston: Houghton Mifflin, 1906.

———. *Collected Poems of Henry Thoreau.* Ed. Carl Bode. Baltimore: Johns Hopkins University Press, 1964.

———. *The Correspondence of Henry David Thoreau.* Ed. Walter Harding and Carl Bode. New York: New York University Press, 1958.

———. *Faith in a Seed: The Dispersion of Seeds and Other Late Natural History Writings.* Ed. Bradley P. Dean. Washington, D.C.: Island Press, Shearwater Books, 1993.

———. Henry D. Thoreau to Henry Vose, May 28, 1838. Printed in *American Transcendental Quarterly* 8 (fall 1970): 6.

———. *Journal.* Ed. John C. Broderick, Elizabeth Hall Witherall, William L. Howarth, Robert Sattelmeyer, Thomas Blanding, Mark R. Patterson, William Rossi. 5 vols. to date. Princeton: Princeton University Press, 1981–.

———. "Natural History of Massachusetts." In *Writings.* Vol. 5. Boston: Houghton, Mifflin, 1906.

———. *Reform Papers,* ed. Wendell Glick. Princeton: Princeton University Press, 1973.

———. "Some Unpublished Letters of Henry D. and Sophia E. Thoreau," ed. Samuel Arthur Jones. *Emerson Society Quarterly,* no. 61, part 2 (1970): 27–59.

———. *Walden.* Ed. J. Lyndon Shanley. Princeton: Princeton University Press, 1971.

———. *A Week on the Concord and Merrimack Rivers.* Ed. Carl F. Hovde. Princeton: Princeton University Press, 1980.

———. *The Writings of Henry David Thoreau.* Boston: Houghton Mifflin, 1906.

Thoreau, Man of Concord. Ed. Walter Harding. New York: Holt, Rinehart, and Winston, 1960.

Thurin, Erik. "Love and Friendship: Emerson and the Platonic Tradition." Ph.D. diss., University of Minnesota, June 1970. Ann Arbor, Mich.: University Microfilms.

Tilton, Eleanor M. "Emerson's Lecture Schedule (1837–1838) Revised." *Harvard Library Bulletin* 21, no. 4 (October 1973): 382–99.

———. "The True Romance of Anna Hazard Barker and Samuel Gray Ward." In *Studies in the American Renaissance,* ed. Joel Myerson, 53–72. Charlottesville: University Press of Virginia, 1987.

Todd, Mabel Loomis. *The Thoreau Family Two Generations Ago.* Berkeley Heights, N.J.: Oriole Press, 1958.

Tryon, W. S. *Parnassus Corner: A Life of James T. Fields.* Boston: Houghton Mifflin, 1963.

Tucker, Ellen Louisa. *One First Love: The Letters of Ellen Louisa Tucker.* Ed. Edith W. Gregg. Cambridge: Harvard University Press, 1962.

Urbanski, Marie. "Henry David Thoreau and Margaret Fuller." *Thoreau Journal Quarterly* 8, no. 43 (October 1976): 24–29.

Waggoner, Hyatt H. *Emerson As Poet.* Princeton: Princeton University Press, 1974.

Wagner, Vern. "No Tumult of Response: Emerson's Reception As a Lyceum Lecturer." *Western Humanities Review* 6, no. 2 (spring 1952): 129–35.

Walls, Laura Dassow. *Seeing New Worlds: Henry David Thoreau and Nineteenth-Century Natural Science.* Madison: University of Wisconsin Press, 1995.

Warfel, Harry R. "Margaret Fuller and Ralph Waldo Emerson." *Modern Language Association of America* 5 (June 1935): 576–94.

Weiss, John. "Thoreau." *Christian Examiner* 79, no. 1 (July 1865). Reprinted in Kenneth Cameron, "The Solitary Thoreau of the Alumni Notes." *Emerson Society Quarterly,* no. 7 (1957): 2–17.

Wesley, Thomas, J. "John Sullivan Dwight: A Translator of German Romanticism." *American Literature* 21, no. 4 (January 1950): 427–41.

Whicher, Stephen E. *Freedom and Fate: An Inner Life of Ralph Waldo Emerson.* Philadelphia: University of Pennsylvania Press, 1953.

Witherell, Elizabeth Hall. "Thoreau's Watershed Season As a Poet: The Hidden Fruits of the Summer and Fall of 1841." In *Studies in the American Renaissance,* ed. Joel Myerson, 49–106. Charlottesville: University Press of Virginia, 1990.

Woodbury, Charles J. *Talks with Ralph Waldo Emerson.* New York: Baker and Taylor, 1890.

Yannella, Donald, and Kathleen Malone. "Evert Duyckinck's 'Diary': May 29–November 8, 1847." In *Studies in the American Renaissance,* ed. Joel Myerson, 207–58. Boston: Twayne, 1978.

Yoder, R. A. "Toward the 'Titmouse Dimension': The Development of Emerson's Poetic Style." *Publication of the Modern Language Association* 87 (March 1972): 255–70.

Index

Alcott, Abigail, 113
Alcott, Bronson, 73–74, 133, 136
"American Scholar, The" (Emerson), 11

Barker, Anna (Fuller's friend), 38, 40–41;
    and Sam Ward, 41–43, 47–49, 51
Blake, Harrison G. O. (admirer of
    Thoreau), 155–56, 163
Brown, John, 173–76
Brown, Lucy (Lidian Emerson's sister), 5–9

Channing, Ellen, 84, 97–99, 138, 146–47
Channing, William Ellery, 4, 94, 126;
    domestic life of, 97–99, 136–39,
    146–47; as Emerson's protégé, 58,
    66–70, 84–86, 145–46
Cholmondeley, Thomas (admirer of Tho-
    reau), 155–56
Christian doctrine, validity of, explored by
    Emerson, 19–20
"Civil Disobedience" (Thoreau), 118
Concord, Thoreau's "peculiar interest" in,
    16–17
Conduct of Life (Emerson), 172–73

Democratic Review, 83
Dial, 3, 28–29, 31–33, 64–66, 124
Duyckinck, Evert, 108, 110

Emerson, Edward (son), 114, 144–45, 178
Emerson, Ellen (daughter), 159, 171–72

Emerson, Ellen Tucker (first wife), 67, 121
Emerson, Lidian Jackson (wife), 5–7, 54 (see
    also Thoreau, Henry David, relation-
    ship with Lidian Emerson)
    illness of, 119–21, 158–59, 171–72; during
        pregnancy, 59–60, 103
    jealousy of, 4, 67, 120
    and son's death, 61–64
Emerson, Ralph Waldo (see also Thoreau,
    Henry David, relationship with
    Emerson)
    Christian doctrine, validity of, explored
        by, 19–20
    and the Dial, 28–29, 31–33, 64–66
    eulogy by, for Thoreau, 181–83
    Fuller's attachment to, 4, 47–51, 55,
        67–70
    and Fuller's friends: Barker, 38, 40–41,
        47–51; Sturgis, 4, 38–39, 43, 48–51, 69;
        Ward, 38–40, 43–44, 47, 49–51
    and Harpers Ferry raid, 173–76
    and Hawthorne, 70
    home of, described, 7–8, 12, 52–53
    illness of, 4, 166
    lectures by, 6, 71–72; in England, 108,
        110–13, 119–21, 126–27, 129; to generate
        income, 43, 59, 62, 103, 130, 159,
        165–66; at home, 13–15
    money provided by, to Thoreau, 17, 60,
        78–79, 102
    as poet, 102, 104, 107–8, 111

Emerson, Ralph Waldo (*continued*)
protégés of, 2, 8–9, 58–59; Channing, 58, 66–70, 84–86, 145–46; Waldo, 81–82, 87–89
public persona of, 149–52
reaction of, to Thoreau's: illness, 62, 156–57, 177–80; imprisonment, 106–7, 118; lifestyle, 158–61, 164–66; poetry, 22–24, 28–29, 33, 56–58, 60, 95–96; *Week on the Concord and Merrimack Rivers,* 4, 134–36
and son's death, 61–63, 72
success pursued by, 129–31
and transcendental movement, 14–15, 28–29, 31–33, 72–74, 153–54
treatment of, in *Walden,* 149
and Walden Pond property, 99–100, 102–4, 112
works by, 3 (see also *Nature*); "American Scholar, The," 11; *Conduct of Life,* 172–73; *English Traits,* 153, 159; "Experience," 63; "Friendship," 44–47; "Human Culture," 14–15; "Literary Ethics," 139; "Ode to Beauty," 107–8; *Poems,* 107; "Protest, The," 20–22; *Representative Men,* 130
Emerson, Waldo (son), 54–55, 61–63, 72
Emerson, William (brother), 77–81, 94
English Traits (Emerson), 153, 159
"Experience" (Emerson), 63

"Fable for Critics, A" (Lowell), 132–33
family (pencil-making) business, Thoreau, 96–97, 126, 138, 170–71
Fields, James (publisher), 148, 179–80
friendship, views on. *See* Emerson, Ralph Waldo, and Fuller's friends; "Friendship" (Emerson); Thoreau, Henry David, views of, on friendship
"Friendship" (Emerson), 44–47
Fuller, Margaret, 38–40, 99; antipathy of, toward Thoreau, 22–24, 56–57, 68; attachment of, to Emerson, 4, 47–51, 55, 67–70; death of, 139; and the *Dial,* 28–29, 31–33, 64; Lidian's jealousy of, 4, 67, 120; and Sam Ward, 41–43, 47

Greeley, Horace, 99, 125, 144

Harpers Ferry raid, reaction to, 173–76
Harvard, Thoreau at, 9–11
Hawthorne, Nathaniel, 70–71, 176
Hawthorne, Sophia, 70
Hedge, Henry, 29, 31
Hoar, Elizabeth, 13–14, 23, 70, 85
Howells, William Dean, 176–77
"Human Culture" (Emerson), 14–15

"Katahdin and the Maine Woods" (Thoreau), 125, 133

"Landlord, The" (Thoreau), 90, 92
"Literary Ethics" (Emerson), 139
"long book." *See* Week on the Concord and Merrimack Rivers, A (Thoreau), material gathered for
Lowell, James Russell, 132–35, 149

"Natural History of Massachusetts" (Thoreau), 65–66
Nature (Emerson), influence of, on Thoreau, 7, 9, 66, 139–40
"Newness, the." *See* transcendental movement ("the Newness")

"Ode to Beauty" (Emerson), 107–8
O'Sullivan, John (magazine editor), 71, 83–84, 89

pencil-making business, 96–97, 126, 138, 170–71
"Persius" (Thoreau), 31–32, 65
"Plea for Capt. John Brown, A" (Thoreau), 174–75
Poe, Edgar Allan, 83, 85, 92
Poems (Emerson), 107
poll tax, Thoreau's refusal to pay, 105–7, 118
"Protest, The" (Emerson), 20–22

Quincy, Josiah, 9–10, 17

Representative Men (Emerson), 130
Ricketson, Daniel (admirer of Thoreau), 156
Russell, Mary (Lidian Emerson's cousin), 55

Sanborn, Franklin, 156, 174–75
Saturday Club, 159–60
Sewall, Ellen, 25–27, 29–31, 33–36, 38, 160
slavery, Thoreau's opposition to, 105–7, 118, 173–76
Snow, Cyrus (school committee member), 11–12
"special parish," Emerson's. *See* Emerson, Ralph Waldo, protégés of
Staples, Sam (tax collector), 105
Sterling, John, 85
Sturgis, Caroline (Fuller's friend), 4, 38–39, 43, 48–51, 69
"Sympathy" (Thoreau), 28–29, 33

Tappan, Lewis, 81
Tappan, William A., 78, 81–82, 89, 93
Thoreau, Henry David (*see also* Walden Pond property)
    efforts of, to gain employment, 11–12, 16–18, 77–79, 110, 128, 131
    Emerson's protégés resented by, 58–59, 67–70, 135
    and family (pencil-making) business, 96–97, 126, 170–71
    Fuller's antipathy toward, 22–24, 56–57, 68
    funeral of, 181–83
    at Harvard, 9–11
    illness of, 61–62, 156–57, 161–66, 177–81
    lectures by, 131, 156
    and New York literary market, 82–84, 89–92
    as poet, 22–24, 28–29, 33, 55–58, 60, 95–96
    public image of, 182–83 (see also *Walden* [Thoreau], self-created image in)
    relationships (*see also* relationship with Emerson; relationship with John Thoreau; relationship with Lidian Emerson): with Alcott, 73–74; with Channing, 97–99, 136–39, 145–47; with Emerson children, 54–55, 114, 144–45, 178; with Hawthorne, 70–71; with mother, 16–17, 34; with Sewall, 25–27, 29–31, 33–36, 38, 160; with Waldo Emerson, 78, 81–82, 89, 93

    relationship with Emerson, 1–4, 51–54, 64, 158–61; development of, 9–15, 18–22, 37; first meeting, 5–9; friction in, 75–79, 108–11, 127–28, 131–32, 136–38, 141–43; intellectual differences, 72–74, 91–92, 129–31, 133–34, 139–41, 152–55; mutual dependence, 167–70
    relationship with John Thoreau (brother), 10–11, 16–17, 22, 26–27, 60–61, 100–101; breach in, 4, 36–37
    relationship with Lidian Emerson, 2, 64, 75–78, 86–87; during Emerson's trip to England, 112–16, 119, 121–22, 125–27
    satirical poem about, 133
    slavery opposed by, 105–7, 118, 173–76
    as teacher (tutor), 22, 27–28, 37, 80–81, 94
    and transcendental movement, 32–33, 72–74, 173
    views of, on friendship, 3–4, 122–25, 141–43, 164–66
    works by, 3, 179–80 (see also *Walden*; *Week on the Concord and Merrimack Rivers, A*); "Civil Disobedience," 118; "Katahdin and the Maine Woods," 125, 133; "Landlord, The," 90, 92; "Natural History of Massachusetts," 65–66; "Persius," 31–32, 65; "Plea for Capt. John Brown, A," 174–75; "Sympathy," 28–29, 33; "Walk to Wachusett, A," 66; "Winter Walk, A," 89–92
Thoreau, John (brother)
    and Henry, 10–11, 16–17, 22, 26–28, 60–61; breach between, 4, 36–37
    and Sewall, 25–27, 29–31, 33–36
Thoreau, John (father), death of, 170
Thoreau, Mrs. John (mother), 86, 146; Thoreau's attachment to, 16–17, 34
Thoreau, Sophia (sister), 6–7, 146, 170–71, 179–81
Ticknor and Fields (publishers), 148
Transcendental Club. *See* transcendental movement
transcendental movement ("the Newness"), 3, 28–29, 31–33, 72–74, 173; burgeoning of, 14–15; dissolution of, 124, 153–54

Very, Jones (Emerson's protégé), 58, 85

Walden (Thoreau), 147–49 (*see also* Walden
    Pond property); self-created image in,
    102, 149–52; success of, 155–57, 180
Walden Pond property, 100–102, 111–12,
    147; Emerson's purchase of, 99–100,
    103–4
Waldo, Giles, 78, 81–82, 87–89, 93
"Walk to Wachusett, A" (Thoreau), 66

Ward, Samuel Gray (Fuller's friend), 38–40,
    43–44; and Anna Barker, 41–43, 47–
    49, 51
Week on the Concord and Merrimack Rivers, A
    (Thoreau)
    marketing of, 108, 110–11, 116–17
    material gathered for, 26–27, 97
    publication of, 132–36, 142–43, 147, 180
    writing of, 100–101, 104–5, 125
"Winter Walk, A" (Thoreau), 89–92